Decolonizing Theory

Decolonizing Theory

Thinking across Traditions

Aditya Nigam

BLOOMSBURY
NEW DELHI • LONDON • OXFORD • NEW YORK • SYDNEY

BLOOMSBURY INDIA
Bloomsbury Publishing India Pvt. Ltd
Second Floor, LSC Building No. 4, DDA Complex, Pocket C – 6 & 7,
Vasant Kunj New Delhi 110070

BLOOMSBURY, BLOOMSBURY ACADEMIC INDIA and the Diana logo are trademarks of
Bloomsbury Publishing Plc

First published in India 2020
This edition published 2020
This paperback edition published 2025

Bloomsbury Academic
An imprint of Bloomsbury Publishing Plc

ISBN: PB: 978-93-69523-96-2; eBook: 978-93-88630-48-1

2 4 6 8 10 9 7 5 3 1

Typeset in Minion Pro by Manipal Technologies Limited
Printed and bound in India

To my mother, Santwana Nigam,
I dedicate this book.

Contents

Acknowledgements

This book has long been in the making in one sense, though I did not know that *this* would be the book I would be writing. At one level, the beginnings of it go back to my early intellectual engagement with the movements against mass dispossession in the early 1990s, movements that ranged from the Narmada Bachao Andolan to the movement in Singrauli where people were to be displaced for the second time in forty years. Coming out of a highly modernist Marxism, this problem of what I now call—borrowing from Ernst Bloch—'non-synchronous' modes of being posed an insurmountable theoretical and philosophical problem. The problem of 'uneven development' in the language of Marxism that was still my language, led to a long and tortuous engagement with the problem of historical time. How do we think of these modes of being that are very much a part of our present? And what do we do? Do we simply sit back and watch them be uprooted, dispossessed and destroyed because that is apparently inevitable according to history's immanent logic? The 1990s was also the decade of neoliberalism, structural adjustment and privatization on an unprecedented scale. It was easy—though immensely disturbing—to see that neoliberalism and Marxism shared a fundamental ground of modernist thinking where it came to these non-synchronous modes of being. Indeed, many Indian Marxists, following the collapse of Soviet bloc state socialism, had even started seeing the collapse as a consequence of the fact that the USSR started building socialism in a society that was not fully capitalist.

From these state-owned mega-developmental projects displacing Adivasi and peasant populations to Singur and Nandigram in 2006 and 2007 in West Bengal, there was a straight line that connected the faith in industrialization and private corporate 'Capital' as the saviours. It did not matter at all that there was a Left or Marxist government in power—Capital had to be wooed and invited to wreak havoc in the name of providing employment. The answer, if one dared ask why, was that that was how it happened in Europe! Something did not seem right at all here and, interestingly, only Marxists who managed to escape this fate of the Bengal Marxists were those who placed their theory of history in abeyance and decided to stand by the peasants and Adivasis. Needless to say, their faith in the 'peasantry' or the 'people' came from Maoism in some form—a non-Western and complex formation that had continued to pay lip service to Marxism but transformed its practice quite a bit.

This was the beginning of a radical questioning of both the Western development and capitalist model as an ideal for others in the non-West to follow, and inextricably tied to it, the philosophy of history that justified it.

The crisis of secularism precisely in the same period, climaxing with the demolition of Babri Masjid, revealed another facet of our naive faith in the very same European model as it did our tendency to mindlessly mimic it. The 'return' of caste—long thought to be dead and a thing of the past—to the centre of our political life, following the implementation of the Mandal Commission, showed that secular/modern discourse was clueless about what it meant. This 'return of caste' too went into constituting the same, extremely complex conjuncture of 1990–1992 and forced a rethink of the narrative of historical progress in another way.

The long and tortuous search for an answer had to go through another, perhaps even more fundamental realization—our entire way of doing theory was of simply setting up the Euro-American experience of modernity as the model, indeed destiny, for the rest of the world. So, has everything been already thought once and for all by Western philosophers and theorists? Is our job simply to apply that theory to our conditions with a modification here or a modification there? What about intellectual activity and thought in all these other parts of the world?

This was where, in a crucial sense, the impetus for those explorations came that have now come together in this book.

It has been a protracted journey of close to thirty years, in twenty of which, my long and immensely formative and productive relationship and partnership with Nivedita Menon has been crucial as it opened me out to new and completely different perspectives. The effects of this long collaboration, intellectually and politically speaking, show throughout the book in different ways. Her reading and comments on the previous draft have also been very useful.

I am also very much indebted to the members of the Reading Group on Non-Western Intellectual Traditions—Rachana Johri, Mohinder Singh, A.K. Ramakrishnan, P.K. Datta and Nivedita—with whom, for five years we collectively read texts from different traditions.

There are, of course, a large number of scholars whose thinking has been very important for opening out new pathways for my own and their debt will be visible in the book at different points. From 2010 on till 2018, I taught courses on Capital and then co-taught a course on Social and Political theory with two other colleagues at the Centre for the Study of Developing Societies (CSDS), where I work. These courses, taught in the CSDS' summer teaching programme, 'Researching the Contemporary', ultimately became the occasion for acquainting myself with works from different intellectual and thought-traditions from different parts of the world. The intense interactions with students in those classes and their queries pushed me to think through some of the issues in greater depth. With regard to familiarizing oneself with the broadly Sanskritik thought traditions, I also received a lot of help and encouragement from Patrick Olivelle and Arindam Chakrabarti during their visits to CSDS. Both of them separately gave us a session with the Reading Group on Non-Western Intellectual Traditions, answering our questions and guiding us.

In the course of this long search, I must also acknowledge my debt to the various social movements of the kind mentioned previously, with whom I have only interacted from a distance but also to movements like the feminist and queer movements and anti-caste activists from different strands of the Dalit movement. I realize how much my thinking has been shaped by trying to engage with the often very contradictory and conflicting impulses of these different movements. The list of friends who have been part of my journey and who have helped in various ways is too big for me to name individually—my gratitude to all of them.

I want to also thank P.K. Datta, Mohinder Singh and an anonymous reviewer for their comments on an earlier draft that helped considerably in improving and texturing the argument.

I am also grateful to my son Anirban and Monobina Gupta for just being there during a very difficult time for them as well. Monobina's astute sense of the field and her journalistic work in Bengal lately has been very illuminating for me. With Anirban, many interesting discussions over the years, especially about race and settler colonialism have been useful in inflecting my thinking.

This book, of course, would not have been possible, in the very difficult period of my mother's terminal illness, had not my sister and her family—Aditi, Shankar, Aranya and Trina—taken on the entire pressure of looking after her. In this entire family of journalists, where everyone is pressed for time, this was not an easy task to accomplish. I thank all of them and Rajinder Nath, who have always been a big support for me.

My mother's illness was most acute during the phase of the writing of this book and she would always ask what I was writing, even when the pain of oral cancer made it difficult for her to speak. I wish she were here to see it. It was through my mother, Santwana Nigam that I actually developed a connection with both Hindi and Bengali languages, which gave me an entry into a thought-world that is crucial for an understanding of what decolonization might mean.

Last but not the least, my very special thanks to Arundhati Ghosh for having been there throughout for sounding out so many of the ideas here—and for the very insightful and delightful conversations on decolonization and the arts and on Bengali culture, in particular, during the writing of the book. I cannot thank her enough for her support in various ways.

Finally, I want to thank the entire staff and faculty of CSDS for their help in different ways in making my work possible. I want to thank Jayasree, our administrative officer, Avinash Jha, our librarian (now retired), Ritwik Gangopadhyay, Hemlata and Raj Karan. I want to thank Mr Natarajan, Jagdeesh Kumar, Ranjeet Negi of the accounts department, Ayodhya, Chandan, Ghanshyam, Vicky, Manoj, Harsh, Vikas and Sachin. Without their spirited support, it would not have been possible to write this book in a hassle-free way.

Chandra Sekhar at Bloomsbury was insistent and forced me to commit to writing this book, which in the end, has turned out to be a very rewarding experience for me.

Introduction

Doing Theory: The Point Is to Change It

The point is to change the way we do theory, we might say, altering Marx's eleventh thesis on Feuerbach.[1] As a matter of fact, the eleventh thesis was not just a crude call to do away with theory and focus on the 'real task' of changing the world, although it has been unfortunately interpreted in that fashion by generations of Marxists. After writing the *Theses on Feuerbach* (1976), which he never intended to publish, Marx did not go and start organizing the working class for the overthrow of capitalism, rather he went on to write huge investigative tomes—*Capital*—only one volume of which could be published in his lifetime. Marx's eleventh thesis should, therefore, be read in a double sense. First, in the context of the first ten theses that were a series of aphoristic comments on the old, mechanical materialism of Feuerbach, where Marx stated his serious philosophical disagreements with that old materialism. The most fundamental of these criticisms is stated in the very first thesis: the old materialism only saw dead matter and could not see practice and practical-critical activity itself as material. In contrast, it was idealism that considered the 'active side' seriously. There is a second sense too, in which one must understand the eleventh thesis—as Marx's break with philosophical essentialism (and metaphysics) and his refusal to discuss matters any more in the older Feuerbachian terms of 'species-being' and the 'alienation of the human essence' that his own youthful *Economic and Philosophical Manuscripts* were shot through with.[2] Marx's insistence now was 'that the human essence was no abstraction inhering in each single individual; in its reality it is the ensemble of social relations.' This was Marx's *aufhebung* of philosophy and the move towards History—still with a capital H however. That is why the *Theses on Feuerbach* has been seen as a kind of 'preface' to *The German Ideology*, where Marx and Engels 'settled accounts with their past philosophical conscience' (Fracchia 1991: 159).

Once this break was made, it was no longer possible to discuss 'Being' except in relation to the social-historical. The 'historical context'—and therefore, historicism—became central and posed a critical challenge to universalism in any form. Of course, what was thus gained was soon lost in Marx's recourse to the Hegelian philosophy of history but that is another matter.

What is important in this episode in the history of thought is that what began with Hegel as the move towards a philosophy of the social-historical reached its culmination in Marx's almost complete break with metaphysics. In a sense, this is what Hegel saw as the realization and transcendence—the *aufhebung* of philosophy.

Does this episode of the move from metaphysical philosophical speculation towards social and political theory (in its broadest and not the Anglo-American sense) hold any significance for the world at large? Is it an episode only in European philosophy? Does it have any significance, for instance, for philosophers and the practice of doing philosophy in India and elsewhere in the global South? My question is not really about what Chakrabarti and Weber call 'hardcore philosophy' (2015: 10–12) and whether it at all remains possible after this epochal shift, for that is really for 'disciplinary' philosophers to answer. My concern here is with the emergence, in the wake of this shift, of a domain of philosophy or philosophical theory that is broadly referred to as social and political philosophy. Political theorist Sudipta Kaviraj has argued strongly—and rightly—that the Indian philosophical tradition never really had any precedent/s of philosophical reflection on social and political matters. In a very profound sense, this is a development that becomes possible only with modernity, when the social and political domains emerge as specific objects of philosophical reflection, in place of the earlier preoccupations with abstract questions of ontology and epistemology. Philosophy can no longer remain insulated from the actual empirical-historical world, its concerns now being largely social and political concerns. The question of power too becomes central now, intricately and constitutively tied as the social and the political are with it.

I should also clarify right away that the term 'political philosophy' as it has been used in the Anglo-American academy is only a 'particular' variant of philosophy, that is, normative philosophy. As we know, normative philosophy, rooted in the analytical tradition, has long managed to insulate itself from the empirical-historical world and argued strongly against any intrusion of the question of power or the empirical into its world, as philosophically illegitimate. However, as Partha Chatterjee (2011) points out, it is not as though normative philosophy is innocent of the empirical-historical; rather, its emergence and existence is predicated on the positing of a 'definite historical past' that he calls 'a time-space of epic proportions' that emerged 'after the victorious conclusion of an epochal struggle' against the absolutist state in Europe (Chatterjee 2011: 1). Normative philosophers usually consign all questions of power and the actual empirical world to the domain of 'social theory', which is supposed to be both empirically oriented and 'explanatory', concerned that is, with what happens and why. Normative philosophy or simply 'political philosophy' in their terms, concerns itself with normative concepts like 'equality', 'justice', 'secularism' and so on, and is primarily interested in elaborating abstract normative principles and is providing justifications for them. It is, however, only one of the ways in which political philosophy is practiced. As is well known, traditions of political philosophy in say, Germany and France follow very different trajectories where the sharp distinctions between the 'empirical-historical' and the 'normative' or between the 'explanatory' and 'normative' are not generally maintained.

In a sense, for the global South or the non-West more generally, it is impossible to keep doing normative philosophy or normative political theory in that sense, for at least two reasons. First, their philosophical-intellectual traditions do not usually maintain this very provincial distinction that is maintained only in the Anglo-American world. So far, we have functioned with the assumption that these traditions are irrelevant to the enterprise of doing theory or philosophy because the latter are separate and specialized disciplines and practices which have a language of their own. Now, this might seem like a legitimate argument given that even in the West, this disciplinary division only took place in the wake of modernity and it would be reasonable to assume that if we are interested in the frontiers of modern knowledge, we must adopt these distinctions. But in retrospect, there could be another way of looking at the problem. If it is true that these distinctions are not universally accepted even in Europe, could this circumstance suggest a more complex relationship than this straightforward one between modernity and the bifurcation of philosophical domains? Is it also possible to understand this state of theoretical thinking in India too, for instance, as a sign of a different mode or tradition of thought, among other things—and not as a sign of its 'underdevelopment'?

Things started changing in this respect only since the 1990s and political science departments, for instance, have started taking something called 'Indian Political Thought' seriously, as far as teaching and research goes. Political theory (aka political philosophy), however, remained unfazed and untouched, as though there was nothing that the study of Indian thought—ancient, medieval or modern—could bring to the table; we could at best use reading techniques and theoretical frames already developed in the metropolitan academies to produce 'interpretations' of Indian texts and thinkers that could be 'liberal', 'Marxist', modernist or secular, or even 'Derridean' and 'Benjaminian' but rarely could the establishments of theory allow any reverse traffic to flow. Things have started to change somewhat at least with respect to some key figures of modern India like Gandhi, Tagore, Iqbal and Ambedkar, whose thought now occasionally enters the practice of theorizing—at least about India.

Second, the practice of theorizing is not and cannot be limited to just how we treat the big names or certain key texts of Indian history. More importantly, it is about going beyond the conception of treating these societies as 'fields' for the collection of academic raw materials and application of theories produced in other climes. We can call this practice the colonial mode of knowledge production, where the raw materials are sourced from these societies and taken into metropolitan academies or their subsidiaries in native countries for production. The theoretical frameworks available in these manufactories are then 'applied' to produce the final products, which are then sold back to the native markets. Breaking out of this colonial mode of knowledge production, of course, requires that we have our own manufactories, our own infrastructure, where the business of knowledge production can take place. This is easier said than done and so there will always be a question of 'the meanwhile'—what do we do in the interregnum? After all the business of doing theory is not simply about setting up machines. Vocabularies, concepts, categories of thought and frameworks emerge in the long and sustained process of theorizing and producing new knowledge in tandem with, drawing upon, and working in languages tied to different non-Western intellectual traditions. It is true that 'postcolonial theory stays within the terrain of Western social theory and very rarely, if at all, draws upon genealogies of intellection from the decolonized world' (Menon 2018: 36). I see this more as a 'predicament' of the Global South (not just of postcolonial theory largely based in the Anglo-American academy). Seeing it as a predicament also means understanding it as an inevitable consequence of the cultural mutilation and epistemic dispossession that follows the long years of colonial rule, where our language and vocabulary itself is made inadequate for such purposes. Yes, it is true that most intellection in the colonized domains henceforth takes place in the colonizer's language. We only have to look at the writings of an Ambedkar, a Nehru or an Aurobindo Ghose among so many others to understand this. This is what philosopher K.C. Bhattacharya (1928), discussed at length in Chapter 1, says about his inability to deliver that particular lecture in his language, Bengali. This is a predicament that continues for reasons discussed in the first chapter, right into our postcolonial history.

It is to deal with this predicament and the question of the 'meanwhile' that we perhaps need to push the parallel with the economy further. We need to appreciate that though we have a vast array of academic and research institutions that could serve as our new manufactories, this domain is also subject to similar pressures as is the economic domain. We could, therefore, opt for one of the two strategies that most postcolonial regimes were faced with: (a) we could produce for the global market, keeping in mind the demands and tastes that are currently in fashion in that academic market, which is what happens most of the time. This is the export-led model. (b) Alternatively, we could think of an intellectual version of the import-substituting industrialization model, where we recognize that there cannot be an overnight transition to a new kind of social science and new theories to take the place of the old colonial ones, but nevertheless prioritize the requirements of our 'home market', while working towards building the required theoretical infrastructure. We can call this the strategy of 'import-substituting theorization.' As discussed at length in Chapter 1, theory should be first and foremost about our being as such, our specific conditions of existence, our choices, our ways of co-living, our relationship with our larger ecology—and only secondarily about being saleable in the global market.

Once we recognize this, it should be evident that our access to 'materials' for knowledge production cannot be about instrumentally visiting a field or an archive, the way a colonizer or an industrialist does, but should be geared to defining another kind of relationship with it. The field, we will then recognize, emerges before us, made up by specific histories, languages and cultures and comprising words, categories and concepts that are 'lived' by people. All of this constitutes the field or the archive and it will begin to have a different resonance once we start relating to these directly. Part of the problem of our instrumental relationship to the field may have to do with modern knowledge itself but there is something very specific that has happened in the colonial world that aggravates our academic disconnect with vocabularies of everyday life. Import-substituting theorization involves the slow and painstaking work of building our own theoretical infrastructures and we must not expect to achieve rapid and 'spectacular' 'growth rates' of the kind that the export-led model can often give us—at the huge cost of being perpetually dependent on the metropolitan centres for theoretical/philosophical sustenance.

Finally, as with the economy, here too we need to abandon any idea of a return to a pristine and pure origin. At this point, we actually enter a very complicated arena. For by now, this much is clear to most people—except rabid 'nationalists'—that a return to some pristine origin is neither possible nor indeed desirable. Import-substitution is not autarky even in the economic domain but in the world of ideas and knowledge, it can be proved to be a cul-de-sac, positively disastrous, as the actual experience of nativistic and indigenist initiatives in the past has shown so clearly.

It is this general recognition that has been recently articulated by two philosophers Jonardon Ganeri (2016) and Arindam Chakrabarti (with Ralph Weber 2015) in their recent interventions. I agree entirely with the argument made by Ganeri (2016), Chakrabarti and Weber (2015) in their attempts to spell out the future directions of philosophers and philosophy in the global South today. Chakrabarti and Weber call for 'comparative philosophy without borders'—that is to say, a philosophy that 'thinks across traditions' in our terms. 'Borderless thinkers', say Chakrabarti and Weber, 'have to be slow travellers who keep leaving and coming back home, even if they have multiple cultural or disciplinary homes' (Chakrabarti and Weber 2015: 227). Borrowing the term 'fusion philosophy' from fellow philosopher Mark Siderits, they say:

> Radically or conservatively, different futures always come from critiques of the present and a re-evaluation of the past. When Western philosophers will recognize that some of the most original ideas of modern or even ancient Western philosophy have come from an interaction with the East, and when the postcolonial and Asian or African philosophers will re-appropriate the riches they have inherited from their colonial 'civilizers' by looking back at their pre-colonial pasts with fearlessly critical but decolonized minds, the future of fusion philosophy will be brighter. (Chakrabarti and Weber 2015: 229)

In outlining their idea of a borderless fusion philosophy, Chakrabarti and Weber talk of three ways of doing such a philosophy. The first way they say 'operates in close proximity to comparative philosophy' in its existing forms 'but purposively and decidedly forgets about questions of sequence—which came first, which is original—or questions of influence or direct refutation'. Almost the opposite of this is the second way that 'maintains a strong commitment to chronological sequence and historical contextualization amounting to a sort of global history of ideas'. This too is a way of being more inclusive of non-European textual traditions even if that happens only formally. As distinct from both of these, is the third way they propose, which they say 'goes beyond the first two ways in the level of assimilation and intertextuality it demands' (Chakrabarti and Weber 2015: 230–231). It is the stance I find closest to my own and it is best we listen to them in their own words.

> Fusion philosophy proceeds with an open eye toward philosophical ideas and thoughts wherever they can be met. It is the conscious

> attempt of filling one's mind in an almost terribly unsystematic manner with whatever one gets out of the study of different styles and traditions. Then, in a subsequent step, one forgets about one's sources. Instead of preserving, quoting and juxtaposing them, one picks up a context, a line of reasoning or some however minor point arising out of years of imaginative rearrangement and cross-fertilization of the ideas retrieved from different cultures, periods, texts and disciplines. Strategic oblivion of one's sources makes an unexpected osmosis of concepts possible. (Chakrabarti and Weber 2015: 231)

In a sense, this is how all great philosophy takes place, its concern being primarily with a concept, a set of concepts and a line of reasoning that the philosopher seeks to develop.

Ganeri though is critical of the enterprise of 'comparative philosophy' despite being fully in sympathy with the Chakrabarti-Weber project of 'borderless philosophy'. Comparative philosophy, says Ganeri, was neither a branch of philosophy nor a philosophical method but 'an expedient heuristic introduced at a particular moment in world history as part of a global movement towards intellectual decolonization' but its ambition was basically, 'to protect thinkers in colonized countries from the peculiar form of servitude that colonialism sought to impose'. Its dual-purpose was 'recognition' and 'integration', where a first generation of philosophers, still in the colonized condition, sought recognition 'for indigenous manners of understanding through demonstration of their comparability with colonial insight' and a second-generation, in the years after the end of colonial rule, 'hoping for assimilation and integration in an internationalized philosophical academy' (Ganeri 2016: 134). 'These projects', he argues, 'aimed either to incorporate indigenous thinking into an unchallenged colonial paradigm or else to reverse colonial asymmetries while leaving a fundamentally colonial structure intact' (Ganeri 2016: 134).

Quite in tandem with what I have argued in the first chapter, Ganeri also believes that the world of academic philosophy 'is entering a new age' that is neither defined by the colonial need for recognition nor the postcolonial wish to integrate. 'We are entering', he claims, 'what we might call the "age of re:emergence"',[3] a new period that is defined by the following features, among others,

> First, philosophies from every region of the world, locally grounded in lived experience and reflection upon it, are finding new autonomous and authentic forms of articulation. Second, the philosophical industry, leaving behind a centre-periphery mode of production, is becoming again polycentric: the philosophical world is returning to a plural and diverse network of productive sites. Third, Europe and other colonial powers have been provincialized, no longer mandatory conversation partners or points of comparison but rather unprivileged participants in a global dialogue. (Ganeri 2016: 136)

Philosophy in the age of re:emergence, Ganeri insists, is 'not a matter of seeking the essence of autochthonous ways of thinking'. 'Essentialism about philosophical traditions' is simply a way of coping with colonial guilt' and 'in this new era every philosophical activity is hybrid and dynamic', he underlines. Philosophers in this age of re:emergence must 'leave to philologists and text-critical historians the attempt to construct an archaeology of past systems of thought, destined only to become specimens in a museum of ideas, for the *once-colonized has to always watch against being made into an ethnographic object*' (Ganeri 2016: 137, emphasis added).

Of course, this difficulty is all the more serious for 'professional' philosophers in countries like India, who have a greater chance of lapsing back into 'their own' philosophical traditions which are always at least a few centuries old, often making those traditions sound quite esoteric. But it is not that even social and political theorists necessarily escape this predicament when they begin to explore even their own 'contemporary' in terms unfamiliar to the hitherto existing world of social theory.

Up till this point, things seem to be relatively simpler—and clearer. What is not so clear and poses perhaps the most intractable methodological problem for theory in the global south is: What then? Where do we now go from here? If hybridity is what marks our existence and we can never reach our 'true selves' by recovering our 'true pasts', do we simply continue with what we are doing, business as usual? Even if we recognize all the problems with modern knowledge and theory that I have discussed in this book, we might still throw up our hands in despair and say that since hybridity is all there is, nothing really can be done. We might be tempted to ask, after all, if any reconfiguration of that knowledge is at all possible. This question becomes pertinent in the wake of postcolonial theory's endeavours over the past couple of decades, given the way it emphasized how Orientalism and colonial discourse have so irrevocably changed the terrain that it is now well nigh impossible to 'really know' what was going on before colonialism came along. At one level, this is very true and as we will see in the first chapter, even those who defined themselves as the standard-bearers of our ancient tradition, were actually operating with a conception of Hinduism or *sanatan dharma* that was already recast by Orientalist scholarship.

However, if we are not to remain forever trapped in the predicament of living life in a way where we are always 'doing things wrong', we do need to break out of it. This 'breaking out' is not something that will take us to the source, but it must be a breaking out that enables us to theorize our own condition adequately for ourselves. To the extent that traditional modes of being and traditional categories undergird contemporary 'traditional' practices, we need to be able to let them speak within our theoretical universe. The 'them' here could be texts of the High Sanskrit or Persian or any other tradition but it could also be concepts and categories that structure and order practices of everyday living that are not always fully legible to the high world of Vedic textuality, even when they are apparently speaking the language of the Puranas and especially of Tantrism. In this 'letting them speak', in setting up this conversation it should be underlined, all we can get access to is how the concepts and categories structuring everyday lives work 'today'. There is little doubt, however, that they 'disclose' before us the world of the Puranic and the paramodern (discussed at length in Chapter 5) that is not otherwise accessible to our world of modern knowledge and theory.

At one level, allowing this encounter to occur within our theoretical world calls for a suspension or 'bracketing' of our preconceived theoretical categories and frameworks. Only then would that world emerge ready for the conversation that it has not set up and perhaps has no interest in setting up. This is a complex area and will perhaps begin to have its maximum impact on the business of knowledge production only when, in the postcolonial world, the business of theorizing is increasingly conducted in the local languages. In other words, this might be a horizon that the practice of 'import-substituting theorization' can aim at, but a horizon that like all horizons are will remain ever-receding.

This book constitutes a modest attempt on my part to 'do' political and social theory in the way I have been advocating so far. The central concern running through all the chapters of the book is what I call, after Ernst Bloch, 'non-synchronous synchronicities', life forms and modes of being consigned to the past. As such the explorations here take the form of a search for an 'outside' to the all-enveloping totalities of modernity and capitalism. These explorations also seek an outside to political and social theory that universalizes the experiences of a small part of the world and sets them up as ideals for the rest of the world.

The first chapter, 'Decolonization of Theory: A New Conjuncture', sets up the larger context of this particular theoretical conjuncture in which there is a global concern and indeed a movement towards 'theory from the South'. Of course, the global scene merely provides a context, for the conjuncture has its own very specific Indian coordinates which the chapter discusses. Chapter 2 unpacks the concept of modernity and its received story by way of an engagement with the revisionist theory of modernity outlined by Sudipta Kaviraj and the idea of coloniality as constitutive of the modern as argued by Anibal Quijano and Walter Mignolo. In doing this, this chapter traces chronologies that go back to different 'timespaces' outside early modern Europe. The argument in the third chapter takes a debate on Slavoj Žižek as the occasion to examine a more general philosophical attitude towards societies and modes of being that lie outside the epistemic fold of Europe. The chapter is not just a critique of Žižek but attempts to set up the question of non-synchronisms that I take up for further exploration in later chapters. Chapter 4 discusses the 'birth of the political' in a way that questions the story of its origins in secularization and the emergence of the political domain and state as objects of independent reflection. This is done in the context of India but also drawing from the larger South and South-East Asian experience which were characterized by dispersed forms of power embodied in the idea of the 'mandala', where notions of sovereignty or a unitary state made little sense. In the fifth chapter, I move on to a discussion of what I call the 'paramodern' and the Puranic mode of being. These are arenas populated by all kinds of beings—humans and non-human spirits that have been banished from the world of the moderns. We could call them the epistemically dispossessed. Finally, Chapter 6 comes to the question of non-synchronisms in the context of the philosophical history of capital and proposes a different way of understanding capital via an engagement with Kalyan Sanyal and Subaltern Studies as well as some Marxists.

Although terms like mandala and the Puranic (pauranik in Sanskrit) are widely used in the relevant literature, my use of the terms does not adhere strictly to their literal meanings. In the way I am using them, they designate forms that are related to but are not reducible to their literal meanings. The mandala as a political form with several different radiating centres of power tied in a loose circle of 'states', is something that has resonances not only in the specifically Hindu universe but also in other political formations in South and South East Asia. Indeed, James Scott (2010) also finds it the most relevant model of political power in the context of his study of the 'Zomia' (or the hill people of India's North-East states, and Bangladesh's Chittagong and Burma). He says, 'each existed as one unit among a galaxy of waxing and waning contending centres' (Scott 2010: 58). The actual empirical form of the mandala obviously varies from context to context, but it does point towards a different model of the political where concepts like sovereignty are irrelevant.

Similarly, the Puranic mode of being in the way I use it has little to do with the texts called the Puranas or with 'Hindu' gods, goddesses and spirits for that matter. As I explain in Chapter 5, it refers to the world in which the Puranas make their appearance—a world that is not Brahmanical and is in fact far more chaotic and unpredictable—even though the texts themselves are Brahmanical, generally. The Puranic mode of being is a mode where humans co-exist with all kinds of spirits—malign and benign—a mode that is pervasive and, in the way, I use the term, not only 'Hindu'. Its pervasiveness can be seen among Muslims as well as among the outcastes as the discussion in that chapter underlines.

Finally, the term 'paramodern' designates the broader domain of those banished and excluded by the rational secular moderns. This space or domain is not just about the Puranic, for it includes all kinds of non-synchronisms, different modes of being that constitute the epistemically dispossessed. The paramodern, additionally, is also related to though distinct from Partha Chatterjee's notion of political society insofar as political society is definitionally limited by its relation to the state and the formal domain of politics.

Hopefully, these terms will make their presence felt more clearly as the argument of the book unfolds. I am also hopeful that the book and the reflections offered here will be taken as an attempt to build on existing scholarship and an invitation to a debate. It is in this spirit that I present it before interested readers.

Notes

1. The eleventh thesis on Feuerbach reads as follows: 'Philosophers have hitherto only *interpreted* the world in various ways; the point is to *change* it.'
2. See Joseph Fracchia (1991) for an interesting and textured discussion of this transformation.
3. The term 're:emergence' that Ganeri uses is part of the name of an art exhibition in Indonesia where the article was first presented as a lecture. Ganeri simply uses the same term to work his ideas around it.

1

Decolonization of Theory

A New Conjuncture

> *Decoloniality 'as decolonization' means epistemic reconstitution, while the horizon of decolonization during the Cold War meant to build native nation-states.*
>
> —Walter D. Mignolo (2018: 382)

Introduction

'Decolonization', in this book, is used precisely in the sense of 'epistemic reconstitution' as indicated in the quote earlier. As such it should be clearly distinguished from the old project of 'decolonization'. However, I prefer to use this term over 'decoloniality' simply because the latter is too closely tied to a particular, if kindred, South American project that has its own discrete history. Although the 'decoloniality' framework has lately been adopted by some African scholars as well, decolonization is a somewhat broader term that has resonances with the work being done in Africa, China and elsewhere.[1] I also do not use the terms 'postcolonialism' and 'postcoloniality' to describe what I intend to do in this book—though, in a sense, there is a clear resonance between all these terms. Mignolo distinguishes between decoloniality and postcolonialism, first and foremost, in terms of the 'geopolitical' backgrounds from where the two tendencies emerge. Postcoloniality, he says, 'emerged from the experience of British colonization (of Egypt and India and of the Palestinian question)'. Moreover, he sees it as enabled by the emergence of postmodernism, especially since the late 1970s. Clearly, the reference here is to the trail-blazing work of Edward Said which opened the pathways for postcolonial theory and postcolonial studies. In contrast, he traces the 'long tradition of decolonial thought' going way back to C.L.R. James, Aime Cesaire and Frantz Fanon (Mignolo 2011: xxvi). Decolonial thinking, he argues, materialized 'at the very moment in which the colonial matrix of power was being put in place, in the sixteenth through the eighteenth centuries' (Ibid.: xxiv).[2] Thus, he says, while South Asia, Australia, South Africa and other former British colonies 'joined postcoloniality', the English- and the French-speaking Caribbean did not (Ibid.: xxvi).

However, the geopolitical difference comprises only a part of Mignolo's argument. He suggests that decoloniality is not simply an intellectual concern that emerges like postcolonialism only in the academy. Rather, he seems to suggest, it is an existential question, which is why it emerges at the very moment when modernity/coloniality comes into existence. I am not quite persuaded by the latter part of his claim that decoloniality emerges at the very moment of the institution of modernity/coloniality—maybe because our experience in India gives a different sense of the emergence of an oppositional discourse to modernity/coloniality. As our discussion further will show, at least in India modernity/coloniality did not produce an oppositional stance in the colonized intelligentsia, to begin with, as large segments of the intelligentsia, in the initial phase, accepted the superiority of Western thought in different ways. It was only with the emergence of nationalist consciousness in the latter part of the nineteenth century that an oppositional discourse began to take shape.[3] Nevertheless, Mignolo is right that postcolonialism *was* more of a trend within the global academy and never had much of a purchase in India, despite the fact that the concern with decolonization of knowledge was very strong through the 1960s and later. Be that as it may, postcolonialism did make a signal contribution in terms of its re-examination and critique of Western knowledge in its relation with the colonized world. That moment has now given way to a different one that Mignolo calls one of 'epistemic reconstitution'. It is in this moment that the present concern with decolonization, as I see it, is located.

Decolonization, in the sense I use it in this book, needs to be understood not as *a particular*, privileged mode of approaching the problem of knowledge or doing theory in the postcolonial world but rather, as referring to a range of possible strategies that might allow us to think our present *independently*—as a necessary preliminary step towards epistemic reconstitution. What I mean by the term *independently* here has to do with our ability to confront our current challenges without looking up to philosophers and theorists from the West to provide us with framing concepts. The idea of decolonization of theory, in the sense in which I use it, while allied to and drawing upon the history of ideas or intellectual history, must be ready to directly address the challenges of our always-turbulent present. It will, of course, be possible to meet this challenge, in its true sense, only when we are able to open out social and political theory to intellectual traditions other than the Western, for that alone can allow us to have a deeper sense of our world. Our efforts, in other words, must be directed not at rejecting Western theory or philosophy but at treating it as one among the many sources of our thinking—that is to say, we must *think across traditions*.[4]

At its most fundamental level then, theoretical decolonization is about standing on our own feet and thinking for our own selves—drawing resources for that thought like intellectual *bricoleurs*, from all manner of sources. That was what theory and philosophy were always meant to help us do. Theory and philosophy are above all modes of intervention in our times; they are not about singing paeans to the glory of a once-great and ancient civilization. Theoretical decolonization is not simply about producing concepts and categories in Sanskrit, Arabic or Chinese instead of English, German or French. At this point, the question can, of course, be asked as to why then do we need *decolonization*? Aren't we doing quite well by 'using' Western theory and philosophy for our purposes? And can we not think for ourselves by mastering the apparatus of Western theory and knowledge? Will we not be better off by doing that job with greater finesse and precision, rather than be drawn into the cul-de-sac of a search for some uncontaminated indigenous intellectual or philosophical tradition?

After all, 'decolonization', beyond its most immediate political sense, *has* often meant an inwardly directed search for some pure, uncontaminated indigenous self. In the domain of thought and knowledge, this translates into a search for some pristine source of authentic knowledge—an indigenous intellectual/philosophical tradition, unfailingly in the singular. And this search has always inevitably been tied to emergent nationalist pride in the colonized world, which saw its domination as being closely related to the new forms of knowledge that colonialism brought in its train. After all, this knowledge came as a part of the practices of the modern state and its legal and juridical paraphernalia that were key elements in the rapid reorganization and bewildering transformation of these societies. But that search for a pure indigenous source turned out to be futile, leading only to violent attempts to get rid of 'impurities' that inevitably become part of life as it moves away from that pristine 'source'. Thus, any search for a pure, unspoilt indigenous knowledge tradition is indeed a cul-de-sac to be avoided at all costs.

But saying this does not prove the converse or legitimize the practice of judging our own societies by conceptual categories that emerged from the specific historical experience of Europe. We are really not doing very well in relying exclusively on Western knowledge and theory if the answer provided by it to all the questions is that the non-West, that is to say about 80 per cent of the world's population living outside Europe and America, does everything wrong. Ask anyone who has been trained in the social sciences (which are constituted by that body of theoretical knowledge) and you will be told that there is something fundamentally wrong with 'us' and our societies: our modernity incomplete, our secularism is distorted, our democracy is immature, our development is arrested and even our capitalism is retarded! A body of theory that tells us that most of the world is *always* doing everything wrong should automatically arouse our suspicion, for that theory is not just innocently 'explanatory'—it does not simply 'explain' what happened in the past (mainly in and via Europe). Equally importantly, it puts in place certain norms and ideals that all societies everywhere must aspire to.

The fact, however, is that far from arousing our suspicion and leading us to re-examine the assumptions of this body of knowledge, we too have long been led by it into believing that the problem lies with 'us' and our societies; that they need the massive intervention of the modern state, armed with Western theory and knowledge to set them right—that is to say, bring them in line with the 'proper'

Western standard. One of the most striking examples of this is the long Marxist debate on capitalist development/underdevelopment in the 'peripheries' through the 1960s, 1970s and 1980s. Long after it had become clear that capitalism in these 'peripheral societies' was not quite 'battering down Chinese walls' and 'building a world in its own image', Marxist scholars kept debating about what was wrong with these societies and why their capitalism continued to be retarded.[5] The answer almost invariably was that the bourgeoisie in these societies was weak and therefore unable to confront 'feudal' structures head-on, thus being forced into a compromise with them. That itself was read as a sign of a 'lack'—of being 'not yet ready' for capitalist progress. In some cases, the idea of the 'relative autonomy of the superstructure/s' was invoked in order to point to the continuing powerful presence of religion and caste in societies like India's, as elements that held back the development of a modern bourgeois ethos. The structure of the theory remained calmly unperturbed by the fact that once again, close to four-fifths of the world showed no interest in obliging it.

Similarly, for decades the modernist criticism was that India's secularism was distorted or diluted because, instead of implementing a robust separation of religion and politics, it talked of *sarvadharma samabhav* or equal respect for all religions and *dharma-nirpekshata* or the state's neutrality between religions. This was why, it was argued, India could not build a strong scientific temper among its people. It was only when the powerful critiques of secularism by scholars like Ashis Nandy and T.N. Madan started resonating with a secular public increasingly besieged by the rise of the Hindu Right that the question of secularism was put under fresh scrutiny in the late 1980s and 1990s. In both the cases, that of capitalism and of secularism, the ideals to which Indian society was supposed to conform were drawn from a certain specific experience (of Europe in the past two centuries) and a specific theorization (that of European thinkers and philosophers) of the challenges that Europe had faced. The actual historical development of Indian society (or other non-Western societies) simply did not figure in these critiques and theorizations except by way of pointing to a constitutive 'lack' that apparently defined them.

It is not that there were no serious scholarly studies of the Indian social formation. There were many, but the questions that were posed to the specifically Indian material by these otherwise rigorous studies were questions that emanated elsewhere: Was there feudalism in India? Were there potentialities of capitalist development in India before colonialism? What was the nature of class struggle or accumulation in premodern India? There were no attempts to excavate, on the basis of a rigorous study of the Indian social formation, what might have been called, in an earlier Marxism, 'laws of motion' internal to any society. Similarly, it did not matter that the question of 'separation' of Church and State in the West arose from within a context of a strong fusion of ecclesiastical and political power in Latin Christendom that simply did not exist elsewhere. It did not matter at all that a deeply diverse society like India's had over millennia—at least from the time of Asoka and the Mauryan Empire—evolved an idiom of coexistence that was not possible to capture in the concept of *secularism as separation* precisely because there was no fusion in the first instance. Even the Sultanate and the Mughal Empire in India were hardly theological states based on Sharia law. We also know from historical research that this coexistence has very long and complex histories (for there isn't a singular history across the Indian subcontinent) that traverse politically different historical regimes on the one hand, and the rise of innumerable heterodox 'religious' reform movements (often clubbed together under the rubric of Bhakti), on the other. This idiom of coexistence was never only an exclusive state affair, as often pointed out by scholars like Nandy but had to do with everyday lived religiosity. To try and fit this into the straitjacket of secularism meant leaving out large areas of life altogether from our understanding of such coexistence.[6]

Now, this relationship to modern Western knowledge is relatively easily understood in the case of those who are explicit modernists of the kind referred to previously. But even those who swear by the Vedas and claim that Vedic India had developed everything from airplanes to plastic surgery technology have the same fascination for smart cities, bullet trains and cashless economies—for the truth of the matter is that these too are colonized minds. This condition of sections of erstwhile colonial populations continuing to live supposedly 'authentic' lives that are actually constituted by colonial knowledge, can be best described in terms of Anibal Quijano's concept of 'coloniality' or the 'colonial matrix of power' (Quijano 2007). Quijano's concept has been taken up by Mignolo and the decolonial theorists and further developed as the 'coloniality of being' (Maldonaldo-Torres 2007) and we will discuss this idea at some length in Chapter 2 but for the moment, it should be underlined that what both Quijano and Mignolo mean by it is that the formal end of colonialism (in the political and economic realm) does not do away with the power relations and the very conditions of 'being' put in place by colonialism. The larger power structure continues to hold sway because the conditions of existence continue to be determined by the ways of seeing and therefore of being that were put in place through colonial knowledge and technologies of colonial governmentality. As Quijano put it, the colonial power structure 'produced the specific social discriminations that were later codified as "racial", "ethnic", "anthropological" or "national"'. Consequently, 'that power structure was, and still is, the framework within which operate the other social relations of classes or estates' (Quijano 2007: 168).

The understanding of Vedic history of the ideologues of the Hindu Right was already one that had been reconstructed under the thrall of the colonial power that had subjugated them. Indeed, it was more than just the thrall of colonial political power, for as scholars have often pointed out, practically every single proposition about Hinduism and the nationalism on which they erected their politics, was drawn directly from Orientalist Indological scholarship.[7] Vedic history, as told by them is the product of a nineteenth and early twentieth-century enterprise that was out to prove to the colonial rulers, and the West in general, that 'we' are not barbarians, that everything that you have today 'we' had from the beginning of Time, that is with the Vedas. The small irony here, of course, is that this is a civilization that claims to be *sanatan* and *shashwat* (that is eternal) and understands Time itself to be without beginning and without end (*anadi anant*). But assisted by the Orientalist scholarship of the likes of Max Muller, the nineteenth-century European Romantic thinkers and philosophers like Scheler and Schopenhauer, our modern Hindu or 'neo-Hindu' thinkers recast their 'history' in remarkable ways.[8] They too now had a revelation (*sruti*) and a beginning in Time, namely the Vedas, even if they still had no God.[9] From the very beginning, then, the neo-Hindu's 'discovery' of his past was a reconstruction mediated by the West, Western scholarship and Christianity.

It is important to underline this point since many intellectuals aligned to the Hindu Right have lately picked up the slogan of 'decolonization' of knowledge. We, therefore, need to be doubly clear about what is at stake here. For about two centuries, Indian intellectuals starting from Raja Ram Mohan Roy to Bhudeb Mukhopadhyay, Bankim Chandra Chattopadhyay and Vivekananda in the nineteenth century or Aurobindo Ghose, Dayanand Saraswati or Bal Gangadhar Tilak in the early decades of the twentieth century, were actively engaged in reconstituting and reconstructing tradition in the light of the new situation inaugurated by colonial modernity and the challenge presented by Christian missionaries. And we cannot but remember here that their efforts were supplemented by the Herculean scholarly initiative undertaken by stalwart social reformists and nationalist scholars like R.G. Bhandarkar, P.V. Kane, V.S. Sukhtankar, U.N. Ghoshal, K.P. Jayaswal, S.N. Dasgupta, S. Radhakrishnan and many others. All these thinkers and scholars were engaged in the reconstitution of tradition in different ways—some in making it commensurate with the demands of modern times by drawing in elements from monotheism (like the Brahmo Samaj), others advocating a return to either a pristine Vedic 'religion' (like the Arya Samaj), which is also an attempt at modernizing through elimination of caste practices, which they saw as a corruption of *shastric dharma*. There were others, conservative and reformists alike, in the North-Western Provinces who avoided all these options but were nonetheless keen to reform their (Hindu) community in significant ways. For instance, in the case of the Hindi literati in North India, Mohinder Singh shows that while they wanted poverty to be eradicated and to that end, virtues of thrift, industry and 'accumulation' to be emulated, they were all equally insistent that instead of blindly adopting modern values, they should 'try to clean up the "old garden of Hindu samaj"' (Singh 2014: 433). Much of the intervention of these thinkers and scholars, notwithstanding the impressive depth of their scholarship, was defensive and apologetic, usually aimed at proving that we too had a robust theological and philosophical tradition. In fact, the popularity of the Vedantic ideal (in its different versions) among nationalists was not at all unrelated to the fact that it came the closest to monotheism, and thus provided the modernizing intellectuals a stance that would be far less embarrassing than the relatively more 'pagan' elements like those prevalent in popular Puranic literature or Tantric practices.[10] Given this, it has to be underlined that the project of decolonization must equally be a project of steering clear of this defensive and profoundly derivative 'nativism' in our scholarly work—but with the added recognition that this is not something that can be accomplished by simply deriding everything of the past as backward and irrational.

The Overture

To be sure, the project of the decolonization of knowledge or the decolonization of thought, or of the imagination in general, is a very old one, certainly in India but also in other parts of the colonial world. Apart from the various scholars and thinkers mentioned earlier, whose work was oriented towards a 'recovery' and reconstruction of traditional thought from the latter half of the nineteenth century onwards, we may rightfully refer here to K.C. Bhattacharya's well known 1928 lecture, 'Svaraj in Ideas', as an early statement of the project. The remarkable thing about Bhattacharya's lecture that is worth recalling even today was the distinction he made between 'cultural subjection' and 'assimilation of alien culture' by the colonized. Cultural subjection, he argued was of an 'unconscious character' and implied 'slavery from the very start'. As opposed to this, assimilation 'may be positively necessary for healthy progress' (Bhattacharya 2011: 103). What was the distinction Bhattacharya was making here? It lay in the fact that cultural subjection occurs when one's 'traditional cast of ideas and sentiments is superseded without comparison or competition by a new cast representing an alien culture'. What happens as a result is that in relation to 'the formation of judgements about our real position in the world', 'we speak of world movements and have a fair acquaintance with the principles and details of Western life and thought, but we do not always sufficiently realize where we actually stand today and how to apply our bookish principles to our situation in life'. As a result, we 'either accept or repeat judgements passed on us by Western culture', or we 'impotently resist them but have hardly any estimates of our own, wrung from an inward perception of the realities of our position' (Ibid.: 104).

In other words, we lose the capacity to make our own judgements about our situation, in a sense because the knowledge that we have at our disposal has no real connection with our lives and thus remains bookish. Bhattacharya then extends this point to the sphere of knowledge and learning, where once again, his point is not about the rejection of the Western knowledge but of having 'distinctively Indian estimates of Western literature and thought'. 'In philosophy hardly anything that has been written by a modern educated Indian that shows that he has achieved a synthesis of Indian and Western thought. There is nothing like a judgement on Western systems from the standpoint of Indian philosophy...' (Ibid.: 104–105).

Bhattacharya thus makes this point amply clear way back in 1928 that svaraj in ideas is not about claiming that Indian philosophical 'systems' are sufficient or have the wherewithal to enable us to deal with the challenges of our times ('realize where we stand today'), that, more importantly, it is about having the confidence to read Western philosophy and theory through 'Indian' eyes, to be able to critically engage with that tradition rather than slavishly follow it and 'apply' its concepts to our realities. In this statement, Bhattacharya identifies what the precise challenge for any project for a svaraj in ideas might be.

However, there are three amendments that I would like to make to Bhattacharya's statement, especially from today's vantage point. First, there is really no single 'Indian' national intellectual or philosophical tradition from where we might critically engage with the West, but only a range of diverse traditions. These traditions range from the various Brahmanical *saddarsanas* (the six philosophical schools, namely Nyaya, Vaishesika, Sankhya, Yoga, Mimamsa and Vedanta) to Charvaka/Lokayata, Buddhism and Jainism on the one hand, and various Islamic and Sufi traditions on the other. And if we recognize that there is no single 'Indian' tradition that we can take recourse to, then just as certain Persian and Arabic currents of thought permeate what is 'Indian', so Buddhism no longer remains 'Indian', having spread from Sri Lanka, Myanmar and Tibet to Japan and China and further east to other Southeast Asian countries. This entire region is a huge melting pot of ideas where different intellectual traditions mingle and produce not one but many traditions, all of which speak to each other and India, happily, stands at the confluence of these different Asian traditions. As a matter of fact, the connections with Iran are in all probability far older, long before Islam came on the scene. To think it possible, therefore, to critically engage with the Western philosophical tradition from the standpoint of 'Indian philosophy', based on such a restricted understanding of the tradition may be a non-starter.

Second, this may also be a non-starter for another reason. To suppose that traditional Indian philosophical systems like the ones mentioned previously might have anything to tell us about the challenges of modernity is itself an unsustainable assumption for two reasons: (a) None of the Indian philosophical traditions, perhaps with the exception of the Lokayata, has ever descended from its metaphysical heights to pronounce anything about the real/empirical world. We might at best find normative or prescriptive texts about proper *dharmic* conduct or ethical conundrums arising out of conflicting dharmas in the context of the varna status of people but that is not really what I mean here. It is, in fact, a question related to the imagination of 'the social' and its ontological status that is at issue here. As Hegel correctly put it, while Indian philosophy had discovered the universal and the infinite and had elaborate disquisitions on it, the finite and the concrete had not even been posited; the finite remained lost in the infinite (cited in Halbfass 1990: 89). Moreover, we cannot forget that what we call modern Western philosophy represented a break, a rupture, even in the West, for that alone could bring Western philosophy to descend from the heights of metaphysical speculation to the world of the finite and the concrete; (b) At an even more concrete level, it was the emergence of the 'socio-political' as a concrete object of philosophical and theoretical reflection that led to the emergence of modern Western social and political philosophy, and this was a fundamentally new phenomenon even in the West. Similar efforts at 'positing the finite' and giving due weight to the 'concrete particularity of the world', begin to take shape only in the nineteenth and early twentieth centuries. It was only partially addressed by thinkers like Vivekananda and Aurobindo Ghose who either reinterpreted 'Maya' or the Advaitic idea of ontological illusion (Vivekananda) or, replaced it with 'Lila' (the Infinite's playful manifestation in the real world), drawing from later Vedantic traditions (Aurobindo; see Bhushan and Garfield 2011, 2017). However, these were just the most rudimentary first steps. Indian philosophical traditions could not have had anything meaningful to say about these matters as long as they continued, even in their modern and contemporary avatars, to bask in the glory of the great spiritual message that they were destined to teach the rest of the world. Having fully conceded that Western thought and philosophy were materialist and made the claim that the uniqueness of India, the secret of its greatness, lay in its spiritual mission, the battle was already lost. For from that point on, Indian philosophy's self-definition made it incapable of dealing with the socio-political world, and the occasional discovery of an *Arthashastra* here or *Sukraniti* there, or the tales of the unique achievements of Indian mathematics and medical science, could hardly help matters.

My third amendment to Bhattacharya's statement has to do with his call to think 'resolutely in our own concepts' that he makes towards the end of his lecture. My point here directly flows from the two points made earlier. Barring the concepts of science, he argues, 'all concepts and ideas have the distinctive character of the particular culture to which they belong' and when we encounter them (that is Western concepts), we must accept them 'as metaphors and symbols to be translated into our own indigenous concepts' for they can be 'properly understood only when we can express them in our own way' (Ibid.: 110). The problem here is twofold. In the first place, this basically still leaves the theoretical/philosophical agency with Western theory, 'our own' task being of continuously translating its concepts into our philosophical language. Second, Bhattacharya assumes that it is a matter of simply translating into a language that already has the wherewithal, in advance, to provide us with concepts with which to think the new context of colonial modernity. If that were the case, we would not have required translating always in one direction. Further, if what I have been arguing previously is correct, then the work still remains to be done at least at the level of the finite/concrete—the social and political world.

However, Bhattacharya's point about our inability to think for ourselves due to our cultural subjection and the need to emerge out of that predicament, though well taken, was clearly not heeded in the decades to come. The situation actually worsened in the period immediately following the attainment of independence, as the newborn nation-state went about building its educational institutions, of higher learning in particular. For, now that India was independent, it had to rapidly develop its capacities, its economy, its pool of technical skills and knowledge. It also had to rapidly train its engineers and social scientists to lay the foundations of modern India. Readily available Western knowledge became the basis of the curricula at different levels. Whatever critical tendencies there had been in our intellectual life earlier, now were pushed aside. That was the logic of nation-states in the modern era and unless you were prepared to 'lag behind', you simply had to follow that logic. This obviously had the most serious consequences especially in the social sciences, and even though small islands of creativity remained, the formal business of higher education could not but take the route of following the model that was already laid out in the West. The question of thinking in our own concepts that Bhattacharya raises presupposes not only the hard labour of theorizing and producing concepts but also a certain degree of 'delinking' from the pressures and demands of the global academy. Bhattacharya of course, does not think of the question in terms of delinking but this kind of strategic withdrawal is in fact undertaken by many intellectuals working in the postcolonial world, especially those who either chose to work only in their vernacular languages and to publish outside circuits of professional peer-reviewed journals while maintaining the highest standards of scholarship and rigour. In the 1980s, at the height of the debate on dependency, development and underdevelopment, Samir Amin (1985) had proposed delinking in the context of the economy and state as the way to a polycentric world. In recent times Walter Mignolo (2007) has argued for a strategy of what he has called 'epistemic delinking' as a way of changing not just the content but the very terms of the conversation between 'colonizer' and the 'colonized' (Mignolo 2007: 459). In a similar vein, making a passionate argument against what he calls 'epistemicide', Boaventura de Sousa Santos calls for an 'epistemological break', proposing a kind of 'rearguard theory' drawing on 'experiences of large marginalized minorities' and 'majorities that struggle against unjustly imposed marginality' (de Sousa Santos 2016: 2). Kuan-Hsing Chen (2010) proposes taking 'Asia' itself 'as a method' in order to deal with the problem of both decolonizing knowledge in general and his specific project of 'decolonizing historical materialism' in particular.

The Current Theoretical Conjuncture

I have mentioned previously that most earlier attempts at something like decolonization of knowledge or theory in India, were undertaken as part of a broadly nationalist discourse which rapidly turned into a project of 'rediscovering' India's past greatness and hence became embroiled in a search for indigenous categories and frameworks. Though this phase yielded some very important work by way of a history of ideas/intellectual history, it not only got trapped within a very narrow, Brahmanical idea of tradition but also remained insulated from the present, from its times. Lower caste challenges to this tendency, notably in Western and Southern India, were quickly marginalized and de-legitimized. They remained in circulation in some circles but found little or no space within the emergent nationalist public.

There is, however, another moment that was not strictly speaking nationalist and where a number of different impulses came together. One strand of it can be linked to an important initiative in the post-independence era that was undertaken during the 1960s, 1970s and 1980s at the Centre for the Study of Developing Societies, Delhi where at least three of the key figures Rajni Kothari, Ashis Nandy and D.L. Sheth formed a nucleus of sorts, enabling a lot of research and intellectual work that was as self-consciously engaged with contemporary politics and culture as it was keen to move away from dominant Western modes of theorizing, based entirely on the Western experience. Although they all started off as intellectuals trained in their respective disciplines of political science, psychology and sociology, their focus was on generating empirical data about political and electoral behaviour that they then attempted to interpret through a deeper sensitivity to the cultural context. By taking this route, they managed to avoid basing their understanding of Indian political behaviour on the high textual tradition of ancient India as though there was a straight line connecting that past with the present. In doing this, they were also able to get a far better handle than many others, on the contemporary changes and transformations in caste consciousness and practices, on the one hand, and the specificity of Indian political culture and democracy, on the other. Ashis Nandy moved towards a deeper engagement with popular culture and cinema as a way of entering the popular psyche. And quite understandably, this exercise was undertaken, perhaps could only have been undertaken at a distance from the academy in the formal sense. Much of the work done by way of a critique of mega Development and mega Science during the 1980s was thus carried out in close collaboration with social movement activists as well as independent intellectuals who worked outside the academy (see Visvanathan 2006). The other important initiative one must mention was the formation of Patriotic and People-Oriented Science and Technology (PPST) movement, formed in 1978 in Madras (now Chennai) by a young group of scientists, who undertook a radical critique of Western/ modern science alongside an exploration of traditional knowledge systems. The interesting thing about this initiative was that it focused not on the so-called 'spiritual mission' of India but on indigenous science, technology and related practices—somewhat in the manner undertaken by Joseph Needham in writing a history of science and technology in China. The group organized three major congresses of traditional Indian sciences and technologies that brought together a large number of people to work and think around these questions. Apart from scientists like C.V. Seshadri, the group also had Gandhian historian Dharampal among its luminaries.[11] It is at this very time that Claude Alvares (1991[1979]) published his *Decolonizing History*, which was about the history of technology and culture in India, China and the West from 1492 onwards. Here too, it was concrete material practices and technology and not India's spirituality that was at the centre of Alvares' concerns. Equally, the inspiration here was not nationalist in any sense but one of retelling the story of science and technology in a perspective that was always-already global. Indeed, it is in Alvares' writings that we see the most sustained concern with the decolonization of knowledge that could already be seen as a precursor to the current conjuncture in some fashion.

This phase flows almost seamlessly into the next—the global one of postcolonial theory, taking off in the wake of Edward Said's work. The story of postcolonial studies is quite well known, and I shall not repeat it here, except make two quick remarks. First, that this was roughly the time when the work of Ashis Nandy that was more directly concerned with a critique of different forms of intellectual hegemony of the West, and that of the Subaltern Studies group of historians opened out new avenues of thinking differently on a number of questions. While Nandy's work was directly concerned with the issue at hand, Subaltern Studies (SS) actually started off as a heterodox Marxist enterprise. The SS scholars started by way of a critique of nationalist historiography and sought to recover the voice of the subaltern—the 'small voice of history', to use Ranajit Guha's expression. The early work of Ranajit Guha, especially his *Elementary Aspects of Peasant Insurgency in Colonial India* in particular, attempted to understand tribal and peasant insurgencies in colonial India largely in terms of their own sense of the world. Partha Chatterjee's *Nationalist Thought in the Colonial World* squarely confronted the question of the relationship of nationalist thought to 'world-conquering' Western knowledge. It was hardly surprising then that this moment in India should tie-up with the rise of postcolonial studies in the global academy. The second point that needs to be made here is that while Ashis Nandy, Subaltern Studies and the later work of Partha Chatterjee were hugely influential in India, postcolonial studies never really had an independent influence within the Indian academy. Nonetheless, there is little doubt that years of postcolonial theory's critique of Western knowledge and theory certainly prepared the ground for the emergence of the current global conjuncture.

There is something distinctly global about the current 'theoretical conjuncture' that is also the point of departure for this book. At one level, this conjuncture is defined by the movements across Africa for the decolonization of knowledge. Starting with the 'Rhodes Must Fall' movement in Cape Town, South Africa, which brought down the statue of the imperial figure of Cecil Rhodes in the University of Cape Town, the movement very rapidly took on the character of a *demand* for affordable education via the Fees Must Fall movement. More importantly, it soon began being articulated as a demand for decolonization of knowledge, echoing once again Ngugi wa Thiong'o's early call for the decolonization of the mind. Between Ngugi wa Thiong'o's 1980s intervention and now, lies an entire period of African scholarship, especially work by African philosophers that paved the way for this moment of decolonization. It does seem though that some strains in the ongoing African decolonization movement (just as in India) are still deeply constituted by *ressentiment* and a desire for some kind of return to the pure source, rejecting the Western heritage altogether, but in another sense, the African moment of intellectual decolonization merges with another that we might call the post-September 11 global moment, which seems to have triggered a veritable earthquake in the field of theory and philosophy. The increased interest in seriously engaging with Arabic/Persian/Islamic philosophical and thought traditions can be seen among scholars of vastly different backgrounds and in different disciplines—philosophy, political theory, art history to name a few (Banaji 2003; Belting 2011; Hobson 2004; Marks 2012; Nusseibeh 2017).

Where we earlier had the postcolonial critique of Western theoretical domination, the present conjuncture saw the emergence of a plethora of new interventions—the 'decolonial option' and 'epistemic disobedience' (Walter Mignolo 2002, 2007, 2011), 'epistemologies of the South' (Boaventura de Sousa Santos 2016), and 'theory from the South' (Comaroff and Comaroff 2016) to name a few of the more recent ones. What marks this moment as unprecedented and new is that unlike postcolonial theory, which focused on critiques of Western knowledge and theory and in an important sense, cleared the way for moving beyond critique, these interventions actually concern themselves with reconstructing social and political theory by drawing on thought-traditions outside the West. There are many other such interventions going on elsewhere in the world, India being one example, where a wide diversity of explorations have been underway for quite some time. One also thinks of Chinese scholars, some of them like Wang Hui, some of whose work is now available in English (though not his *magnum opus*, *The Rise of Modern Chinese Thought*) and many others whose work we only see referred to. Such interventions enable us to understand that there is a larger body of work now, not only being done by scholars steeped in their own linguistic-cultural universes but also that is breaking down disciplinary boundaries like 'political theory' or 'social theory' or 'philosophy'. Precisely because the traditions that they are engaged in excavating acknowledges no such distinction and because the concerns are rather more existential than purely academic, this book too, therefore, uses the term 'theory' as a general term without making any distinction between political theory, social theory or indeed, philosophy.

From some time in the late 1990s, we have also seen the emergence of the new sub-discipline of 'comparative political theory' that has gained many new adherents, especially in the Anglo-American academy (Cooper et al. 2017; Godrej 2009; Tully 2016). Initiated by scholars like Fred Dallmayr (1997), this enterprise also engages with work of the kind referred to previously and has made some significant advances in opening out the hitherto insular discipline of political theory to other, non-Western, traditions. Simultaneously, we have scholars steeped in Sanskrit philosophy, for example, talking of 'comparative philosophy without borders' and 'fusion philosophy' (Chakrabarti and Weber 2015).

In laying out the contours of the proposed field of comparative political theory, Dallmayr positions it in relation to political theory and political philosophy as it is practiced in Western universities and which 'revolves around the canon of Western political thought from Plato to Marx or Nietzsche'—with 'occasional recent concessions to strands of feminism and multiculturalism as found in Western societies'. But he also positions it in relation to the more empirical field of 'comparative politics', which the new field seeks to 'transgress and unsettle', where the very nature of comparative politics (in both its empirical-descriptive avatar and the stylized formal modelling that goes in the name of theory) prevents any questioning of the categories with which it works (Dallmayr 1997: 421). Almost a decade down the line, we have a practitioner lamenting that not much has really happened by way of breaking new methodological paths and making concrete moves in the direction of making comparative political theory really comparative (Godrej 2009: 137). After a decade, we still find another important figure in the field, James Tully (2016) making a passionate case for 'deparochializing political theory.' Tully sees his projects as parallel, if not allied to, projects of decolonization and provincialization, at least insofar as the initial move in all of them is one of 'reparochializing [actually existing] political theory' (Tully 2016: 56). The primary thrust of Tully's proposal for deparochializing is of making political theory dialogical in its true sense and the main bulk of his essay is concerned with suggestions as to how to make the enterprise more democratic and dialogic. He even proposes doing away with the term 'political theory' and calling the project 'comparative political thought' as that will, he argues, take away the weight of a highly specialized academic discipline and make it more open for dialogue (Ibid.: 56–57). While Tully's proposals are well-intentioned, it is perhaps no longer a matter of the Western academy becoming more open and dialogic in relation to other thought-traditions but more importantly a question of agency. Who determines what the agenda of the day for theory will be? What is it that we mean by theory? Is the division between an empirical-explanatory 'social' theory and a non-empirical normative 'political' theory even a valid one for all times and all places? What are the possible reconfigurations that theory might have to undergo, with a whole range of life experiences entering the agenda that were hitherto exiled into the world of empirical history writing? What will the history of modernity and capitalism look like when the bulk of our social and political theorists are either indigenous Americans or Blacks transported during the Atlantic slave trade to the US? Will the cherished narratives of modernity and capitalism as historical progress hold any more? All these—and many more—questions are likely to come centre-stage in place of anodyne notions of 'Justice as Fairness' that refuse to talk of historical injustices that undergird the very Progress that makes such abstract normative theory possible. Liberal political philosophy's insistence on the individual as the centrepiece of all theorizing may actually appear, at least in certain contexts, as a way of excising factors such as the ones mentioned earlier (mass dispossession and genocide) from the discourse of political theory/political philosophy, blocking their very entry into the hallowed precincts of normative theory. However, that will be a different discussion which we cannot undertake here.

Let us return to our point about the current theoretical conjuncture. We can see that a wide range of approaches, methods and even styles and genres all come together in some fashion in constituting this conjuncture of decolonization of theory. Though not in agreement with all of them, this book nevertheless, sees these different impulses as crucial to the success of the project.[12] The need for an alternative body of knowledge, theories, philosophies—not *an* alternative theory in the singular—arises thus from an immense dissatisfaction with the way dominant, hegemonic Theory pronounces its judgement on the rest of the world. Though equally diverse internally, the different components of this Theory share certain common assumptions about modernity, capitalism, secularism and progress and their intrinsic relationship with the West. If it is true, as mentioned earlier that what our social science knowledge, erected on the edifice of this Theory, teaches us about ourselves is (that four-fifths of the world always gets things wrong), then the difficulty has to do with the categories that we deploy in order to understand these societies. As I indicated previously in relation to capitalism and secularism, without going into *specific* philosophies or philosophers, we can say that these categories do not simply innocently 'explain' what happened in the past but also carry huge normative baggage about what *should* be. So, the point really is to turn the question around and ask why is it that 'we' must be studied and understood through these categories? Perhaps we are not doing what you think we are doing or should be doing. Sudipta Kaviraj once remarked in another context, that such a theorization led to a kind of 'ontological depletion' of the non-West. I should clarify at this point, that 'Non-West' is my term and I use it quite unabashedly—*not* as a residual category to refer to something that is 'not West' but more like an Advaitin would say about Brahman—'not this, not this' (*neti neti*, in Sanskrit). This is the Advaitin's way of saying that Brahman is indescribable in positive terms but you can say what it is not. We could call it the global South, or the 'Third World' or the 'postcolonial world'—but all these terms refer to 'us' in a very specific way, a very specific context. So, if we were to talk about the world that has suffered from the consequences of the 'epistemic violence' (borrowing Gayatri Spivak's term) meted out by the modern West, we will find that it is not simply the 'Three Continents' (Asia, Africa and Latin America) that the 'Non-West' must refer to here: it must also include all the indigenous populations that were virtually exterminated in genocides carried out by the civilizers in the USA or Australia, or the Blacks who were transported *en masse* from Africa —who despite being geographically part of the 'First World'/the West or the global North form part of our Non-West, epistemically speaking.

If postcolonial political elites today are chasing the chimera of 'smart cities' and 'cashless economies', it is no less because the only language, the only knowledge, the only theories available to them are those purveyed by the dominant language of the social sciences and of social and political theory that tells them that there is only one way to the Future (also in the singular)—and that is the future that passes through the present of the West. As a result, these elites are always running to 'catch up' but effectively, to stay in the same place—and the cost of this is borne by the poorer populations who are being dispossessed every day, to clear the way for this dream. On the other hand, those who actually live in the United States of America—the indigenous and black people—continue to suffer as second-class citizens. They are not just political victims of a vicious capitalist machine, they are equally the epistemically dispossessed, victims of an equally vicious epistemic machine and hence part of the generic Non-West that I talk of in this book.

This is why the 'Euro-normality' of the social sciences and theory needs to be rectified, that is why it is a part of the larger problematic of decolonization. And the difficulty is that there is no easy solution here as I have already indicated—we cannot simply argue that all Non-Western scholars and thinkers are pure while all Western scholars are imbricated in the hegemonic colonial project. On the contrary, we will find in the course of the book that often it is safer to rely on the scholarship of Western scholars who have devoted decades, immersed in Indian/Sanskrit texts, and understand shifts in their nuances over time than supposedly 'Indian' scholars, who are driven by explicit political agenda. It is not that the Western scholars I am referring to (certainly not all) have no agendas but those are often academic agendas one obviously has to work around those. On the other hand, as outsiders from a different culture, they are often able to discern what is distinctive and different in the culture that they are studying. A case in point is the long and endless debate on 'history' and whether Hindus had a history. Most Indian scholars, even the most respected and serious of them, seem to have had a deep aversion to what they are quick to decry as some kind of an 'Orientalist construction' about India and Hindus. Then we have a whole range of writings which attempt to show that from Kalhana's *Rajatarangini* to the vernacular *buranjis*, we have 'history' everywhere. The point, however, is completely missed—if not obfuscated—if we do not recognize that even for any mainstream text like the *Natyashastra* or the *Arthashastra* or *Manusmriti* or the *Mulamadhyamakarika*, we know little about their authors or the contexts of their production. All we can tell is a range of three centuries within which these authors may have lived and produced their texts. The point is also lost if we do not recognize that there might be something uniquely interesting about a civilization, namely the Vedic that does not leave behind any traces—'no objects or images' but only words. Words—'verses and formulas that marked out rituals' (Calasso 2015: 3). The Vedic people built no temples and left literally nothing except words. This is something worth much more serious exploration than seems to have happened, one suspects, because of the tendency to dismiss the very idea that Hindus had no history. Seen from another angle, this need not have been understood as a 'lack' but as a pointer to a very different cosmology. This is a lack modern Indians start feeling much more intensely in the nineteenth and twentieth centuries, as they embark on their journey of self-discovery. As Sudipta Kaviraj says in [his] study of Bankim Chandra Chattopadhyay, there is a veritable 'outbreak of history' in the nineteenth century—precisely because its lack is felt with such intensity.[13] We cannot pursue this issue here and I bring it up simply to underline that there is no easy way out when it comes to decolonizing thought.

Some Methodological Considerations

This book does not constitute yet another attempt to lay down an agenda for the decolonization of knowledge or theory. It is not a programmatic statement—for the time for programmatic statements is long over. It is rather, an attempt to think through a range of critical theoretical issues by stepping away from the received wisdom of academic social sciences and theory. It, therefore, deliberately refrains from framing similar-looking or similar-sounding phenomena in the Indian context in terms of readily available theorizations from other times and places—an exercise that has so often proved misleading. This attempt comes out of a long and tortuous engagement with our times, undertaken in a context where the academic world has repeatedly disappointed in providing the language, the concepts and the tools adequate for understanding the bewildering world we live in. As indicated earlier, my increasing realization that the academic answer to every question I had was that we were 'not quite there' yet (not-yet modern, not-yet secular, not-yet democratic and so on) was extremely dissatisfying.

Trying to go back to political thinkers of modern India for help was not of much use; indeed, it was so often frustrating. If one went to them with the expectation that these great thinkers would give us alternative visions of modernity, secularism or capitalism, then the experience was inevitably disappointing. Given that with the rare exception of a Gandhi or an Ambedkar here or a Tagore or Iqbal there, most of them seemed to be pretty much in the thrall of modernity as they encountered it 'empirically' as given, and of the idea of 'Progress' as they received it 'normatively' (as a desired goal that led to the modern West), this experience was bound to be disappointing. For one thing, these thinkers were people in the midst of battle, in a life-and-death struggle of sorts, and theorizing in the academic sense was hardly a priority for them. For another, reading them 'historically' and 'contextually' did not seem always the best strategy to adopt. Reading Gandhi and

Ambedkar 'in their context', for instance, seemed to tie us down to endless unproductive restaging of their specific historical battles, without allowing us the opportunity to extract what was of significance in their thought beyond that moment, which had larger implications for understanding the specific character of our modernity. Thus, apart from the caste question that obviously separated the two, there is much more to both Ambedkar and Gandhi, say their very different but very prescient critiques of both the nation and democracy. This 'more' is also evident in their search for some kind of a moral-ethical community beyond the state, well known in Gandhi's case and evident in Ambedkar's later turn to Buddhism. It was important, then, from the point of view adopted in this book, *to contemporize, that is, de-historicize texts and concepts*—not just with regard to modern thinkers but also with respect to concepts from an earlier time. Of course, with ancient texts, we hardly have an option given that we really know next to nothing about the conditions of the production of those texts. By this, I do not mean that the historical context is unimportant. Far from it, it is crucial in understanding the way in which a thinker's thought proceeds, responding to his or her times. It is, in fact, only when we know a thinker intimately in her or his context that we can really get what is of context-transcending significance in her thought. We can summon up different aspects of their thought in our contemporary only when we have thus established a conversation with them.

The situation is worse confounded by the fact that dominant academic modes of reading modern Indian thinkers tend to either reduce them to some recognizable category from within Western thought (for example Ambedkar the liberal or modernist, Gandhi the anti-modernist or anarchist) or frame them within the thought of some Western philosopher/s or the other. From the point of view of the task undertaken in this book, these strategies are hardly helpful, for the simple reason that the questions that are often posed to these thinkers are most often not their questions. It is important, therefore, to maintain some fidelity to the text as well as to the significant shifts and turns in the thinker's thought.

In political thinkers like Gandhi, there is a good deal that is simply implicit in his practice and his scattered and cryptic, though theoretically potent remarks. These are not simply available as theoretical statements or formulations to be 'used', for they have to be excavated and elaborated. Tagore and Iqbal, both primarily poets, do have a somewhat 'philosophical' response to modernity, in Tagore's case drawing on Upanishadic thought and in Iqbal's, on a combination of the Islamic thought and some Western philosophers like Bergson or Nietzsche. Despite his deep investment in the modern, Ambedkar went into it with open eyes and was ever ready to subject its categories to interrogation and presents us with interesting surprises in his own way.[14] Just as Gandhi has his own 'other West' which he admires, so do Tagore and Iqbal connect with a certain West. But even in their case, it is not possible to simply lay our hands on the concepts or formulations they use, in order to develop something like an alternative theory of modernity or secularism. Though all four of them have very different takes, in each of them there is available, an interesting non-Western response to modernity. However, once again, from the standpoint of this book, these would still remain at the level of *a response* to what they perceived as a fundamentally new situation arising out of a Western-manufactured modernity that was given. Gandhi's response was to reject it lock, stock and barrel, while Tagore and Iqbal wanted to inflect this modernity with their own traditional ways of being, transform tradition and yet not surrender to the modern unconditionally. Ambedkar sought to actively intervene to shape it while retaining a critical stance regarding it. However, none of them provide us with a proper critique, let alone alternative theorization of modernity. Among most thinkers in colonial India, what we get by way of critique is a rejection of whatever was understood to be related to 'materialism' of the West, namely its individualism and reduction of human relations to the cash nexus as it were. Indeed, for many of them, believers in *varnashramadharma*, equality too was a Western idea that didn't sit well with Indian tradition.[15]

For there to be anything more than *a response* to an emerging given situation—something like a critique or an alternative theorization—we would have to look outside the field of political action and thinkers who were primarily articulating their ideas in the political field. This would be the field of philosophical thought and scholarship but here too, those who thought they were not really enchanted by the dazzling light of Western modernity, felt more at home with Romantic thinkers of the West and remained obsessed with the idea of 'India's spiritual mission'—an obsession that M.N. Roy had called 'heady wine'.[16] For most of the scholars went back to excavate India's ancient intellectual heritage in the mode of panegyrists, not as critics.[17] Those who went as critics, like Roy himself in his later phase, when he withdrew from politics, were still inclined to read Indian intellectual and philosophical history in terms already understood through their study of Western philosophy. There was little chance in that stance too of coming up with any alternative theorization.

On a somewhat personal note then, my intellectual-political journey started as a Marxist and most of my questions came up, rather, in the course of dealing with the veritable dead-end that I encountered in our political life. If the frameworks and concepts provided by academic social sciences and by theories/philosophies like Marxism failed to illuminate, where should one start looking for answers? Some fascinating new perspectives opened up via feminist theory in some crucial respects especially where questions of 'the political' (the personal is political), production and reproduction, the masculinist nature of most theorization, masculinist nature of nation-states as such, the inherent constructedness of sexual identity and 'experience' were all being thought afresh. While feminists opened up new avenues in one respect, the decisive moment in another sense, came via a 'decentring' of the Western philosophical tradition and its relentless interrogation and critique by poststructuralist thinkers and philosophers. The entrenched orthodoxies in the Western philosophical tradition, let us be clear, were not shaken by any serious challenge posed from the outside but came really from within. Poststructuralism—or what was often derisively labelled 'postmodernism' in the Indian intellectual universe—constituted an internal critique of the Western metaphysical tradition; it was not meant to do our job of thinking our tradition and our challenges for us. However, it did open out a space within which also emerged postcolonial theory in the Western academy and where some of the work being done in countries like India, discussed earlier (for instance Subaltern Studies and Ashis Nandy), found resonance. It should be clarified here that Nandy is by no means a postmodernist or poststructuralist as many people often tended to label him. Nandy's view of South Asian/Indian/Indic cultures is often charmingly essentialist and he is quite unconcerned about dispelling any doubts about his supposed valorization of tradition. When I say his work found resonance within the general atmosphere created by postcolonial theory in the Western academy, post-Edward Said, it should be understood in the specific sense that Nandy's sustained critiques of colonialism and his reading of the 'loss and recovery of the self' under colonialism resonated with critiques of colonial knowledge that were becoming quite influential at that time.

Newer perspectives opened out with the work of these scholars and increasingly the critiques of nationalism, the nation-state, of mega Development and mega Science (or the science establishment) or of secularism by Nandy, invoking Gandhi and Tagore, pointed towards other ways of thinking that came from some of these thinkers. Nandy, in a way, engages Gandhi and Tagore in a contemporary dialogue; he does not simply do a textual exegesis of their writings. Rather, by the time Nandy brings them before us, they have become parts of his own apparatus of thinking, providing him conceptual resources for his own interventions. But here we find elements of a properly theoretical critique, not yet systematic it is true, of certain dominant Western concepts and categories, which are mounted from the standpoint of a radically different cultural-historical context. Such, for example, is Nandy's critique of secularism (drawing on Gandhi) and nationalism (drawing on Tagore).

This then is where this book's concern with decolonization of thought comes in. It draws from all these different strands of scholarly work, drawing unapologetically on modes of engagement wherein concepts, categories and figures from other times and other contexts that become part of our own mode of thinking. After all, we do use concepts from Western theory which ironically appear less foreign to us than say Nagarjuna's *pratitya samutpada* (co-emergence, co-arising) and *sunyata* (emptiness)—two concepts that are silently at work in my understanding of a number of things in this book. When using concepts, irrespective of where they are drawn from, we rarely remain faithful to their original meanings, for quite often the meanings of concepts too fall in the category of *dhvani*, or suggestion which has to do with how it is received in any given context.[18] So when Nagarjuna insists that there is 'no self' (*anatta*) because everything has dependently arisen or co-arisen, he certainly does not mean that I, Nagarjuna, do not exist. This is not a statement about the empirical person but about what we could call the essential self or the self as some ultimate reality. This is not very unlike Marx, in the sixth thesis on Feuerbach (Marx 1976), where he insists that 'the human essence is not an abstraction inhering in each individual' and that, 'In its reality it is the ensemble of social relations'. For Nagarjuna, however, it is not simply about social relations—for a term like that makes no sense in his times—but about everything: Everything is co-arisen and therefore without any substantial, independent identity of its own insofar as its 'ultimate truth' is concerned. Hence *sunyata* or emptiness becomes a general ontological claim.

Given that the continuous running theme in all explorations and theorizations of our 'postcolonial condition' is that of a constitutive 'lack', all theorizations about the postcolonial world are naturally hemmed in by this sense of 'incompleteness'. The postcolonial condition thus is marked by the fact that it remains forever suspended in the space between 'tradition' and modernity', 'religious' and 'secular' or 'precapital and capital'. For a long time, this was understood to be a transitional condition populated by forms that would eventually give way to a full blown modernity, a proper secularism and an unadulterated capitalism. That faith has long been given up—after a brief flicker of hope in some quarters, in the 1990s, when in the wake of 'globalization', it was believed that all the barriers to accumulation would finally be washed away, and along with the advent of this full-blooded new capitalism, the last vestiges of 'pre-modern'/traditional life forms too would be wiped out. Nobody now seriously believes that any such transition is anywhere on the cards.

So scholars suggested we move away from teleological understandings of a single/singular modernity towards notions of 'multiple' and 'alternative' modernities (Eisenstadt, Shmuel, Schluchter 1998). Some of these theoretical moves were supplemented later by a vast range of historical scholarship that began to excavate the erased histories of the non-West—intellectual as well as material/economic—arguing forcefully that much of what went into the making of modernity in the West came from different parts of the world. If John Hobson (2004) spoke of the 'Eastern origins of Western civilization', others like Jack Goody (2006) talked of the 'theft of history, theft of civilization and theft of capitalism' by the West from the East. There were other scholars like Jairus Banaji (2007) who traced the beginnings of capitalism to the massive networks of trade across the Mediterranean, enabled by Islam. The focus of both Hobson and Goody was on the great developments in science and technology in the Arab world and China. Some other revisionist historiography also emerged in roughly the same period that, basing on Catholic Christian accounts of the Crusades, began retelling the story of the renaissance in Europe, consequent upon the discovery of the great storehouses of knowledge that were the libraries of Toledo and Cordoba. They told us a story that had long been lost to the world of how, when intellectual activity in Latin Christendom was completely under the thrall of the Church, giant strides in philosophy and science were being made in the Arab/Islamic world (see Chapter 2). All this work opened out new possibilities, new ways of understanding modernity as not simply a Western product.

While all that scholarship points in the right direction, it was hamstrung, in my opinion, by the fact that it could only rescue non-Western/postcolonial societies by claiming that they too were modern, if in a different way. Here, I do not intend to discuss works like Chris Bayly's (2004) that in exploring the global roots of modernity almost makes it sound like it was some grand collaborative project. At least, the scholarship mentioned previously makes no such claim; on the contrary, it is deeply aware of the violence of the erasure of these other antecedents of the modern. Nonetheless, the difficulty with this line of thinking is that it does not really question modernity as a normative ideal, which remains more or less secure in its place, as defined by the Western discourse on it.

The non-West's deliverance was only possible, it seemed when it made its claim to the normative universe defined by Western modernity. Proponents of notions of alternative and/or multiple modernities, however, took a slightly different tack by taking the more conventional starting point: while 'the common starting point of many of these developments was indeed the cultural program of modernity as it developed in Europe, its creative appropriation by those that followed inaugurated multiple modernities' (Eisenstadt 2000: 1; Eisenstadt and Schluchter 1998: 5). At one level, the truth is somewhere in between but in a way that is very different from the way both these positions assume something called 'modernity', which in itself is not unpacked. In Chapter 2, I undertake a detailed discussion of this question but for the moment let me state the following.

I do remain indebted to the work of the kind mentioned earlier in attempting to think the questions of modernity, capitalism and secularism afresh. However, I take my cue from Anibal Quijano's argument that if the concept of modernity only or primarily refers to the idea of newness, the rational-scientific or the secular, then we cannot get away from the fact that it is possible to find such modernity in all cultures, *across* historical epochs (Quijano 2000: 543). It will, therefore, be my argument in this book that what has colonized the world in the period we identify as the modern is a particular assemblage of ideas, knowledges, technologies and practices sourced from different parts of the world but framed within a discourse of Progress and Reason, characterized by individual rights, the bourgeois property right in particular and the endless creation of wealth as a mark of civilization. This discourse is an exclusively Western product and is very closely tied to the emergence of 'capitalism' as a mode of being. I explain this point at greater length in Chapter 6 but for the moment suffice it to say that as distinct from a 'mode of production', I use 'capitalism' in the way we use terms like 'individualism' or 'nationalism' or 'secularism'—as ways of relating to the world. This discourse, it can be argued, is embodied in the unique apparatus of the State in such a way that it may not be an exaggeration to say that it is really the State (and the Law) that is the peculiarly modern invention that comes to colonize our imagination in this period. In other words, it is important not to conflate everything, from science, technology and reason to different forms of religious coexistence, with the modern or with modernity. Modernity, in this sense, must be seen primarily as a disposition, a way of being that is closely tied to 'capitalism' in the sense previously mentioned and the emergence of the modern State.

It with this understanding that I explore the very idea of modernity and along with it, notions of 'the political'/state, the 'secular' and capital/ism in the chapters that follow. One of the chapters (Chapter 5) deals with the 'secular' and its peculiar afterlife in India but more so in order to also enter the problem of what I call the *paramodern*, for this seems to me to be the most difficult question facing us today. The paramodern, I argue, can be seen as a world at a distance from, or 'outside', modernity so to speak, in the sense in which we use the prefix 'para' in parascience or parapsychology or paranormal. The paramodern in that sense is a world populated by the non-rational or even the irrational, animated by apparitions, hauntings, fear/s, anxieties and of course, by spiritual and religious experiences—all the creatures that had been banished by the moderns from their sanitized world. It was long assumed that what marked Western modernity as truly modern was precisely that it had done away with these beings and ushered in an entirely new era of Reason. In that sense, the paramodern, to the extent it was recognized, remained a question specific only to non-Western/postcolonial societies, where modernity was yet to develop properly enough to be able to transform the unruly, inchoate mass into the *demos*, and into proper individual citizens. In the era of Donald Trumps and Boris Johnsons, this does not seem to be an issue of 'underdevelopment' alone. The figures of Donald Trump and Boris Johnson are mere symptoms of that fact that the paramodern was actually alive, teeming with all the beings banished from modern society.

While I have stated at the outset that there isn't and cannot be any single approach to decolonization, I do need to state my own position a little more clearly. I will do this via a brief engagement with some recent articulations—globally and within India.

Let me begin by simply recalling the opening passages of Dipesh Chakrabarty's (2000) *Provincializing Europe* to underline where my starting point differs. Chakrabarty starts by underscoring the indispensability of the categories like state, bureaucracy, capitalism or civil society, citizenship, democracy, popular sovereignty and so on in thinking the phenomenon 'political modernity' (Chakrabarty 2000: 4). Indeed, he even goes on to say that these 'concepts entail an unavoidable—and in a sense indispensable—universal and secular vision of the human' (Ibid.). Chakrabarty then follows this statement up by listing names of illustrious figures from the non-West who 'warmly embraced themes of rationalism, science, equality, and human rights that the European Enlightenment promulgated', ranging from Indians like Raja Ram Mohan Roy and M.N. Roy to Tunisian philosopher Hichem Djait and of course, Frantz Fanon (2000: 4–5). For me, however, the problem begins precisely because these categories and frameworks are responsible, despite their indispensability, for what I have called following Sudipta Kaviraj, the ontological depletion of the non-West. To be fair to Chakrabarty, he agrees that European thought has 'a contradictory relationship' to the experience of political modernity in India: that it turns out to be 'both indispensable and inadequate' (Chakrabarty 2000: 6).

However, my problem with Chakrabarty's argument will become clear from the way he reads and affirms Ranajit Guha's argument about the 'political nature' of peasant and Adivasi insurgencies in colonial India, in contradistinction to Hobsbawm's claim about the 'prepolitical' nature of such revolts. Guha's critique of the category of the 'prepolitical', says Chakrabarty, 'fundamentally pluralizes the history of power in global modernity' (Chakrabarty 2000: 14), and that 'his point is that what seemed "traditional" in this modernity [of peasants in revolt] were "traditional only in so far as [their] roots could be traced back to pre-colonial times, but they were by no means archaic in the sense of being outmoded"' says Chakrabarty (Ibid.: 15). My problem here with both Guha and Chakrabarty is with their attempt to claim both being modern and being political on behalf of the tribal or peasant populations in revolt, as their justification of the rebellion of the peasants. It is as though without being able to make that double claim of being both *modern and political*, the peasants—and with them, Subaltern historians—were destined to be doomed. To 'pluralize the history of power in global modernity' you do not have to first show that your peasants are modern and political. As the discussion in the subsequent parts of this book will try to argue, it is precisely the assumption that the only thing that 'seemed traditional' about the peasants was that their 'roots could be traced back to precolonial times' that is problematic from my point of view. It fails to even pose the question of 'the outside' of both modernity and capital/ism: once touched by Western colonialism, we simply become modern, virtually without residue; only the roots 'can be traced back', perhaps with great difficulty, to precolonial times. In a sense, it is precisely in order to deal with this modern/traditional binary that I have taken recourse to the category of the paramodern mentioned earlier. Or take Chakrabarty's criticism of Ernest Mandel and Frederic Jameson: 'From Mandel to Jameson, nobody sees "late capitalism" as a system whose driving engine may be in the third world' (Ibid.: 7). Once again, there seems to be no redemption for the non-West until, in Chakrabarty's terms, it can claim to be capitalist, not just modern and political—and the driving engine, no less!

This is the understanding that I move away from in this book. Methodologically, it is, therefore, important for the argument of this book to conceptualize what I am tentatively calling 'the outside' of both modernity and capitalism. In a manner of speaking, we might say that the driving engine of both modernity *and* capitalism lies in the third world or the non-West—in the sense that it constitutes a kind of 'constitutive outside' of these phenomena. Colonialism and slavery then and the immigrants trooping into the 'metropolises' now certainly 'drive' both modernity and capitalism but in a sense very different from Chakrabarty's.

More recently, Jean and John Comaroff (2016) have made a case for 'theory from the South', where they argue (as the subtitle of their book itself suggests) 'Euro-America is evolving toward Africa'. What they mean by this phrase is explained by them at length in the opening chapter. Here, their claim is that 'modernity was almost from the start, a north-south collaboration—indeed a world-historical production—albeit a sharply asymmetrical one' (Comaroff and Comaroff 2016: 6). 'Collaboration', even asymmetrical, is a very strange choice of a word to describe what was an unprecedented process of violent colonization—though once again, in all fairness one should recognize that the Comaroffs do not elide the question of the violence of colonialism generally. But the point of their argument is that to the extent that 'the making of modernity' was 'a world-historical process', its story 'can as well be narrated from its undersides as it can from its self-proclaimed centres' (Ibid.: 6–7). So far so good and one cannot possibly have any problem with this claim. What seems problematic in their rendering is that everything that was once seen as a sign of the 'underdevelopment' and 'tradition' or worse, deformed modernity, is now seen by them as the direction in which Euro-America is now moving. Almost as if, by saying that Africa is the world's destiny, you somehow exalt it. And despite their protestations to the contrary, the picture is quite dark. Thus, 'Hurricane Katrina revealed to middle Americans the extreme poverty, abjection, and inequality in their midst, the hidden effects on infrastructure of the retraction of the resources of the state…the ruthlessness of police in dealing with the indigent…'. Further,

> (B)rutal conflict in the *banlieues* of Paris, attacks on immigrants in the United Kingdom, and the repression of Muslims in the Netherlands have played out similar themes, making clear how, despite the triumphal fetishism of democracy and human rights, of neoliberal deregulation and the freedom to be, the nations of the north are witnessing rising tides of ethnic conflict, racism, and xenophobia, of violent criminality, social exclusion and alienation… Africa, it seems is becoming a global condition.' (Comaroff and Comaroff 2016: 18)

So we realize that when the Comaroffs say that Euro-America is evolving toward Africa, it is not anything positive really nor does it have anything to do with Africa's own achievements in any field—for the way Africa has been theorized, there isn't anything positive to talk about.

However, we can understand the claim that the Comaroffs make in another sense. The point can be made by partially reversing Marx's well-known claim that 'human anatomy is key to the anatomy of the ape' and that 'bourgeois economy supplies the key to the ancient': instead of assuming that the higher form (anatomy of man, bourgeois economy) simply supplanted the lower without residue, these are instances where the 'lower form' so to speak, continues to live a subterranean existence within what were considered 'higher' or modern forms.

Let me conclude this chapter then, by referring Partha Chatterjee's (2011) delineation of the tasks of the postcolonial political theorist. Chatterjee's earlier interventions, where he had elaborated his concept of 'political society', made two simultaneous moves: First, they rejected the dominant narrative of modernity and modern politics as being grounded in the formal discourse of rights and individual citizenship and insisted that there are other modes in which politics takes place 'in most of the world', that need to be seriously contended with, theoretically speaking. These modes of politics, Chatterjee argued, were a constitutive part of the story of postcolonial modernity and were not just prior stages on the way to our final arrival into real modernity. Second, in doing so, Chatterjee did not take recourse to arcane notions of 'indigenous tradition' as have many theorists in the past. In other words, even while recognizing the cultural and historical specificity of the Indian/postcolonial situations, Chatterjee's interventions underlined the ineluctable modernity of the experience of politics that the postcolonial theorist needed to confront. This implied that even in arenas not yet colonized by it, modernity nevertheless remained the 'background condition' of politics.[19] This also meant a recognition of the fact that no body of traditional political and social thought could be equal to the task of theorizing the contemporary experience of politics and that political theory in our parts of the world had a twofold task: Even while challenging the universalist pretensions of Western thought, it would have to desist from the easy option of simply valorizing 'our' cultural difference in some essentialist sense and would have to take seriously the task of producing a body of theoretical concepts that would be context-transcending—though not universalist—in their ambition.

Much of this was implicit in Partha Chatterjee's earlier work. In his subsequent *Lineages of Political Society* (2011), he makes them explicit for the first time and in fact, produces a critique of the dominant mode of doing political theory in the West, especially normative theory. Chatterjee begins by critiquing what he calls 'the mythical time-space of normative theory' that is often assumed to take place in 'an ahistorical and timeless space where perennial questions about the right and the good are debated' (Chatterjee 2011: 1). But as a matter of fact, it is not any abstract ahistorical time-space, says Chatterjee, but that 'these normative debates take place in a time-space of epic proportions which emerged fully formed only after the epochal struggle against an old order of absolutist, despotic, or tyrannical power'; they posit a definite historical past as the era that has been left behind (Ibid.: 1). This allows Chatterjee to undertake a detailed examination of the trajectory of normative theory where empirical-historical difference leads to piling up of exceptions to the theory. He argues,

> The actual practices of modern political life have resulted not in the abandonment of those norms but in the piling up of exceptions in the course of the administration of the law… The relation between norms and practices has resulted in a series of improvisations. *It is the theorization of these improvisations that has become the task of postcolonial political theory.*' (Chaterjee 2011: 19, emphasis added).

The theoretical challenge then is not simply to break the abstract homogeneity of the mythical time-space of Western normative theory; the even greater challenge is to redefine the normative standards of modern politics in the light of the considerable accumulation of new practices that may at present be described in the language of exceptions but which might contain the core of a richer and more diverse set of norms (Ibid.: 22).

To a large extent, I agree with Chatterjee's line of thinking with regard to the challenge for political theorists in our parts of the world today and we need to confront one of the most important implications of this argument straightaway. Going by this line of argument, the world of theory, *even normative theory*, can no longer be kept insulated and protected from the messy and chaotic empirical world. Political theory (or simply theory), if it has to be decolonized, must engage with the empirical—both in the historical mode and the anthropological. It is certainly not necessary that the political theorist become a historian or an anthropologist, but it is of critical importance that s/he engages with the work done by them. This book attempts to, therefore, 'do theory' in the only mode that seems possible to us today from our vantage point.

I would like to add one crucial point to Chatterjee's argument mentioned earlier that relies almost entirely on the conceptual paraphernalia of Western theory and philosophy. And this point obviously has to do with a central contention of this book—that the enterprise of theory or philosophy in the non-West today has to be one of thinking across traditions. The point is emphasized in different ways throughout the book that traditional categories and concepts do not simply die away and are part of the ways of being of ordinary people—even if sometimes in drastically modified forms and those alone give us a way of understanding practices at different levels as well as allow us to see things from perspectives that have now been made invisible in the formal domains of knowledge.

A final point, in conclusion, may be required here. The central *theoretical* concern of the book, any discerning reader will easily see, is with the problem of the '*outside*'. The way we have come to understand the modern world, irrespective of whether we espouse totalizing 'structuralist' philosophies or individual-centric liberal ontologies, they leave us with no space 'outside' the modern. There is no outside to capital, there is no outside to the modern, there is no outside to politics and so on. What I am referring to tentatively, as the 'outside', is the space, however, that most of the world inhabits but believes it is in a world where it cannot but obey 'laws' of the modern, or of capital ending up in creating more problems for itself than it can solve. I put 'outside' within quotes, of course, for the simple reason that the notion of the outside actually presupposes a totality or a structure that I move away from. Nonetheless, it is still a useful term at this stage to draw attention to the specific problem that I want to flesh out.

The next chapter will start by looking at modernity—the key master-concept of social and political theory—from the outside. It will prepare us then to move on to a discussion of other key concepts that I want to discuss in this book.

Notes

1. See, for instance, Ndlovu-Gateshemi (2015) and Nkenkana (2015) that directly adopt the framework of decoloniality in relation to African development and women's liberation respectively.

2. I discuss the idea of the colonial matrix of power a little further in the chapter.
3. This is not to say that there was no opposition, in terms of peasant and Adivasi revolts during the early years of colonial oppression, for example; what we are talking of here is more the response from within the literati. It is, of course, also to be kept in mind that such a generalization does not imply that there were no oppositional intellectuals in the nineteenth century or that everyone in the twentieth, after the hegemony of nationalism was established, was an opponent of colonial rule. What it does mean is that in some form or the other, most intellectuals in the nineteenth century were keen to identify the weaknesses of their own respective communities or society, and to find ways of reforming them so as to make them able to face the challenge of the new times.
4. The expression 'thinking across traditions' was first suggested by Nivedita Menon, as the subtitle for a long essay that I was writing on violence and the political. It was subsequently used as a part of a course title that I was co-teaching with two other colleagues in CSDS. The idea of 'thinking across traditions', for me, was a way of steering clear of the dead-end of indigenism while simultaneously transforming our relationship to Western theory and philosophy—treating it as *one* of the sources for doing theory.
5. Both the expressions in quotes are from *The Communist Manifesto*, written by Marx and Engels and published in 1848.
6. To be sure, as Nandy keeps pointing out, this co-living or coexistence was not about syncretism or about 'loving thy neighbour' but was often about what he calls 'epic consciousness' where the other may be ignored, even despised but whose presence would be essential for the very being of the self.
7. For a recent argument that deals specifically with the RSS and its ideological antecedents, see Jyotirmaya Sharma (2015, 2019). Though one need not agree with all the details in Sharma's elaboration of the argument, it is one of the rarer species of writings that takes the thought-world of the RSS and Hindutva seriously.
8. I borrow the term 'neo-Hinduism' from Wilhelm Halbfass (1990), who in turn borrowed it from the work of Paul Hacker. As a way of differentiating them from the more orthodox '*sanatan dharmi*' Hindus, this is a useful term—though as Halbfass and others have shown at length, even the *sanatanis* and their use of the term *dharma* as religion is not quite as orthodox as is often claimed by the *sanatanis*.

9. Vivekananda (2018) actually says it in so many words in his famous presentation to the World Parliament on Religions (1893). And he says both things in the same breath:

   > The Hindus have received their religion through revelation, the Vedas. They hold that the Vedas are without beginning and without end. It may sound ludicrous to this audience, how a book can be without beginning or end. But by the Vedas no books are meant. They mean an accumulated treasury of spiritual laws....' (Vivekananda 2018: 7)

   In this same lecture Vivekananda continuously invokes 'the Almighty' and 'God' but simultaneously goes into complex acrobatics in trying to determine the relationship between the creator and creation but that is a discussion we cannot go into here. Unlike Sharma (2015, 2019) referred to earlier (Note 2), I do not believe that Vivekananda is a direct ancestor of the Hindu Right. Rather, he is part of a larger milieu in which a churning is taking place in Hindu society and where many of the ideas that eventually go into the fashioning of Hindutva discourse are produced. But they are not all directly compatible in every respect with Hindutva ideology; rather Hindutva ideology draws elements from different sources, systematizes and produces a mix that would perhaps have been strongly disavowed by their authors.
10. It should also be underlined here that just below this vast scholarly enterprise, there began to flourish what one can call a popular neo-Hinduism where a large number of cock and bull stories regarding the 'scientific and technological achievements' of the Vedic people were produced and circulated. Some of these built upon actual developments—for example, reconstructive surgery in which ancient Indians achieved great heights as part of the overall development of medical knowledge, the *Susruta* and *Charak Samhita*. Much of this 'Puranic' or popular neo-Hindu common sense was manufactured, it seems, at a distance from the more serious intellectual work that was being done at the scholarly level.
11. Unfortunately, there is virtually no history of the PPST available anywhere to my knowledge, though one can sift through about a decade and a half of PPST Bulletins (available in the CSDS library) in order to get a sense of the work and debates that engaged the group. Obviously as always happens, different people come together with different inclinations and so it was with a group within the PPST that seemed to have been more drawn

towards the more virulent strands of indigenism, eventually parting ways and going over to the Hindu Right. I am grateful to our former CSDS Librarian and scholar Avinash Jha for sharing his intimate knowledge and insights about the PPST with me.

12. The enterprise of this book is, therefore, very different from the one undertaken by Mahajan (2013) or even Rathore (2017) though there may be points of common interest.
13. I take a different stance here from Thomas Trautmann's (2012) otherwise very illuminating and useful argument. My understanding here is that while Trautmann is correct that the 'Indian' understanding of Time is not necessarily the one we get in the great texts—I am not interested here in going back to the Mesopotamian origin point when all were but one, and there was no difference between Europe and the Rest. My reference point here is the way people relate to time at an everyday level, where Mircea Eliade perhaps gets it better—though we do not need to make a very sharp division between linear versus cyclical time. It is these lived practices that perhaps account for a complete lack of interest in preserving records, making archives, recording history—which is what made Bankim Chandra Chattopadhyay exclaim that the sahebs write even the history of their killing birds, but alas! Bengalis have no history. This void that is felt by people like Bankim is actually a much more prevalent feeling in the late nineteenth and twentieth centuries and needs to be taken seriously. It is precisely in this sense that Ashis Nandy talks of 'millions of people who live "outside" history' (Nandy 2003: 83).
14. His last act of mass conversion to Buddhism is interesting in two ways. First, he did not think of individual exit like most modernists would do but was always thinking from the standpoint of the community. Second, he was in this instance going beyond demanding 'rights' for the community in the domain of Law and the State but transiting to a new community as part of his quest for radical social ethics.
15. This is, in fact, a stated position of the Rashtriya Swayamsevak Sangh even now.
16. M.N. Roy, in his *India's Message: Fragments of a Prisoner's Diary* had noted (in the Preface to the 1950 edition) noted: 'The belief in India's spiritual message to the materialist West is a heady wine. It is time to realize that the pleasant inebriation offered solace to proud intellectuals with an inferiority complex. The legacy of that psychological aggressiveness is not

an asset, but a liability' (Roy 1950: vii). That psychological aggressiveness continues to be a liability today and has in fact led to a closure.

17. Once again, I borrow this distinction from Roy, who said of Sir S. Radhakrishnan, that though he is a recognized authority on Indian philosophy, 'he is a panegyrist, not a critic' (Roy 1950: 181).
18. The concept of *dhvani* or suggestion/reverberation emerges in the course of medieval commentaries and debates on the *Natyashastra*. Says Kapila Vatsyayan: 'Now [post Anandvardhana's *Dhvanyaloka*] the concern is both with the nature of aesthetic experience, the quality of experience, the poetic form, the relationship of 'word' and 'meaning', as also the response of the reader or hearer' (Vatsyayan 1996: 132).
19. The term 'background condition' is Charles Taylor's (2007).

2

Modernity and Coloniality

Beyond Kaviraj's Revisionist Theory

Introduction

This chapter deals with what one might call modernity's 'origin myth'—and the narrative of its rise that Western modernity gives itself. We know the official story 'by heart' by now. This is the story of the heroic struggle through which the modern world emerges from the darkness of the past, of the 'Dark Middle Ages' and the thraldom of the Church. The story begins, characteristically, with the Renaissance in the fifteenth century, passes through the Reformation and finally reaches its apogee with the Enlightenment. It is in the course of these five centuries, with some ups and downs, that the modern world comes into its own, instituting in the process, the sovereignty of Reason, and establishing 'Man' at the centre of the universe. It is in the course of this heroic struggle that Europe itself comes into being, reclaiming its great past in Classical Greece, drawing a seamless 'historical' connection with between that past and the heroic present, whence the dazzling light of the Enlightenment shone on the world, illuminating it and liberating it from the darkness of superstition and blind faith.

Charles Taylor (2007) has complicated the story of what he calls the 'secular age' in recent years but even in his narrative, this part of the story is not contested; at best it is textured and 'put in its place' by explicitly underlining that the story he is telling us is that of Europe alone.[1] Now that is an important corrective and I will return to some aspects of Taylor's argument and narrative later in this chapter but for the moment, I want to underline that the problem with this official, and now, common sense narrative was not just that it presented the European story as a universal one that can be simply rectified by saying that his is merely a story of Europe—or what Taylor calls 'Latin Christendom' (in its premodern avatar). It was certainly problematic and incorrect to claim that the entire world lay mired in darkness, superstition and stagnation till the light of the Enlightenment fell on it and that part is rectified *indirectly* by Taylor's insistence that he is only telling us a European and not a global story. I use the term 'indirectly' because his claim leaves space for other stories to be told but given over two centuries of overlay of the official narrative, it does not really give us a sense of what else was going on in the rest of world and how the European developments themselves might have been affected by them. Taylor himself seems to be quite at sea in this regard. That is why his work remains profoundly Eurocentric in other respects for he cannot get away by not claiming universality on behalf of European modernity. What is really striking, though perhaps not quite surprising, is that in this massive and majestic volume, Taylor remains blissfully unaware of, or refuses to acknowledge, the fact that neither intellectual resources of Europe's Renaissance nor of Europe's scientific and technological development were entirely endogenous in origin. Indeed, even the direct and seamless connection between classical 'Greece' and modern 'Europe' presented by the official narrative, is simply there at work in his text, uninterrogated and unproblematized. Writing two decades after Martin Bernal published *Black Athena* (1987) and a whole host of scholarship in its wake, Taylor nevertheless manages to hold on to the naive idea of classical Athens and Greece being unproblematically part of Europe. After all, it is reasonably well acknowledged by now that 'the roots of Athens were much more in Asia Minor, Persia, Central Asia and other parts of Asia'; they are certainly Afro-Asian (Frank 1998: 8). That ancient Athens belonged to an intellectual geography which was entirely different from what the later European appropriation of it suggests is now fairly widely acknowledged.

I want to emphasize that here I am not talking about colonialism or complaining that Taylor ignores this important constitutive aspect of European modernity; rather, I am concerned with the intellectual, scientific and technological resources that went into the making of modern Europe and what constitutes 'Europe'. Taylor's book was published as late as in 2007 and yet it remains totally untouched by recent scholarship that has opened out some critical dimensions of the European story itself. Before we proceed to look at some of the new insights and information made available by this scholarship, I want to refer briefly to a text by an early Indian Marxist, M.N. Roy, written in the early 1930s. This slim book, *The Historical Role of Islam* (originally published in 1939) is interesting because, unlike Taylor, it displays deep awareness, not only of the historical role of Islam in general but also because it recognizes something that seems to have been forgotten over time—Islam's and the Arab world's contribution to the making of European modernity. Underlining the state of the world at the time of the rise of Islam, Roy says,

> The rich spiritual legacy of the glorious civilization of ancient Greece was almost buried under the dreary ruins of the Roman Empire, and lost in the darkness of Christian superstition. The grand mission of rescuing the invaluable patrimony, which eventually enabled the peoples of Europe to emerge from the depressing gloom of the holy middle-ages and build the marvellous monument of modern civilization, belonged to Saracen arms and the socio-political structure erected on the basis of Islamic Monotheism. (Roy 1981: 9)

One need not agree with everything that Roy says or with the specific deductions that he makes here and there, but there is little doubt that he had grasped what was critical in this story of the rise of Islam and its relationship to the emergence of the modern world. Thus,

> There is no end of testimonies to prove that even in the predominantly martial period of their history, the Saracens were far from being barbaric bands of fanatical marauders, spreading pillage and rapine, death and destruction in the name of religion. Then, the period of conquest was short, as compared to the long era of learning and culture that flourished subsequently under the patronage of the Khalifs [sic].... (Roy 1981: 14)

Roy then goes on to emphasize that Islam 'contributed to the forging of new ideological instruments' which brought about the subsequent social revolution. And what were these instruments? 'The instruments were experimental science and rationalist philosophy. It stands to the credit of Islamic culture to have been instrumental in the promotion of the ideology of the new social revolution' (Roy 1981: 21). It may be interesting to note that to Muhammad Iqbal too, the rise of Islam signified the 'rise of the inductive intellect' (Iqbal 2011: 140).

This is a crucial issue for Roy, who goes on to say, citing Averroes (Ibn Rushd):

> The distinctive merit of the Arab scholars was the zeal to acquire knowledge through observation. They discarded the vanity of airy speculation, and stood firmly on the ground known to them. That great merit of Arabian learning is decisively evidenced in the following view of its doyen Averroes: 'The religion peculiar to philosophers is the study of that which is; for no sublimer [sic] worship can be given to God than the knowledge of his works, which leads to the knowledge of him and his reality....'
>
> [Yet], *the heretic movements of Europe, during the twelfth, thirteenth and fourteenth centuries drew inspiration from the suppressed teachings of the Arab philosopher; and it was the heretic movement that shook the foundation of the Catholic Church* which had held Europe in spiritual subordination throughout the middle ages. (Roy 1981: 68–69, emphasis added)

I have cited at some length from Roy's book in order to underline that this was not an unknown story even in the 1930s. Even to someone like Roy, who was not a professional scholar but an active revolutionary, this perspective was not unavailable—though it was far removed from the dominant self-presentation of European modernity.

In this chapter, I do not want to go into the official narrative of European modernity at any length as it is very well known. Rather, in the next section, I will discuss, in some detail, the 'revisionist theory of modernity' proposed by Sudipta Kaviraj, in order to set the stage to return to the story that is indicated by Roy mentioned previously. Strictly speaking, it is incorrect to say that we will 'return' to that story because we now have, thanks to new historical research and new theorizations, possibilities of a dramatic reorganization of the very idea of 'modernity'. The two sections that follow the next, therefore, will bring in some counter theorizations from different parts of the world to show that: (a) that the official narrative doesn't quite hold, and (b) to the extent that it does, it is an account that makes sense only from the inside.

Official Theory and the 'Sequentiality' Argument

Sudipta Kaviraj (2005) proposes an alternative, 'revisionist theory of modernity' (only in outline though) that builds on an argument that he began making in the mid-1990s, especially in the wake of the rapid dismantling of the old import-substituting industrialization (ISI) model in India as well as in many other parts of the world, under the aegis of neoliberalism. In two companion articles (Kaviraj 1995, 1996), he takes up the relationship between 'democracy' and 'development' (the latter term actually standing in for the violent process of industrialization) for examination. In the early days of neoliberal 'reforms' in India, a massive assault was launched on the ISI model for having held back India's development through active state intervention that meant among many other things, highly regulated 'labour markets', where it was neither possible to leave the determination of wages to the market, nor hire and fire workers at will. This apparently distorted the wage, cost and price structure and held back accumulation. The assault was therefore directly on workers' unions and of course, on employment, especially in public enterprises. The advocates of neoliberalism held up instances of South Korea and Brazil as models of rapid development for the former colonies—both highly authoritarian states that had achieved high growth rates by stifling democratic institutions and crushing the labour movement. It was from here that the question arose as to what the relationship between these two components of modernity might be: Would they always be functionally related to each other, working in tandem, for example, as suggested by the Marxist characterization of democracy as '*bourgeois* democracy'? Could they also be actually acting at cross purposes in some conditions? If so, under what conditions could that happen? And from these questions arose the idea of sequentiality that was later proposed as a key argument in the 'revisionist theory of modernity'. The sequentiality argument, very briefly, claimed that the relationship between democracy and development actually depended upon the contingent fact of which of these arose first, historically, in any particular society. Depending upon the sequence in which they arose, the earlier element could not but impact on how the later elements took shape. In Britain (and Europe generally), where industrialization had already taken place and the dispossessed working class had no rights, so to speak, the demand for democracy arose through the struggles of the workers—and working women. By the time that happened, however, the workforce had already been disciplined in ways conducive to factory regimes and the so-called capitalist 'work ethic'. Perhaps they had already been disciplined into being 'responsible citizens' as well. In contrast, in India, democratic practices and institutions, going beyond just elections, emerged much earlier during the complex course of the anticolonial struggle and eventually impeded the kind of ruthless industrialization that was possible in Europe and Britain. The nature of its capitalism too, therefore, could not but be different. So, the conclusion was inescapable that far from being functionally related to each other, democracy and development had a fragile and contingent relation to each other, which was often antagonistic.[2]

From here, Kaviraj obviously could not but take the next step of asking what this meant for the very concept of 'modernity'. Can 'modernity' be seen as a singular, teleological process that would eventually lead all societies to the same destination? Would not the character of each society, modern in its own way, actually be determined by the actual historical sequence in which these different processes arose within it? And even more significantly, was it at all possible to discuss this differential character of modernity without reference to the other constituent elements that constituted the modern, for example, individuation, secularization, capitalism and so on? If not, how do we then understand this highly heterogeneous and contingent process? Actually, further questions lurk here that Kaviraj does not ask but which I will come to later in the discussion.

By the time Kaviraj came to outline his 'revisionist theory of modernity', his exposition now came to be centred almost entirely on Europe. This has to do with his belief that modernity was an entirely European phenomenon and if one had to theorize about it one had to go back to the story of where it came from. To that extent, the fact that now he was theorizing about 'modernity' that was inescapably European, recourse to the dominant/official narrative seems like the most natural thing to do.

At this point, it may be useful to flag a point of methodological concern that animates Kaviraj's quest though he does not quite put it thus: Can phenomena like 'modernity' or 'capitalism' or 'nationalism' that originated in the West and travelled outward thereafter, be understood to have acquired the fullness of their meaning at the time of their birth itself, or only as long as they remain within the geographical confines of the West? If the shape and form these phenomena acquire in their outward journey are of any consequence; if that journey plays a role in shaping them differently, then their meaning cannot be determined in advance of subsequent historical development.

In the remainder of this section, I want to enter into a discussion on the 'revisionist theory' in order to both underline its strengths and highlight what seems to me to be some of the weaknesses that might allow us to then move to a consideration of the counter-theorizations referred to previously.

Strictly speaking, it is not correct to say that Kaviraj takes recourse to the dominant, or what he calls the received narrative in any straightforward or unproblematic way. For, if that were to be the case, he certainly would not need to articulate a revisionist theory. In marking out his point of departure, therefore, Kaviraj identifies two kinds of difficulties. First, he argued, that the received theory 'expected processual outcomes of modernity to become increasingly uniform', which he felt, despite being true in general terms, appeared quite doubtful on a closer analysis (Kaviraj 2005: 500). Thus, for instance, he says, even though the *modern* state would be quite central to the writing of any political history of India after the mid-nineteenth century, it is equally true that here the bureaucracy, 'one of the modern state's principal institutions', behaved very differently from its European counterparts. It, by no means fits into the theoretical model of a rational-legal authority constructed by Max Weber (Ibid.: 500). Second, he claimed that the very success of democratic politics in India was 'giving rise to patterns of political conduct, trends in collective political behaviour, modes of critical thinking, and evaluative judgement that are impossible to fold back into recognisable European forms' (Ibid.: 500). The 'historical extensions of Indian democracy', though certainly a part of Indian modernity, he suggested, are playing out in completely unexpected ways. Thus,

> Our major theoretical problem, arising out of the restrictive structure of the received theory, was simple but intractable. The easy binary distinction between "traditional" and "modern" habituated social scientists to think of these two as exclusive and exhaustive such that anything not modern was taken to be traditional. (Kaviraj 2005: 501)

To make matters worse, everything modern was so closely identified with being Western, where forms of politics and economic and social behaviour were concerned, that it led to even more serious difficulties. Hence, the theoretical task:

> To recognise the unfamiliar behaviour of Indian democracy, the unfamiliar evolutions of the Indian state, the un-Western urbanity of our cities, and surprisingly unaccustomed twists in economic behaviour, *we required a theory of modernity that could cut itself from its points of origin in European history and conceive of these trends as modern.* (Kaviraj 2005: 501, emphasis added)

So here was the challenge: Even though modernity originated in Europe, its trajectory in the wider, especially non-Western world, required a theory that could describe and explain the modernity of each such society not as something other than modern (distorted, incomplete, corrupted by tradition and so on) but recognizing it as a different kind of modernity. But in order to accomplish this task, it is necessary for Kaviraj to move towards 'disaggregating' the general theory of modernity (Ibid.: 502). The first step towards this is accomplished by mapping out the major conceptual shift that occurs in Europe and its understanding about what was new about its being 'civilized', in contradistinction to the uncivilized or 'rude' and inferior—societies that would have in earlier times be simply understood as different civilizations. In this way, this new discourse produced a homogeneous picture, not only of European civilization but also of the 'inferior', pre-modern societies. 'By this conceptual re-description', says Kaviraj, 'this new theory recast the relation between Europe and other parts of the world' (Ibid.: 503). It also emerged most powerfully in the writings of Karl Marx and Max Weber that this was not just a universal civilization in the sense that it was based on the principles of a universal reason but also that it could in principle, be achieved by other societies as well as it spread outside the boundaries of Europe. 'This common theory reflected with greater accuracy the new relation of power that had emerged between modern Europe and its colonial possessions', says Kaviraj (2005: 504). By the end of the nineteenth century, not only did this theory have an explanatory dimension about modernity in and its future trends in Europe but it also had prognostications about its power to destroy earlier social forms and 'install a universal form'—that would obviously be more desirable (Ibid.: 504).

Here is where the problems begin. Kaviraj's proposal is that we should adopt explanatory aspect and reject the normative 'diffusionist teleology' of this theory, 'in the light of our constant difficulties'. This is fine as far as it goes but what exactly does Kaviraj propose? Instead of the normative teleology, we should '*install in its place a theory which holds that there is a logic of self-differentiation in modernity*. The more modernity expands and spreads to different parts of the world, the more it becomes differentiated and plural' (Ibid.: 504, emphasis added). It is interesting that on other occasions when Kaviraj discusses the problem of democracy or modernity in India for instance, he is very careful to point out the ways in which Indian society itself and its cultural-historical practices are the critical vectors that end up transforming both democracy and modernity. How then does he claim, in this crisp theoretical formulation, that the agent of this entire logic of differentiation is modernity itself? What else can the term 'self-differentiation' mean? I submit that the problem here is with Kaviraj's residual structuralism (and Marxism) that cannot but think of entities like modernity and capitalism as structures that are governed by an internal logic. Thus, while it would make perfect sense for him to speak of the agential role of Indian society and its antecedent practices in the purely empirical sense, the minute he starts theorizing, it is the logic of the structure or totality that must take precedence.

However, that is still not my main issue with Kaviraj's argument so let us now move to the key sections of his essay and the central and most important move that he makes in understanding modernity. Here is what he says:

> Theorists who analyse modern European history acknowledge that the phenomenon called *modernity is not a single, homogeneous process*, but a

> combination of several which can be isolated and distinguished. When we are talking about modernity, we are talking about a number of processes of social change which can be studied or analysed independently of each other—such as, capitalist industrialisation, the increasing centrality of the state in the social order (Foucault's 'governmentality'), urbanisation, sociological individuation, secularisation in politics and ethics, the creation of a new order of knowledge, vast changes in the organisation of family and intimacy, and changes in the fields of artistic and literary culture. *If modernity can be shown to be analytically decomposable into these constituent processes, that raises a further and crucial question: how should we view the relationship between them*? (Kaviraj 2005: 508–509, emphasis added)

In this remarkable passage, Kaviraj lays bare the key question about the relationship between these several different processes that can, in fact, be studied and analyzed independently. Notice the use of the term 'combination': If modernity is not a single, homogeneous process but a combination of several...'. Now, a combination defines an external relationship in contradistinction to a totality or a structure. A combination is a contingent coming together of various different processes or elements and unlike a structure or a totality need not have any logic of coherence—a logic of the whole—at all. So, the question that immediately presents itself is that of the precise relationship between say capitalist industrialization, governmentality, secularization, individuation, democracy and so on—between any two of them and between them together. Are they all coeval? Do they have the same origins? Are all processes that are coeval necessarily governed by the same logic? Schematically, Kaviraj identifies two ways of conceiving their relationship—*symmetrical* and *sequential*. The dominant view in the social sciences sees these relations as symmetrical because it sees them as being functionally related to each other such that 'either all of them would emerge, evolve and survive interdependently, or none at all'. Further, 'the emergence of any one or more of these constituents creates conditions for the emergence of others, leading eventually to the establishment of the whole constellations' (Ibid.: 508–509).

As opposed to this, it is the sequential view, he argues, that can and does allow us to see that if one process precedes the other historically, it actually becomes an antecedent condition for the ones that follow and therefore, it cannot but determine the form and shape that the subsequent ones will acquire.

The interesting thing, however, is that once Kaviraj has made this point, it will actually be difficult to find any serious theorist in the West who has actually ever undertaken to provide a comprehensive theory of something called *modernity*—except perhaps modernism in the domain of art theory and art practice. In a footnote (note 38) Kaviraj points out that interestingly, 'practically every single separate process in this complex has been given its 'proper' theory—Smith and Marx on industrialization, Guizot and Foucault on what is now called governmentality, Weber on rationalization of bureaucracy and secularization, Tocqueville on democracy, Toennies on individuation, supplemented by various theories of the city, of modern art and the novel, gleaned from the works of Baudelaire, Benjamin, Bakhtin and many others' (Ibid.: 508).

What Kaviraj finds interesting is that all these other processes have their own theorists but it is no less interesting that beyond all the processes and theories (and theorists) that he identifies, it will perhaps be impossible to find a single theorist who has studied and provided a comprehensive 'theory of modernity'. Even the works that have 'modernity' as their explicit object of inquiry do not really provide us with any comprehensive theory as such in the way we have the development of theories of capitalism or secularization for instance. To take but the most obvious example: Neither in *The Philosophical Discourse of Modernity* (1987, hereafter PDM) nor in the celebrated 1980 acceptance speech he delivered at the award of the Theodor Adorno Prize, 'Modernity: An Unfinished Project' (see D'Entreves and Benhabib 1996, hereafter MUP) does Jurgen Habermas actually seek to define or provide any comprehensive theory of modernity. In MUP, Habermas focuses almost exclusively on aesthetic and cultural modernity, referring to *social modernization* only in passing, largely through a discussion of scholars like Daniel Bell and Peter Steinfels. Apart from these, he devotes a section of the lecture to the 'project of Enlightenment' where the maximum that we get is his very brief summary of the project of modernity as it was formulated by the *philosophes*:

> The project of modernity as it was formulated by the philosophers of the Enlightenment in the eighteenth century consists in the relentless development of the objectivating sciences, of the universalistic foundations of morality and law, and of autonomous art, all in accord with their own immanent logic. But at the same time it also results in releasing the cognitive potentials accumulated in the process from their esoteric high forms and attempting to apply them in the sphere of praxis, that is, *to encourage the rational organization of social relations.* (D'Entreves and Benhabib 1996: 45, emphasis added)

That is the maximum that we can get here—the rational organization of social relations. Immediately after this, he goes on to discuss how very little of the optimism of the Enlightenment remains in the twentieth century. In the grander project of PDM, where Habermas mounts his systematic defence of modernity, seeking to rescue it from the hands of the 'postmodernists' and their forebears, the critics of the Enlightenment—Nietzsche, Heidegger, Bataille, Horkheimer and Adorno, Foucault, Derrida and others—through a series of lectures, too he neither defines nor presents a comprehensive theory of modernity for his readers. He discusses modernity's consciousness of time and lets us be content with a full lecture devoted to 'Hegel's concept of modernity'. It is by way of Hegel's critique of subjectivity and the 'authoritarian embodiments of a subject-centred reason' that we are given a glimpse of Habermas' own concept of communicative reason (Habermas 1987: 30–31). If there is any theory or concept of modernity that Habermas provides us in PDM, it has to do with the new time-consciousness of modernity, its orientation to the future, evident in the 'dynamic concepts' that emerged together with the 'modern age' or 'new age' in the eighteenth century or acquired new meaning then that continue to have meaning in our time—words like revolution, progress, emancipation, development, crisis and *Zeitgeist*.[3] Alongside, Habermas insists on the idea, specific only to the modern age, that 'modernity has to create its normativity out of itself' (Ibid.: 7).

It seems then that most often the concept of modernity is assumed to be the state that emerges once universal reason establishes its dominion, or as Habermas put it, 'rational organization of social relations'. Secularization, disenchantment, rational-legal authority, individuation and indeed, civil society and capitalism—all emerge as consequences of this key, all-important development in Europe.

This does not mean, however, that Kaviraj's insight that modernity is not a single, homogenous process becomes any less important for us. On the contrary, it allows us to see it as a constellation in the most literal sense. After all, a constellation like the Ursa Major or Ursa Minor does not actually exist. It is only by convention that we discern that particular shape, made by connecting seven stars together into a figure. By breaking down the constellation of modernity into its constituent processes or phenomena, Kaviraj opens out a pathway that ironically also reveals the limits of his theorization.

Complex Chronologies: Beyond Sequentiality

Once we have performed the Kavirajian operation of disaggregation of modernity, another set of questions arise. Unlike many scholars who have lately been arguing that modernity is and has always been a global project, I agree with Kaviraj that modernity as this particular constellation, this assemblage that he has just taken apart is of entirely European provenance. But if we look at the elements more closely, we will find that each of the different elements has a discrete history that goes way beyond the borders of Europe and to remote and distant times. In other words, the singular linear chronology that the idea of sequentiality entails is immediately put into crisis as soon as Kaviraj has finished with his operation. In the brief discussion of M.N. Roy mentioned earlier, we have already encountered one such genealogy—that of Reason that connected classical Greece via the Arab *falasufs* and Ibn Rushd in particular, to the beginnings of rationalism in Europe. The endogenous story of the secular age that we learned from Charles Taylor, tracked the particular developments within Christianity but seemed completely oblivious of the long history of reason and where it tied up with the fate of modern Europe. But there are other histories as well—the history of science and technology where both China and the Arab world were centuries ahead of Europe that lay prostrate before the power of the Catholic Church.

In this section, I want to track some such genealogies of the processes and phenomena that went into the making of modernity—genealogies that have been made available to us thanks to a huge and continuously expanding body of historical research.

Since the question of the spread of Reason and rationalism is so central to this autobiography of Western modernity, it may perhaps be best to start precisely with the story of its difficult emergence that will give us an altogether different picture from that painted by Charles Taylor and the dominant narrative, as well as from Kaviraj's account.

The story actually begins around the time of the Crusades with figures like Adelard of Barth and Michael Scot who went out in search of Arab learning (Lyons 2010; O'Brien 2011). Thus, for instance, drawing on contemporary Catholic accounts, Peter O'Brien tells us:

> The Crusades opened Latins' eyes to further dimensions of Islamic superiority beyond military prowess. Reports and tales of what the Crusaders experienced in the far off lands were immensely popular back home. This literature overflowed with descriptions of splendors unknown to Latin Christians. The Arab cities were larger, the palaces lovelier, the merchants wealthier, the wares finer, the food tastier. In point of fact, many of the most coveted luxuries in Europe—rubies, emeralds, carpets, ceramics, silk, damask, sugar, bananas—reached Europe via major ports in the Near East where European merchants conducted business with worldlier Muslim traders connected to the Far East.' (O'Brien 2011: 20)

However, O'Brien tells us, it wasn't simply the material advances that caught the medieval Christian but more importantly,

> *Perhaps the most stunning, and humiliating, revelation of Islamic superiority occurred in philosophy, natural and metaphysical.* By the time of Charlemagne (742–814), medieval Latins had lost all but the thinnest contact with the tradition of ancient learning. The Church became the sole (official) authority of what counted as knowledge...
>
> By contrast, cultivated Muslims embraced ancient learning. Not only did they preserve and venerate the works of Greek masters such as Plato, Aristotle and Euclid that were lost to the Latins, Islamic and Jewish sages the likes of Musa al-Khwârizmî, al-Farabi, al-Ghazzali, Abu Ma'shar (Albumasar), Ibn Sina (Avicenna), Ibn Rushd (Averroës),

> and Maimonides augmented and improved the inherited storehouse of knowledge. No wonder, then, that exposure to this corpus stunned the less mature Western mind 'like a bombshell'. (O'Brien 2011: 21, emphasis added)

Jonathon Lyons' (2010) masterful and fascinating reconstruction of this story details the role played by two central characters—among many others of the time—in bringing Arabic learning to Europe, namely Adelard of Barth and Michael Scot in the twelfth and thirteenth centuries respectively. Adelard of Barth is, of course, the pioneering figure to have begun the enterprise of acquisition of Arab knowledge and Lyons tells us that although he had managed to get access to a very large number of works in Antioch, 'nothing had prepared Adelard for what he found in his dogged pursuit of what he called *studia Arabum*, learning from the Arabs.' How he came to acquire many of these works itself forms an interesting story. Sometime before Adelard arrived in Antioch from England, 'combined Norman and Genoese forces' says Lyons, 'had captured the city of Tripoli' and cites *The Damascus Chronicle of the Crusades*, a contemporary Arab account, to tell us that in the booty carried off from Tripoli 'by the victorious Christians were "the books of its college and libraries of private collectors"'. Thousands of these works, says Lyons, 'ended up in the hands of Antioch's merchants, now within easy reach of the man from Bath' (Lyons 2010: 3).

Pioneering though they were, Adelard of Bath's scholarly explorations, Lyons informs us, largely ignored philosophical or theoretical texts. 'For his translation of Albumazar, after all, Adelard chose the author's abbreviated text, without its philosophical core. His strong leaning towards the more technical disciplines of Arab astronomy and astrology set the direction of the first wave of the Latin translations carried out in Spain' (Lyons 2010: 157). As Western scholars dug their teeth into the new knowledge becoming available to them, they acquired greater and greater sophistication and 'it was a matter of time before they would venture from the mildly problematic matter of astronomy and astrology ... to the downright dangerous learning of Arab and Greek cosmology and metaphysics.' Bridging this gap between the two, says Lyons, is the figure of the Michael Scot (Ibid.: 157–158).

The reign of Frederick II (1198–1250) constitutes a significant milestone of sorts—an unprecedented moment in the opening out of a certain Europe to the broader world and to the world of ideas. Frederick II emerged as a patron of the sciences and of philosophy, supporting Muslim and European Christian but also Jewish scholars and corresponding with 'learned figures and rulers throughout North Africa, Al-Andalus, and other centres of Arab science' (Ibid.: 168). Michael Scot, we are told, joined Frederick II's court sometime in the mid-1220s 'on the strength of a reputation earned in Spain', whereupon arrival in Toledo around 1217, he had 'set about translating an important Arab treatise on the heavens and three of Aristotle's most influential works, *On Animals*, *On the Heavens*, and *On the Soul*, from the Arabic versions' (Lyons 2010: 169).

Before we proceed any further, it might be of some interest to see the way the Arab thinkers related to Greek philosophy and Aristotle, who was without doubt greatly revered. This will also help us understand what these *falasufs* were doing with Aristotle's work almost fifteen centuries down the line. In the ninth century, the philosopher al-Kindi, the first among a line of great *falasufs*, while acknowledging his debt to the Greeks, 'also makes it clear that the Arab thinkers were intent on advancing classical wisdom and adapting it to the needs of Muslim culture.' Thus, says al-Kindi:

> It is fitting then to remain faithful to the principle we have followed in all our works, which is first to record in complete quotations all that the Ancients have said on the subject, secondly, to complete what the Ancients have not fully expressed, and this according to the usage of our Arabic language, the customs of our age, and our own ability. (cited in Lyons 2010: 175)

What seems quite remarkable is that the Greeks are here simply referred to as 'the Ancients', almost as though there is a direct connection between that world and the contemporary Arab world—temporal distance is all that separates them. And no less remarkable is the fact that al-Kindi goes on to underline that '"research, logic, preparatory sciences, and a long period of instruction" are the only way for ordinary people—meaning those who are not blessed by God with prophecy—to attain knowledge' (Ibid.: 175).

Michael Scot, in the event, became the key translator and transmitter of the works of Ibn Rushd (Averroes) to the world of Latin Christendom. It was his translations, 'underwritten, transcribed, and forwarded to the universities at Frederick's command, that did more than anything to bring the Commentator's [that is Averroes'] comprehensive views on philosophy, particularly his reading of Aristotle, to the immediate attention of the Latin-speaking world' (Lyons 2010: 173). Among Averroes' 'most incendiary philosophical teachings' was the idea of 'the Eternity of the World, in contradiction to the traditional Muslim, Christian, and Jewish understanding that God made the universe at a time of his choosing and then controlled each and every event in it' (Ibid.: 174). As opposed to this, the Arab philosophers held that though God created the universe, he left it to human beings, his supreme creation so to speak, to understand, follow and execute his purpose as Iqbal too was to put it centuries later.

And with the availability of Averroes' works in Europe, a whole new ferment of ideas began to take shape. He died in 1198 and as Lyons puts it,

> Within little more than half a century of his death, he was the undisputed star of an intellectual drama playing out along Paris's Street of straw, the legendary scholars' lane that ran through the theological heart of western Christendom (Lyons 2010: 183)

Further:

> By the time of Thomas Aquinas's arrival in the late 1260s, things in Paris had deteriorated still further. Many among the arts masters [in university arts faculties] were openly asserting their right to pursue philosophical speculation wherever it might take them. This generally meant incursions into territory the theologians guarded jealously for themselves, including speculation on the Creation, the soul, and the attributes of God. (Lyons 2010: 189)

The rest, as they say, is history. It would be interesting to actually delve a bit into the actual philosophical issues at stake but that is not possible within the scope of this chapter. However, one thing seems to be quite clear—virtually all the key issues related to the existence of God, the meaning of Creation and the Eternity of the universe that were to dominate the struggle against the Church's authority in Europe, were all pretty much in the centre of the *falasuf's* concerns. It is as misleading, however, to assume that this is all they were debating, as it is to see these philosophers as just 'Aristotleans', who did no more than interpret the master, so to speak.[4] Their concerns, given the context of monotheistic Islam, within which they were writing, and the central concern of a tenth-century philosopher like Al-Farabi with his ideas of the 'virtuous city' (*al-Madinah al-fadila*) and the role of the new ruler who founds the new political community (as opposed to the traditional ruler), are already shot through with matters that would be later designated as 'secular' in Europe, several centuries down the line. Christopher Colmo (1998), in fact, likens al Farabi's enterprise to that of Machiavelli's concern with the Prince—or the founder of a political order. 'The founder of religious community can use religion to bind the community together, uniting it towards a single goal', says Colmo paraphrasing al Farabi. He adds that '(T)o affirm this truth while placing prudent limitations on the universal claims of religion is al Farabi's intention in the *Book of Religion*' (Colmo 1998: 719). al Farabi recognizes the place of both, religion and philosophy but accords a higher place to philosophy on the basis of a novel and interesting argument. He bases his argument on the claim that there are also false prophecies and false prophets and it is only philosophy that allows us to distinguish which one is genuine and which not.

Majid Fakhry, in his fascinating study of Ibn Rushd/Averroes (Fakhry 2001) gives us a glimpse of the subsequent trajectory of what Ernst Renan has called 'Averroism' in Europe. In order to give a sense of the impact and of the figures involved, let us cite Fakhry himself:

> Before long, however, there grew around Averroes' name a large and determined circle of followers, first at Paris and subsequently at Padua and elsewhere in Italy, known as Latin Averroists. Their leaders in Paris were Siger of Brabant (d. 1281) and Boethius of Dacia (d. 1284), whose influence in theological circles was such that the church authorities at Paris were compelled to intervene. Thus in 1270, Etienne Tempier, Bishop of Paris, issued a condemnation of fifteen propositions which

> were in conflict with Catholic doctrine, according to him. (Fakhry 2001: 134)

However, he continues,

> Averroism continued to gain ground in Italy, especially at Padua. The great Florentine poet, Dante Alighieri (d. 1321), himself based upon Averroes' theory of the possible intellect a whole new secularist theory of the state in his *De Monarchia.* This theory was intended as a challenge of the Papal claim that the emperor receives his authority from 'the Vicar of Christ', rather than directly from God. (Fakhry 2001: 135)

During the first half of the fourteenth century, the leading Italian teachers at Padua 'carried the torch of Averroism, whether in philosophy or medicine'. Among these figures were teachers like 'Gregory of Rimini, Jerome Ferrari, Fra Urbano of Bologna, Marsilius of Padua, John of Jandun and Pierre of Abano'. 'John of Jandun (7. 1328) was the most famous of those teachers' and as a 'thoroughgoing Averroist, John of Jandun upheld the eternity of the world, the unity of the intellect and the impossibility of personal immortality, on philosophical grounds, in an unqualified manner' (Fakhry 2001: 136). A close friend of John of Jandun was Marsilius of Padua (d. 1343) with whom he jointly published a political treatise entitled *Defensor Pacis* (Defender of Peace) that had 'profound Averroist undertones', says Fakhry. 'In this treatise, Marsilius defends the thesis of the separation of reason and faith, at the philosophical level, and that of the church and the state, at the political level—a thesis that was thought to follow from the teaching of Averroes' (Ibid.: 136). This tradition continues right into the sixteenth century and among other Italian masters, Fakhry names 'Gaetano of Tiene, Michael Savonarola and Pietro Pompanazzi (d. 1525) about whom he cites Renan as saying:

> If we apply the name Averroist to this family of thinkers who were troubled and exasperated by [religious] constraints, so numerous in Italy during the Renaissance, and who hid behind the name of the Commentator [that is Averroes], Pompanazzi must be placed in the forefront of Averroists. (Fakhry 2001: 137)

This genealogy of reason and 'secular' thought, we can see, tells us a very different story of the accounts of both Charles Taylor and Sudipta Kaviraj, both of whom present us with a story of modernity's rise that is entirely internal to Europe's development. It is also worth remarking here that any such internal-to-Europe account of the rise of the modern age, almost inevitably ends up reproducing what is by now the received common sense about the rest of the world, which too is presented as lying submerged in superstition and darkness till the light of the Enlightenment fell on them and redeemed them in some fashion. Janet Abu-Lughod, in recalling the backdrop to her landmark *Before European Hegemony* (1989), remarks that her work on the history of Cairo had convinced her that the Eurocentric view of the Dark Ages was ill-conceived.

> If the lights went out of Europe, they were still shining brightly in the Middle East. Visiting and studying most of the major cities in that region of the world reassured me that Cairo was only one apex of a highly developed system of urban civilization.' (Abu-Lughod 1989: ix–x)

We have so far seen one aspect—that of the intellectual-philosophical developments in the Muslim world that fed into the making of modern Europe. Let us now take a brief look at the developments in science and technology, where again Europe drew on major and critical developments in the Islamic world as well as in China.

It is obviously not possible here to recount all the ways in which the developments in science and technology elsewhere went into the making of the modern age. At best, one can only indicate very broadly here. The reference to astronomy has already come up a few times, starting with our discussion of M.N. Roy's views but it might perhaps be of some interest to indicatively cite an episode from George Saliba's work (2007). This episode pertains to the discovery of Ibn-al-Shatir's work and the role it played in the formation of the Copernican heliocentric view of the world. Saliba's book devotes fairly long sections to the preoccupations of the Arab astronomers with Ptolemy's work—which they even corrected in crucial respects (Saliba 2007: 67). A sheer accident in 1957, Saliba tells us, brought to the attention of

Otto Neugebauer, 'who was then working on the mathematical astronomy of Copernicus, a text that contained the theoretical astronomy of the famous Damascene astronomer Ibn al-Shatir (1375).' It did not take Neugebauer great effort to figure out, despite unfamiliarity with Arabic 'that Ibn l-Shatir's lunar model was indeed identical, in every respect, to that of Copernicus' (Saliba 2007: 196). Edward Kennedy, a friend of Neugebauer, who was then a professor of mathematics at the American University of Beirut and himself 'a distinguished historian of Islamic astronomy', actually brought the model in Ibn al-Shatir's text to the latter's attention. Kennedy had encountered the work of al-Shatir while working in the Bodleian Library at Oxford and it was a student of his, Victor Roberts who then published an article titled, 'The Solar and Lunar Theory of Ibn al-Shatir: A pre-Copernican Copernican Model' (Ibid.: 196).

> For Neugebauer to find that there was a direct connection between the works of Copernicus and the Arab planetary theories, which were produced in the Islamic world about 200–300 years before, was a discovery that was shocking in its own time and has not been fully digested yet in the secondary sources dealing with the history of science in general. (Saliba 2007: 196)

The setting up in Baghdad of the Bayt al-Hikma or the House of Wisdom, under the aegis of the Caliph al-Mamun was a landmark event in the intellectual history of the world as that was the place that functioned for almost four hundred years, till the 'sack of Baghdad' after the Mongol attack, as the centre where knowledge from all over the world was translated, debated and stored. But the story actually begins even earlier, with the shifting of the capital of the Abbasid Caliphate to Baghdad in 762 CE by the second Khalifa, al-Mansur. Already, al-Mansur had begun the process of drawing from all sources of knowledge and learning from across the world—Chinese, Persian and Hindu and so on. It is during his reign, in 771 CE that a delegation of 'Hindu sages' arrived in Baghdad that changed the course of subsequent intellectual history in a manner of speaking:

> At the caliph's invitation an Indian scholarly delegation skilled in the movement of the stars arrived in Baghdad bearing Hindu scientific

> texts, an important jumping-off point for early Arab astronomy and mathematics. The Hindu sages understood how to solve equations based on the trigonometric sine function and had devised ingenious ways to predict eclipses. The caliph ordered an official translation of the Hindu material into Arabic, part of an increasingly organized effort to absorb Persian and Indian knowledge. (Lyons 2010: 62)

It is not quite true either that the efforts of al-Mansur were initially directed at translating classical Greek works into Arabic—an impression sought to be conveyed by a certain narrative that while acknowledging the great strides made by Arab science and philosophy, still represents them as being in the thrall of Greek learning. In fact, it seems that the approach towards Persian and Hindu knowledge—its translation, 'accompanied by original research, would soon be applied with great effect to the third important strand of ancient learning, that of the Greeks' (Lyons 2010: 62).

It was to 'accommodate the vast scale of work needed to translate, copy, study, and store the swelling volume of Persian, Sanskrit and Greek texts' that al-Mansur established a royal library 'modelled after those of the great Persian kings, which eventually became the basis of the famous Bayt al-Hikma (Lyons 2010: 63). But still, long before the Bayt al-Hikma was set up, 'the visit of the Hindu delegation to the Abbasid court, around 771, marked a turning point in Arab intellectual history'.

> The Indian sages brought with them prized Sanskrit scientific texts, believed to be in part the work of the seventh-century scholar Brahmagupta and known as the *siddhanta*. According to a tenth-century account by the widely travelled geographer, al-Masudi, the documents contained all Hindu knowledge of the spheres, the stars, mathematics and other sciences. Another account notes the heavy reliance in the *siddhanta* on the sine function—an invaluable contribution developed by the Hindus and later seized upon and refined by the Arabs—as the basis for all its calculations. By the ninth century, all six trigonometric functions—sine and cosine, tangent and cotangent, secant and cosecant were known. Only the former was an import; the other five were Arab discoveries. (Lyons 2010: 70–71)

Around the same time as the transmission of Hindu astronomy, Indian mathematics, fundamental to which was the decimal place system with nine numerals and a zero, too came to be known in the Arab world. The key figure here was that of al-Khwarizmi, based in the Bayt al-Hikma, who 'produced a successful treatise on the use of the new system, *The Book of Addition and Subtraction According to the Hindu Calculation*, the first known Arabic work on the subject' (Lyons 2010: 73).

The interesting point to note here is that while this new system was adopted by Arab scholars and its use proliferated between the eighth and tenth centuries, Europeans took another couple of centuries to adopt it. It was in 1202 that a Pisan merchant Leonardo Fibonacci, significantly, living in Tunis and 'persuaded by the new Eastern concepts', 'wrote a book rejecting the old abacus system in favour of the new Hindu-Arabic system. The new system finally emerged within the Italian merchant communes' (Hobson 2004: 176–177). And it is hardly controversial now, remarks John Hobson, citing Charles Singer, that 'the European adoption of this Eastern numerical system "was a major factor in the rise of [Western] science, and was not without effect in determining the relations of science and technology in the sixteenth and seventeenth centuries"' (Ibid.: 177). We could also note here in passing that neither complex capitalist methods of accounting nor the colonial drive for enumeration and classification would have been possible without this numerical system having become the general system of calculations.

Hobson also tells us that

> Al-Khwarizmi's work on algebra was equally important and was translated into Latin in 1145 by the Englishman Robert of Ketton as well as the Italian, Gerard of Cremona. Ketton's translation of al-Khwarizmi's work was 'Algorithmi' (hence the term 'algorithm'). And the term 'algebra' came from the title of one of al-Khwarizmi's books *Al-Jabr W'almuqalah* (given that al-jabr was translated as algebra). (Hobson 2004: 177)

It is also worth registering here that Al Khwarizmi's book remained the major text on its subject in Europe right down to the sixteenth century.

Hobson cites Francis Bacon who 'famously claimed in his *Novum Organum* (1620) that the three most important world discoveries were printing, gunpowder and the compass' and observes that strikingly, 'all three were invented in China' (Ibid.: 57). We might add, that strikingly without these three, there might have been no colonialism! The Chinese also discovered, around 1000 CE that the magnetic north and true north were not the same, a knowledge that by the fifteenth century 'enabled the construction of the most accurate maps then known' (Hobson 2004: 57).

'By 1100 the leading edge of global intensive power', says Hobson, 'had shifted across to China and remained there till the nineteenth century. China also developed considerable extensive power and came to dominate in this respect after the fifteenth century...' (Ibid.: 50). Hobson designates the economic advances made by China in the eleventh century, in the period of the Sung dynasty, as the 'first industrial miracle', where 'many of the characteristics that we associate with the eighteenth century British industrial revolution had emerged by 1100' (Ibid.: 50). 'China's "industrial miracle" occurred over a period of 1500 years says Hobson, and culminated in the Sung revolution—some six hundred years before Britain entered its industrialization phase.' Hobson's claim is that 'it was the diffusion of many Sung Chinese technological and ideational breakthroughs that significantly informed the rise of the West' (Ibid.: 51).

It is impossible to detail the developments in China in economic terms during this long period but it is true that Hobson is not the only one making such a claim about the Chinese miracle. In recent years, following upon the work of economic historians such as Bin R. Wong (1997) and Kenneth Pomeranz (2000), a lively debate has come up as to why, despite this mind-boggling level of development, it wasn't China but Europe that took the course of capitalist development and embarked on the road to 'modernity'. However, two points made by Hobson (among many others) are interesting from our point of view. First, 'China's iron and steel miracle goes back to 600 BCE with the first cast-iron object dating from 513 BCE, and steel being produced by the second century BCE.' In terms of the gross annual production of steel, China produced 13,500 tons of iron in 806, about 90,400 tons by 1064 and as much as 125,000 by 1078. In contrast, Europe as a whole would only produce greater volumes by 1700 and that even as late as 1788, Britain was producing only 76,000 tons (Hobson 2004: 51) Second, one particular Sung innovation 'was the creation of a tax system based on cash. While paper money was invented around the ninth century for credit purposes, by the early tenth century it evolved into "true" paper money as a medium of exchange.' 'By 1161 the state was issuing ten million notes a year. Significantly, these pioneering developments were later copied by the Europeans, with the English catching up only as late as 1797' (Hobson 2004: 54).

In terms of the advances in commerce and trade, it is by now well recognized that long before the rise of Islam, there were complex mechanisms in place that facilitated the long-distance movement of goods and money and instruments for money transfer as well. These acquired considerable sophistication after the rise and consolidation of Islam. 'Sumaria invented some of them and the Sassanids were using 'banks', 'cheques', and 'bills of exchange' before Islam was introduced (Abu-Lughod 1989: 216–217). Mechanisms and practices like partnerships, contracts and *commenda* were known to be commonly used. Many scholars, including Janet Abu-Lughod, have even seen the *commenda* as 'a capitalist instrument par excellence .... Through it, capital could be invested either in commerce, or unlike Europe, in industrial production' (Ibid.: 220). Further, 'where there is money, there must be money changers. The bankers (who, as in Europe, were often merchants as well) not only assayed and certified the money but changed local and foreign currencies. Goitein suggests that money changers were ubiquitous' (Ibid.: 223).

'Furthermore', says Abu-Lughod, 'although European bankers did not develop the full bill of exchange, its precursor the *suftaja*, of Persian origin, was in full use in Middle Eastern trade' (Ibid.: 223).

One can go on cataloguing more and more instances of the fact that not only was the world before the rise of Western modernity not a world of darkness and ignorance, it indeed provided many of the critical elements in the world of knowledge and material practices that Europe then built on, developed and transformed to break even newer ground. It is clearly not possible to detail and catalogue all such connections in all the fields concerned. However, in drawing this section to a close, it may be important to underline that we have perhaps only begun scraping the surface of the layers of connection that lie between these different worlds. Much exciting work is coming out by the day and much more will become available to us in the not-so-distant future. If we have seen Laura Marks (2012) trace for us the connection between the thought of an Ibn Sina (Avicenna) and Gilles Deleuze via Duns Scotus, we have had the no less exciting work of Hans Belting (2011) in the domain of art history that traces in detail, the ways in which the Arab theory of Optics went into the shaping of the idea of 'perspective' in Renaissance art. Belting's book focuses on the work of Abu Ali al-Hasan Ibn al-Haytham, also known in the Latinized form as Alhazen, and his *Kitab al-Manazir* or *The Book of Optics* in particular, though Ibn Haytham was by no means the author of this single book. He is supposed to have authored ninety-two books and as Belting puts it, '(I)n the theory of optics, which will occupy us above all, he had an influence on Western science up to the era of Kepler and Galileo, who built on Alhazen's work and at the same time took the first steps beyond it' (Belting 2011: 91–92).

What Laura Marks (2012) calls the 'ethnic cleansing of philosophy', through which all traces of its past connections with the non-European world were erased and Greece appropriated as the prehistory of modern Europe, will take a long time to overcome, largely because over the last two centuries or more, the version that has been established is this 'ethnically cleansed one'. As Peter J. Park (2013) observes, the 'development of the modern discipline of philosophy and the exclusion of non-European philosophies from the history of philosophy are related phenomena but scholarly inquiry into their connection has so far yielded little explanation' (Park 2013: 5). The difficulty, in my view, arises from the fact that the story of the rise of modern thought and philosophy as told in the dominant narrative is inextricably tied to its larger narrative of the rise of [Western] modernity. One of the reasons why things don't seem to change is related to what Anibal Quijano calls the 'coloniality of power'—the continuation of the matrix of power that was put in place by the modern/colonial beyond the actual demise of colonialism.

In a sense, this brings us to the last section of this chapter, on coloniality. The problem of coloniality is important to engage with for another reason. Now that we have unpacked one aspect of the autobiographical narrative of Western modernity, we still have one task remaining. This is the task of looking at another erasure—that of colonialism/coloniality—as integral to the story of modernity.

Modernity and the Coloniality of Being

I have already used the concept of coloniality as formulated by Anibal Quijano and elaborated by Mignolo in the opening section of Chapter 1. Rather than repeating that discussion, in this section, I will briefly look at the ramifications of the idea of coloniality. In his now-classic formulation, Quijano starts with the observation that Europe had established a relation of direct political, social and cultural domination 'over the conquered of all continents' (Quijano 2007: 168). He then goes on to underline that although defeated in its formal and political aspects everywhere, 'that colonial structure of power produced the specific social discriminations which were later codified as "racial", "ethnic", "anthropological" or "national", according to the times, agents and populations involved' (Ibid.: 168). He argues that if we look at the 'main lines of exploitation and social domination on a global scale', it will be clear that the logic of that exploitation and domination is still directed against 'members of the "races", "ethnies" or "nations" into which the colonial populations were categorized', from the conquest of America and onward (Ibid.: 169). Seen from this point of view, it is necessary to see the massive dislocation of populations that colonialism entailed, as parts of a structure of power that continues to structure contemporary relations of exploitation/domination. The massive dislocations include the Atlantic slave trade, the transportation of indentured labour across continents, settler colonialism and the genocide of the indigenous populations in the Americas and Australia and New Zealand or apartheid through the colonization of South Africa, to name some of the historical instances. The continuing discrimination against the blacks in the USA or Europe, the genocidal wars in West Asia, the demonization of immigrant populations across the Western world—all these constitute the mechanisms of the coloniality of power. What is more, as indicated in Chapter 1, even the ways in which Hindutva politics plays out a 'politics of the self' constituted through colonial knowledge, is indicative of this coloniality of power. In other words, the 'coloniality of power' is actually about the transformation of the very conditions of being and has also been theorized as the 'coloniality of being' (Maldonaldo-Torres 2007). Drawing on the work of Enrique Dussel and Mignolo, Maldonaldo-Torres (2007) points out that the idea was that 'colonial relations of power left profound marked [sic] not only in the areas of authority, sexuality, knowledge and the economy, but on the general understanding of being as well'. While

> the coloniality of power referred to the interrelation among modern forms of exploitation and domination (power), and the coloniality of knowledge had to do with impact of colonization on the different areas of knowledge production, coloniality of being would make primary reference to the lived experience of colonization and its impact on language. (Maldonaldo-Torres 2007: 242)

This distinction to my mind seems a bit overdrawn for the coloniality of power and knowledge already implies fundamental transformations in conditions of being as such. I will, therefore, use the expression 'coloniality of being' as the more general condition that structures life after colonialism as such.

The 'forms and effects' of 'cultural coloniality', argues Quijano, have varied across different continents with Latin America facing the worst, the massive extermination of the natives, 'mainly by their use as expendable labour force, in addition to the violence and conquest', not to mention the diseases brought by the Europeans. Between the Aztec-, Maya-Caribbean and the Tawantinsuyana (Inca) areas, more than 65 million inhabitants were exterminated over the course of about fifty years. Africa too faced a similar 'cultural destruction', though somewhat less than in America, while the high cultures of Asia and the Middle East could never be destroyed in such a way, though they too were placed in a subordinate relation to the European (Anibal Quijano 2007: 169–170). The important point that Quijano makes is that it is precisely in this period when European colonial domination was consolidating itself, that 'the cultural complex known as European modernity/rationality was being constituted'. Thus,

> The intersubjective universe produced by the entire Eurocentered capitalist colonial power was elaborated and formalized by the Europeans and established in the world as an exclusively European product and a universal paradigm of knowledge and of the relation between humanity and the rest of the world. Such confluence between coloniality and the elaboration of rationality/modernity was not in any way accidental, as is shown by the very manner in which the European paradigm of rational knowledge was elaborated. (Quijano 2007: 171–172)

It is the conjunction of the two processes, their simultaneity and the fact that they together put in place a world of the sort that Quijano describes that is important, and not whether the process was accidental or in any way entailed by what we understand as modernity. Indeed, the idea of a necessary connection between the two processes implies that they were a consequence of the same logic—something like the logic of an internal movement of a totality. As I will argue below, this is a highly problematic idea and I would like to steer clear of it. Moreover, it is also unnecessary: Even if we were to claim that their conjunction was contingent, there is enough evidence that the two processes mutually reinforce each other: colonization/coloniality on the one hand and the institutionalization of 'European modernity/rationality' on the other.

Worth registering at this point is the expression 'European modernity/rationality', for it serves to emphasize that in itself, the earlier history of rationality or reason and science that we have encountered in the previous section was not accomplice to the violence of colonization in the way that the modern European avatar of Reason (now with a capital R) became. It is not that there weren't violent wars conducted by the Islamic rulers of the various empires that dot its history but those wars were not legitimized by a secular discourse of Reason that divided the world between the 'savage/barbaric people' and the 'civilized' ones, whose civilization lay precisely in transforming the world in its own image—whatever the cost of that transformation. If that meant that the philosophers of Reason must justify, in racial terms, the project of colonization, or in the best case, simply look the other way, then so be it. The important point at issue here is to recognize that reason, science or what we now call secularity, are not in any way exclusively European products but that with their becoming part of a particular European discourse of Reason ('European modernity/rationality'), they acquire a new dimension as they become the signs of Progress and Civilization.

In a subsequent article, Quijano takes head-on the question of modernity as such and raises an important question that is worth thinking about seriously.

> If the concept of modernity only, or fundamentally, refers to the ideas of newness, the advanced, the rational-scientific, the secular (which are the ideas normally associated with it), then there is no doubt that one must admit that *it is a phenomenon possible in all cultures and historical epochs*. (Quijano 2000: 543, emphasis added)

Thus, he says, despite all their particularities and differences, China, India, Egypt, Greece, Maya-Aztec, and Tawantinsuyo, 'all exhibit signs of that modernity, including rational science, and the secularization of thought' (Quijano 2000: 543). The point of this last rhetorical flourish is really that if there has to be any specificity to the concept of 'modernity', it cannot be sought in these different constituents that came to be associated with it through the institution of European modernity/rationality and the discursive constellation that produced this complex.

Strictly speaking, what the earlier societies/cultures identified by Quijano did not have was what one can call the 'philosophy of the individual'—the specific idea of a person who was the Cartesian thinking subject par excellence, who also became the central figure of the emergent discourse of rights. The individual as the bearer of rights—and of freedom and autonomy—was also the individual who was, at the same time, the owner of property. Indeed, it was the right to property that ensured the full personhood of the individual. Quijano discusses this subject and criticizes it in insofar as 'the "subject" is a category referring to the isolated individual because it constitutes itself in itself and for itself, in its discourse and in its capacity of reflection' (Quijano 2007: 172). He also goes on to criticize the concept of the subject, which he positions against 'intersubjectivity and social totality as the production sites of all knowledge' (Ibid.: 172). While the first part of his criticism of the subject is important, it does not seem at all necessary to invoke the highly problematic concept of social totality, which soon ties Quijano up in knots from which he makes desperate attempts to break away. After making various kinds of justification for the idea of totality (Quijano 2007: 174–175), Quijano is ultimately left with the difficulty of extricating himself from it. His investment in the idea of totality is understandable in so far as it makes it possible to incorporate the dissonant Other within the same social reality, but he is very soon confronted with the inescapable difficulty immanent in this concept, namely that it must be defined in terms of a necessary internal logic which leads to other serious problems. Thus, soon after justifying the need for the concept of totality, he has to say:

> In this way, finally, the ideas of totality, which elaborated an image of society as a closed structure articulated in a hierarchic order with functional relations between its parts, presupposed a unique historical logic to the historical totality, and a rationality consisting in the subjection of every part to that unique total logic. This leads to conceiving society as a macro-historical subject, endowed with a historical rationality, with a lawfulness that permits predictions of the behavior of the whole and of all its part, as well as the direction and the finality of its development in time. The ruling part of the totality incarnated, in some way, that historical logic, with respect to the colonial world i.e. Europe. (Quijano 2007: 176)

This is precisely why it is unnecessary and even counter-productive to replace the concept of the individual thinking subject with any kind of idea of totality or structure, where often the individual is reduced to the status of the 'bearer' of the structure and where the logic of totality takes over in the manner explained in the quote above. It is enough, from our point of view, to insist that the individual (subject) is always-already embedded in her world—a world of commitments and attachments, so to speak. Her knowledge, consequently, does not begin with the 'I think' but is produced either by simply being imbricated in a world that is prior to 'thinking' (in a somewhat Heideggerian sense) or is discursively produced, especially in the context of modern knowledge institutions (somewhat in the manner of Michel Foucault). To that extent, Mignolo's axiom ('I am where I think' or 'I am where I do') can be suitably modified to 'I think where I am' or 'I think where I do' (Mignolo 2011: 80–81).

Being-thinking-doing aren't in that sense quite separable. Of course, Quijano's question then might still remain and we can now pose it in a modified form thus: Can we still account for the Other if we do away with the idea of a totality? Perhaps the idea that one can account for 'identity and difference' in the same breath, providing the space for the Other, only by positing the idea of a totality is nothing more than a Hegelian ruse. The recognition of the Other, strictly speaking, does not require any reference to any larger reality, which in the event, always turns out to be a version of the theological One. In the history of Marxism, too, this has been a thorny issue and we know of Louis Althusser's interrogations of the Hegelian idea of what he called a 'simple totality' whose internal development was determined by a single contradiction and its logic of *auhfebung* or sublation. Althusser, we may recall, had posited the idea of a 'complex totality', via Mao Zedong's idea of a multiplicity of contradictions, whence arose his adaptation of Freud's idea of 'overdetermination'. In this rendering, there was never a simple logic of the totality or structure possible for there is no simple/single contradiction that could determine its internal movement. Given a multiplicity of contradictions, there can only ever be contingent piling up of contradictions whose conjunction would open up different possibilities of change—instead of a teleological movement. In this kind of a schema, the logic of Self and Other as two sides of the identity/difference model no longer works. Similarly, feminist theory too never felt the need to posit 'patriarchy' as a totality. Though there are different philosophical currents within feminism, by and large, the most radical strands within it destabilize the very notion of identity by moving away from the male/female binary to an understanding of a range of sexual identities, often at once male and female. The Self and the Other appear equally unstable in that context. Thus, we can see that there are different ways of thinking about identity/difference or the Self and Other that do not need to invoke the metaphysical category of the totality.

This is not the place for a more detailed discussion on this issue, but it bears repetition that the idea of a totality or a structure is best avoided as a solution to the vexed question of subjectivity. Rather, my interest in this chapter—and this section in particular—is to take up another aspect of this autonomous individual subject that impinges on the question we were discussing earlier. This was the question of the specificity of European modernity/rationality as distinct from reason and science in earlier and other cultures.

To be a little more specific, I want to suggest that it is with the institution of 'bourgeois private property', that there comes into view a whole new constellation that I would like to call 'capital/ism'. But this 'bourgeois private property' is not to be confused with some 'thing' called 'capital' or a system/mode of production, which by its own internal logic went about accumulating and devouring older forms of life. Bourgeois private property should be seen rather, as the name for the newly instituted relationship to the world—that of the bourgeois self—which we may also call the Lockean self, whose 'ontology' C.B. Macpherson (1962) laid out in the early 1960s, in his *The Political Theory of Possessive Individualism*, as follows:

1. What makes man human is freedom from dependence on the wills of others.
2. Freedom from dependence on others means freedom from any relations except those that are voluntarily chosen by an individual with a view to his own interest.
3. The individual is essentially the proprietor of his own person and capacities, for which he owes nothing to society.
4. Although the individual cannot alienate the whole of his property in his person, *he may alienate his capacity to labour*—as that alone is alienable. (And quite remarkably Locke of course, never considered 'servants' as persons.)
5. Human society consists of a series of market relations.
6. Since freedom from the will of others is what makes a man human, each individual's freedom can rightfully be limited only by such obligations and rules as are necessary for securing the same freedom for others.
7. Political society is a human contrivance for the protection of the individual's property in his person and goods, and therefore for the maintenance of orderly relations of exchange between such individuals regarded as proprietors of themselves (Macpherson 1962: 263–264).

To these seven propositions, one also needs to add an eighth one that explicitly recognizes accumulation—beyond what can be taken if enough were to be left for others. This eighth proposition is crucially Lockean and as Macpherson shows at great length, Locke here actually annuls his own principle (that of leaving enough for others) by bringing in a fresh new principle—that of money and wage labour (Ibid.: 204–221). Locke's claim that 'a man's labour was his own', Macpherson underlines, had virtually the opposite significance from what we might think it could mean, for 'it provides a moral foundation for bourgeois appropriation' (Ibid.: 221). It is this new relationship to the world, formally entrenched via the language of rights, individual autonomy and freedom, that opens out the space for the emergence of *capitalism* as a *mode of being*—as something that is not reducible to capital in the sense of being anything substantial like wealth or money, nor even to capital as a social relation in Marx's sense. Although Marx too says that capital is not a thing but a social relation, but his sense is very different from what I am suggesting here. Thus, for instance, in *Capital Vol. III*, he says that,

> However, capital is not a thing, but rather a definite social production relation, belonging to a definite historical formation of society, which is manifested in a thing and lends this thing a specific social character. Capital is not the sum of the material and produced means of production. *Capital is rather the means of production transformed into capital*, which in themselves are no more capital than gold or silver in itself is money. *It is the means of production monopolised by a certain section of society*, confronting living labour-power as products and working conditions rendered independent of this very labour-power, which are personified through this antithesis in capital. (Marx 1971: 814, emphasis added)

Now the idea of 'a definite social production relation, belonging to a definite historical formation of society' is in itself not problematic but its explication in the passage, later on, reduces it to 'the means of production monopolized by a certain section of society', and thus narrows its sense down to little more than 'a thing' that accounts for the power capital enjoys vis-à-vis the workers.

To say that capitalism represents a *new mode of being* is to insist on its being something much more than a production relation and ownership of means of production. It is to claim that it is not merely an economic system but a disposition towards the world that morally justifies individual bourgeois appropriation of land and nature and is in turn enabled by virtue of having become a part of that new constellation that we are calling modernity. Thus, for example, had the disenchantment of the world, a part of the longer-term secularization process, not occurred in Europe, it would have been difficult to transform everything in the world into a saleable commodity. This apparently very simple transformation (the commodification of everything) conceals behind it certain epochal changes: the emptying of all other meanings from entities/beings in the natural world, the emergence of the autonomous individual, the philosophical justification for the creation and accumulation of wealth, the institution of the abstract model of market exchange, which in turn assumed its disembedding from social relations in Polanyi's sense.

Here one part of Charles Taylor's argument can help us understand how this process was accomplished in Europe. In a very significant sense, he tells us, disenchantment was accomplished not by secular or atheistic thought but by the long drawn out struggle of the Reformation. By positing an alternative religiosity in the form of a transcendent God, already by the eighteenth century, the Reformation had divested the natural world of its spiritual meanings. With what Taylor calls the 'Great Disembedding',

> the newly remade society was to embody unequivocally the demands of the gospel in a stable and, as it was increasingly understood, a rational order. This had no place for the ambivalent complementarities of the older enchanted world: between worldly life and monastic renunciation, between proper order and its periodic suspension in carnival, between the acknowledged power of spirits and forces and their relegation by divine power. *The new order was coherent, uncompromising, all of a piece. Disenchantment brought a new uniformity of purpose and principle.* (Taylor 2007: 146, emphasis added)

This 'Great Disembedding', says Taylor, was implicit in the Axial revolution; indeed, it was its logical conclusion (Ibid.: 146). Taylor links the primacy of the individual in modern Western culture to the 'earlier radical attempts to transform society along the principles of Axial spirituality', which eventually leads to the more secular conceptions of the moral order, paving the way for making the great disembedding a full-on revolution. This revolution, he says, 'disembeds us from the cosmic sacred; altogether, and not just for certain people as in earlier post-Axial moves' (Ibid.: 157).

With John Locke, the move towards what we might call a new ontology of the economic is already in evidence. God gave us powers of reason and discipline and we must use them to improve the human situation by being 'Industrious and Rational'. 'The imposition of order by human will' is a direct consequence of the Lockean scheme' (Taylor 2007: 167). Thus, argues Taylor, 'we can already see in Locke's formulation that the 'economic', defined as 'ordered, peaceful, productive activity', becomes the model for human behaviour (Ibid.: 167). Soon thereafter, the idea that 'commerce and economic activity is the path to peace and orderly existence' becomes 'more and more accredited'. What is more, this 'new economically-centred notion of natural order' comes to undergird 'doctrines of harmony and interest' and even came to be projected on to the universe 'for *it is this which is reflected in eighteenth century vision of cosmic order*, not as a hierarchy of form-at-work but as a chain of beings whose purposes mesh with each other' (Ibid.: 180, emphasis added).

And of course, like Macpherson, Taylor too has no doubt that the idea that this economic model of the universe is itself undergirded by the even more fundamental idea of an exchange between autonomous individuals as the basis of human interactions. It can be seen here that nothing like capitalism has yet emerged and yet, the philosophical, intellectual and even material preconditions (in the form of the great disembedding) are already in place. These are the conditions of possibility of the emergence of capitalism in Marx's sense though this is the new mode of being that eventually starts directing the state's interventions in society, *is* the disposition I am calling capitalism. And this new 'economically-centred notion of natural order' is what we can safely identify as the 'modern (European) episteme'. The term 'European' is superfluous here because it is really with this overarching new philosophical discourse, the specific European contribution that modernity becomes modernity.

Quijano also elaborates the idea of modernity, as seen from his end of the world by arguing that 'America was constituted as the first space/time of the new model of power of global vocation' and two historical processes associated in the production of that space/time converged, establishing 'two fundamental axes of the two models of power'. One was the 'codification of the differences between the conquerors and conquered in the idea of "race", a supposedly different biological structure that placed some in a natural position of inferiority to others'. The second was a new structure of control and its resources and products. Crucially, this new structure was an articulation of all historically known previous forms of control of labour, slavery, serfdom, small independent commodity production, and reciprocity, together around and upon the basis of capital and the world market (Quijano 2007: 533–534). Central to this new model of power is the new ontology of the economic and as a matter of fact the designation of some populations as inferior too initially was a matter of defining as uncivilized, barbaric and savage, populations who lived close to natural existence—who did not create wealth, accumulate and thereby contribute to the Progress of 'mankind'.[5] In a significant sense, the advent of the modern is felt as this new ontology of the economic invades societies that lay outside Europe. It is not accidental then that most theorizations of modernity from Latin America take the 'discovery' of the Americas and the 'world-system' as their starting point, which Dussel sees as 'a response to the first Eurocentrism, which thought that Europe, since its supposed Greek and Medieval Latin origins, produced "from within" the values' that were universalized in the last five centuries, that is, in the time of modernity (Dussel 2002: 222). Though differing with the world-system perspective in significant ways, both Dussel and Mignolo take it as their reference point in moving towards a global, rather than European, history of modernity.

In conclusion, it should be emphasized that while all these perspectives (Dussel, Quijano and Mignolo) open up the question of modernity/coloniality in interesting ways, it is necessary to emphasize that while drawing from different sources, it is in Europe that modernity as we know it was fashioned. Central to this fashioning of modernity was the enunciation of the European episteme that placed the economic at the centre of its understanding of the universe. In that sense, despite the fact that histories of reason, secular statecraft, science and technology, among other things, go back to longer histories in different parts of the world, it may not really make sense to call them 'early modernity'—for modernity is not any of these things individually but rather the name of that constellation that emerges with the mode of being I am calling capitalism. Driving the world to adopt this mode of being is the might of a powerful epistemic machine. In the next chapter, I discuss the figure of Slavoj Žižek and some of his work to underline that this machine is driven by assumptions of a theoretical nature in which all manner of people, including radical thinkers, participate.

Notes

1. Actually, Charles Taylor is almost exclusively concerned, in this volume, with the question of what he calls 'secularity', of which he identifies three senses, in order to disaggregate the idea of 'secularism' and through it explains more clearly in what precise sense the modern age could be called a secular age. This part of his exercise is very important and clarifies many things—both historically and theoretically, in particular, about the continued existence of belief/faith in modern society. To that extent, it would be unfair to expect Taylor to delve deeply into an exploration of the non-West's relationship to European modernity. However, to the extent that some of these histories enter directly into the making of modern Europe, one would have expected at least some awareness of those relationships.
2. I should state here that much of what I have said previously is my own free rendering of Kaviraj's argument—including the detailing of the examples.
3. Habermas draws a large part of his argument including this from the groundbreaking work of Reinhart Koselleck (1985).
4. For an account of the philosophical debates in the Islamic world and the internal logic of those debates as opposed to say, being mere commentators on Aristotle or Plato, see Nasr (2006).
5. It may not be out of place to mention here that in the first decade of the twentieth century, an important Hindi literary figure, Mahavir Prasad Dwivedi was passionately advocating the study of political economy and accumulation of wealth/capital, primarily because he thought that in India

people save money 'only for future security', which he held responsible 'for the reign of poverty'. If only they would invest their money/capital productively, there would be no poverty. That accumulation is a mark of civilization comes through very clearly in his writing when he says, that despite these limitations, 'Neither are our countrymen like the uncivilized and ignorant forest dwellers of Australia, Fiji or Africa, who are incapable of thinking about the needs of the future'. Again, in the chapter on 'Capital' in his *Sampattishastra* (Science of Property), 'Those who are uncivilized (*asabhya*) or ignorant have a weak desire for accumulation because they don't have any knowledge of pleasure and pain of the future' (cited in Singh 2014: 440–441).

3

Marxism and Non-Western Thought

Apropos a Debate on Slavoj Žižek

Introduction

It may be useful to begin this chapter with an anecdotal account of a conference I attended over ten years ago. It was 13 March 2009. A whole galaxy of philosophers and theorists had gathered for a three-day conference, 'On the Idea of Communism', under the auspices of the Birkbeck Institute for the Humanities, London University. The conference opened to a jam-packed hall where all tickets had sold out—this was a ticketed show where philosophers like Alain Badiou, Slavoj Žižek, Jean-Luc Nancy, Antonio Negri, Jacques Ranciere, Terry Eagleton and many others were to 'perform' on the 'idea of communism'. Nancy could not eventually attend because he was unwell. The huge Logan hall was so overflowing with people, including gate-crashers like me, that the organizers had to arrange video streaming in a neighbouring hall which too was almost full! It was certainly very encouraging to see such an overwhelming turnout in those bleak days.

The conference began in the afternoon with brief opening remarks by Alain Badiou and Slavoj Žižek. Badiou made a general point about the continuing relevance of the 'communist hypothesis'. It was a staid and philosopher-like intervention. And then Slavoj Žižek came up to speak. In the five brief minutes he spoke, it was clear that he was the star—a rock star playing to the gallery. Indeed, Žižek and his audience seemed already tied to one another in a bond of performing for each other. This once post-Marxist, now relapsed Marxist philosopher-theorist spoke animatedly: 'We must resist the temptation to act. We must refuse being told that children are dying of hunger in Africa or in the slums of India, for this is the philosophy of the present times. They don't want us to think.'

And he went on, amidst cheers from the audience,

> We must do, you must do what Lenin did in 1915, after the war broke out, after the failure of the Social Democratic parties. He went to the library and started to read Hegel's *Logic*. And this conference should be our moment of reading Hegel's *Logic*.

How much polemic is compressed in this one statement was, of course, evident only to those who have followed Žižek's intellectual trajectory, for he was not just making a simple point about reading and thinking, as opposed to mindless 'doing' that is the mantra of our neoliberal times; he was also polemicizing against all kinds of anti-Hegelians: Althusserians, post-Marxists like Laclau and Mouffe, poststructuralists, Deleuzians and so on.

The background to the conference was an ongoing exchange between Alain Badiou and Žižek on the idea of communism. Badiou's piece that kick-started this debate appeared in the *New Left Review*, shortly after Sarkozy's electoral victory in France. It seems to have quickly become a major reference point for Left-wing discussions, given the political-intellectual climate of our times, as it argued for the continued relevance of the communist idea. Badiou argued in this piece that Communism—or what he calls the 'communist hypothesis' whose history stretches from the revolt of Spartacus to the present—is still relevant today. It's relevance, however, is as a regulative ideal, not as a programme and many of its earlier beliefs (like the party-form) had become redundant. Žižek enters, at this point. Žižek, it may be recalled, rapidly reinvented himself after his initial post-Marxist forays into theory. He took up cudgels on behalf of Marxism and revolution, claimed to 'repeat Lenin' and unabashedly proclaimed that the Truth of Marxism is only visible from the truly proletarian standpoint. Lest I be misunderstood, I quote Žižek directly:

> Lenin's wager—today, in our era of postmodern relativism, more actual than ever—is that universal truth and partisanship, the gesture of taking sides, are not only not mutually exclusive, but condition each other: in a concrete situation, its *universal* truth can only be articulated

> from a thoroughly *partisan* position—truth is by definition one-sided. (Žižek 2000: 550, emphasis original)

This could well be said of Islam or Hindutva—that its 'universal truth' can only be articulated or grasped through the partisan standpoint of the believer. And this is merely one of the many such statements that Žižek has made in this infamous 'plea for Leninist intolerance'.

Žižek could not obviously accept the mild 'philosopherliness' of Badiou's position and entered into a debate with him. What was the issue of contestation? Žižek's contention was against Badiou's claim of communism being 'a mere horizon', that is to say, without a programme. Doesn't this reduce communism to a mere Kantian regulative ideal? Truth to tell, Badiou's essay itself is pretty orthodox, philosophically speaking, but Žižek would have none of that. Communism is not just the horizon; *it is a programme*, he had proclaimed in his intervention. And thus, the backdrop for the present conference was set up. I was left wondering then as to how this philosopher could within a short five to ten minutes intervention maintain that we must refuse the temptation to act, we must think; and yet, with equal vehemence argue that communism is nothing if not a programme. A programme, to my mind, is nothing if not a call to action. It is, of course, a different matter that on two occasions, more than 20 years apart, Marx himself defined communism as 'the real movement that will set free the forces that have already taken birth in the womb of bourgeois society'—it was in other words, *not* a programme. 'It has no ideals to realize, no blueprint to which the world must conform', was the powerful statement after the Paris Commune.

From my point of view, the problem is not just one of Žižek's fidelity or otherwise to Marx but rather, the emperor's new clothes type of question: Who formulated the programme? What vision does it embody? Does it include the innumerable national liberation/anticolonial struggles of the twentieth century in Asia and Africa in particular that were conducted under the sign of Marxism, especially in its Leninist version? After once having made his infamous 'Leftist plea for Eurocentrism' (Žižek 1998), does he consider Non-Europeans as having any thought and agency in the matter of formulating the programme? On the other hand, if many of the national liberation struggles met the same disastrous fate that befell 'actually existing socialism' (which included the part of Europe to which Žižek himself belongs) and turned into monstrosities, how does Žižek understand them? If they are part of Žižek's communist programme, then the programme certainly fails to inspire any confidence about the future, for it only means that the full implications of such a programme have neither been thought through nor its actual historical experience analyzed and understood.

If the idea of communism has to have any meaning, even as a horizon, if it has to have any relevance at all, it can hardly be elaborated without reference to the 'real movements' of our times and a ruthless examination of past failures. The conference displayed virtually no awareness of the fact that in our times, issues were much more complicated than mere capital-labour conflicts. Take for instance the new Left-wing formations in South America where the indigenous leadership has led the re-emergence of the Left, representing interests of indigenous people and cocoa growers, and on issues such as water privatization and the 'rights of nature' so to say. Islam and Empire constitute yet another pole of the contemporary which was far away from the minds of both the speakers and the audience who asked questions (except one questioner). At which point I turned to take a look at the composition of the audience. Not one black person in the entire audience. Some four or five East Asians and an equal number of South Asians were all I could see in that audience. And why not? After all, it was a conference where white men alone and (one or two token women apart) were on the dais, talking about the world from their very narrow, European experience.[1]

Does this composition say something about the direction in which our thought is going? Does the radicalism of the white radical have anything to offer to the non-white, global South? Some years ago, in 2006, I had heard Alain Badiou speak in Princeton. There the audience was not communist. And it was not a ticketed show but free. There were Palestinians, North Africans and many others in the hall and Cornell West on the dais, chairing. Badiou, the French radical philosopher found himself besieged after his talk during the question-answer session. Badiou had spoken grandly of why '9/11 was not an Event because it did not enunciate anything new'—a particularly Badiouan notion of 'Event'. Half an hour into his talk, he was smuggling in old universalisms into his exposition, representing 9/11 as Evil. A Palestinian woman student got up to ask him if he had any idea why in that case Osama bin Laden was considered a hero among a large number of people across the world. I had learned only a few days ago that pictures of bin Laden and Che Guevara could be seen together in many places in the Bolivian capital.[2] Badiou tried in vain to answer her, giving rise to more and more questions in the process till someone asked: 'What then does your universalism say regarding this complete lack of ability to understand the other?'

No such questioning or interrogation was possible today. It was a comfortable gathering of similar people—brought up in the same traditions. The only other person who was to attend but was not allowed to because he did not have the appropriate visa (so Žižek informed the audience) was Wang Hui from China. One wonders, however, what a single token presence of Wang Hui could have done to the direction of the conference.

It is this huge gulf of incomprehension across people otherwise speaking the same language of social sciences and often equally invested in universalism, that one must bear in mind when trying to grasp what is at stake in what follows in the rest of this chapter. The fate of Slavoj Žižek is important to understand here. For, it is precisely his passionate espousal of Universalism—a muscular, messianic Universalism—that ultimately consigns him to his very provincial and fortified European existence.

Postcolonialism and the Postnational

In a recent article provocatively titled 'Can Non-Europeans Think?' published in *Al Jazeera*, Hamid Dabashi posed the question of the very possibility of thought outside Europe and in the non-Western world more generally.[3] Dabashi's piece was in response to an article by Santiago Zabala, entitled 'Slavoj Žižek and the Role of the Philosopher', where

Zabala attempted to read in Žižek's persona and oeuvre, the possible implications for the philosopher-figure as such.[4] He dwelt on Žižek as a figure who is at once a philosopher and a public intellectual—a role not very easily available, he argues, to academic philosophers.

If most significant philosophers become points of reference within the philosophical community, he says, 'few have managed to overcome its boundaries and become public intellectuals intensely engaged in our cultural and political life as did Hannah Arendt (with the Eichmann trial), Jean-Paul Sartre (in the protests of May 1968) and Michel Foucault (with the Iranian revolution).' Zabala explains this rare ability/possibility by invoking Edward Said on the 'outsider' status of the intellectual and by underlining the direct engagement of the thought of such philosophers with contemporary events.

'These philosophers' says Zabala, 'became public intellectuals not simply because of their original philosophical projects or the exceptional political events of their epochs, but rather because their thoughts were drawn by these events.' He asks what enables an intellectual to respond to events of his epoch in a manner that s/he can contribute productively.

'In order to respond', he continues, quoting Edward Said, 'the intellectual has to be "an outsider, living in self-imposed exile, and on the margins of society", that is, free from academic, religious and political establishments; otherwise, he or she will simply submit to the inevitability of events.'

This is an interesting issue that is of great relevance for the question Dabashi takes up in his response, namely that of non-European thought, especially because for a long time after gaining independence, the nation-building project often roped in many of the best intellectuals and thinkers, leaving little space 'outside' that project. Unfortunately, Dabashi does not go into this question at all—though it is very much at the heart of the issue of intellectual life outside 'the West'. This issue is also important in another sense that might have been worth exploring further—in later phases, the pressure of continuous public-political engagement often left (or leaves) little space for doing the kind of academic philosophy that Zabala has in mind.

One cannot really blame Dabashi for not having any particular interest in Žižek's persona or oeuvre, for, as Walter Mignolo points out in his contribution to the debate, the non-European thinker may have 'better things to do'.[5] Thus, a contemporary non-European thinker or scholar might prefer to engage with her times in more direct ways—that is to say, without the necessary mediation of Western philosophers and thinkers or reading them on her own terms; she might find, as many indeed do, the elaborate invocation of the (Western) philosophical pantheon before embarking on any journey of thought, irrelevant if not positively irritating. S/he may not find discourses on 'communism' and the 'truth of the proletariat'—as in the thought of a Slavoj Žižek or an Alain Badiou—relevant at all to her condition. For these are discourses which, with each successive defeat in the real world, retreat one more step into abstract metaphysics, till there is no relation left whatsoever between the actually existing 'working class' and the Žižekian proletariat.[6]

This is not to say, of course, that intellectuals in the East are not interested in the struggle against capital and the questions posed by Marx's thought. They are, but perhaps in a very different way. After all, in the current form, both the 'theory' of 'capital' as well as of the struggle against it, is entirely based on the Western story, drawing on available bodies of knowledge there. For one thing, many postcolonial scholars and thinkers today would argue that more than any reified notion of 'the logic of capital' the battle might actually lie in the domain of knowledge and thought. It is here that 'capitalist relations' acquire a justification that makes it of a piece with the question of colonial domination. Thus, for instance, Walter Mignolo (2002) writes,

> The following argument is built on the assumption...that the history of capitalism as told by Fernand Braudel, Wallerstein, and Giovanni Arrighi and the history of Western epistemology as it has been constructed since the European Renaissance run parallel to and complement each other. The expansion of Western capitalism implied the expansion of Western epistemology in all its ramifications, from the instrumental reason that went along with capitalism and the industrial revolution, to the theories of the state, to the criticism of both capitalism and the state...

> And at the moment when capitalism began to be displaced from the Mediterranean to the North Atlantic (Holland, Britain), the organization of knowledge was established in its universal scope. 'There can be no others'[7] inscribed a conceptualization of knowledge to a geopolitical space (Western Europe) and erased the possibility of even thinking about a conceptualization and distribution of knowledge 'emanating' from other local histories (China, India, Islam, etc). (Mignolo 2002: 59)

This is why most contemporary struggles against capital in many parts of the world including India take the form of struggle against land acquisition or the philosophy underlying big dams and nuclear power.

This is a battle that has to be fought at the level of challenging this complex body of disciplinary knowledges and nobody knows better than the former colonial subjects that there is no immanent logic of capital that pushes in the direction of capitalist development but the force of a formidable 'epistemic machine' backed by the naked power of the state. Žižek too is a product of that very same epistemic machine and is fully constituted by the understanding that Mignolo points towards. Thus, elsewhere, in response to Evo Morales' claim that 'Everything began with the industrial revolution in 1750, which gave birth to the capitalist system.... Under capitalism, Mother Earth does not exist, instead there are raw materials,' Žižek can only chuckle: 'one is tempted to add that, if there is one good thing about capitalism, it is that under it Mother Earth no longer exists' (Žižek 2010: 97). It is not difficult to see that the logic behind this claim is precisely that this destruction of indigenous life-forms by capitalism is progress—that until the whole earth has been transformed to a 'disenchanted' saleable commodity, we cannot claim to be truly modern. The whole point of many contemporary critiques of capitalism, however, is precisely that they reject, implicitly or explicitly, this narrative of progress.

The difficulty is that even when the theorist produced by this epistemic machine turns his or her gaze to the non-West, she can only see instances of 'retardation'.[8] The European trajectory remains the norm and so every other story has to be narrated in terms of its deviation from that norm. This is what Sudipta Kaviraj refers to as the 'Euro-normality' of the social sciences—the fact that Europe constitutes the natural 'north' of the compass of social and political theory (Kaviraj 2009: 189). The fact that ruling elites in these postcolonial societies too partake of this vision and are therefore constantly engaged in the game of 'catching up', only exacerbates the situation. In fact, it gives a certain urgency to the need to break with this Euro-normality, given that this 'catching up' is never benign and involves massive levels of dislocation and violence—as one sees for example, in the restructuring of Indian cities or the sharp conflicts around land acquisition.

This Euro-normality is not merely an affliction of the ruling elites of the postcolonial world but structures, equally, the vision and thought of most Marxists. Thus, most Indian Marxists too believe that it is necessary for societies like India to catch up with the West, economically speaking. They too believe that the whole world must first become capitalist in the western way, for any socialist project to succeed.[9] Theory for us in the non-West has been a Western inheritance, all the more so for Marxists whose understanding of Marxism's history still remains woefully tied to the story of its European/Western episode. This despite the fact that it was in the non-West that Marxism actually found its most enduring habitat. Even today this story remains to be written.[10]

Breaking with this Euro-normality demands that thought in the three continents finally emerge from its 'self-incurred immaturity', creating its own concepts and categories, and stop looking to the West for theoretical guidance at every turn.

It is in this spirit that Dabashi joins issues with an implicit assumption in Zabala's piece. This assumption—that all thought, in a manner of speaking, begins in Athens and ends in Paris—is of course, no longer stated as explicitly these days as it used to be in earlier times, thanks to the powerful intervention of postcolonial studies in the last couple of decades.[11] Nonetheless, it remains a widely shared assumption in the self-satisfied world of Western philosophy/theory.

The End of Postcolonialism?

Let me turn to Dabashi's response that essentially reacted against the following opening paragraph in Zabala's piece.

> There are many important and active philosophers today: Judith Butler in the United States, Simon Critchley in England, Victoria Camps in Spain, Jean-Luc Nancy in France, Chantal Mouffe in Belgium, Gianni Vattimo in Italy, Peter Sloterdijk in Germany and in Slovenia, Slavoj Žižek, not to mention others working in Brazil, Australia and China.

Hamid Dabashi is legitimately irritated by what he terms 'the unabashedly European character and disposition of the thing the author calls "philosophy today"—thus laying a claim on both the subject and time that is peculiar and, in fact, an exclusive property of Europe.' Dabashi is also annoyed at the cavalier fashion in which philosophers from other parts of the world are referred to ('"working in Brazil, Australia and China", not meriting even a specific name'). But in letting his legitimate irritation get the better of him, Dabashi misses an opportunity of posing a question that we all need to contend with: Why is 'philosophy' today, always-already Western? Is it merely a question of Zabala's arbitrary selection of names that is at issue here, or is there something more?

To put the matter slightly differently, why is all thought in the 'non-West' always colonized by the political? If one looks at the situation in India, for instance, there is little doubt that there were long and robust traditions of abstract philosophical thought—preoccupied with questions of logic, epistemology, causation and being, disquisitions on language and meaning and similar questions—through more than two thousand years preceding the advent of colonialism. Why is it that from the late nineteenth century on, 'politics' takes centre stage?[12] It is not just that 'politics' becomes the key object of inquiry; rather it is that all inquiry and thought comes to be *colonized* by it. In the 'cramped space' of colonized life, politics alone provides the site from where a challenge to the colonizers' knowledge can be mounted. Philosophy retreats into the mists of time—taking on the form, in the Indian case, of an excavation of Buddhist, Vedic or Vedantic philosophy, except where it concedes defeat and adopts various forms of colonizers' philosophies (positivism, utilitarianism and so on). Marxism perhaps was an exception because, for the Indian—and I suspect generally colonial—subjects, Marxism is not philosophy properly speaking but a discourse *on* politics and history, that provided at once a language to critique colonialism and one's own tradition.[13]

Dabashi ends up spending a lot of time and energy in supplying specific names from the three continents. He marshals a formidable list of names which include Ashis Nandy, Partha Chatterjee, Wang Hui, Sudipta Kaviraj, Henry Odera Oruka, Ngugi wa Thiong'o, Wole Soyinka, Chinua Achebe, Okot p'Bitek, Taban Lo Liyong, Achille Mbembe, Emmanuel Chukwudi Eze, Azmi Bishara, Sadeq Jalal Al-Azm, Fawwaz Traboulsi, Abdallah Laroui, Michel Kilo, Abdolkarim Soroush. They are undoubtedly very important thinkers but are they actually doing philosophy? I think some of them are, but most of them self-professedly think *at the borders of philosophy*. In an ironic twist, the Hegelian/Marxist project of the *aufhebung* of philosophy is realized here, in the colonial world. Philosophy is faced with its own negation. Thought can no longer take self-referential exegesis as its model; nor can it be content with the conduct of an endless internal dialogue with a Plato, an Aristotle, a Kant or a Hegel. For thought must confront the fact of colonialism and confront it at a new level of urgency.

At one level, politics becomes *the* key issue—one that defines the oppositional character of thought of the colonized in relation to that of the colonizer. Politics comes to define not merely issues that are explicitly political but for a subject population, often comes to provide a route to thought in other domains as well.[14]

One consequence of Dabashi's exercise is that it draws him into the same West *versus* Non-West binary that in a sense, he has himself been trying to question over the past few years, laying his intervention open to attacks like the one by Michael Marder.[15] It is certainly not enough to claim that philosophy is not a European preserve and somewhat self-defeating to produce a list of people who we claim are 'doing philosophy', for it seems to push Dabashi into a defensive mode, without delineating the impact of colonialism's epistemic violence upon thought itself. Needless to say, Marder's is an attack that depends to a large extent on caricature and oversimplification. Consider this:

> In contrast to this simplistic construal, *post-colonial theorists agree that there is no strict division between the colonizer and the colonized*; that

> both colonial and post-colonial structures of power and domination are complex and multilayered, as they are shot through with class, gender and other differences; that claims to a rightful political representation of the subaltern are usually ungrounded, as they are voiced by those most privileged in the colonial or post-colonial societies—men, wealthy elites and so forth. (Marder 2013, emphasis added)

We are, of course, not told who these postcolonial theorists are who 'agree' that '*there is no strict division between the colonizer and the colonized*'. Nor are we told about what precisely is meant by the statement that, 'claims to a rightful representation of the subaltern are usually ungrounded, as they are voiced by those most privileged in the colonial or postcolonial societies—men, wealthy elites' and so forth. While there is a grain of truth in each of these statements, the sweeping assertion of the order suggested in them—almost implying that therefore, there is really no difference between the colonizer and the colonized—is nothing short of a caricature. A recognition of the many layers of power and domination *within* ex-colonial societies does not by any stretch of imagination exonerate colonialism from the multiple layers of violence that it has perpetrated on the societies it colonized. Nor does it exonerate Western theorists and philosophers of the charge of smugness—even those who have lately begun to recognize that *some* thought possibly takes place outside the precincts of their world and their academies, but who seem to be content with making some superficial gestures to that effect, without letting that thought disturb their philosophical apparatus in any way.

A good example of this would be Žižek himself, whose *Living in the End Times* (2011), published after a flying visit to India, displays characteristic audacity in making theoretical pronouncements about India and Indian tradition (from Tantrism and Vedic rituals to Maoism), all on the basis of a superficial reading of just one book on each of these subjects.

In other words, despite the multi-layered and complex nature of both colonial and post-colonial structures of power and domination, the divide *is* quite stark. And radicalism of any sort is no guarantee that a Western/European philosopher will even attempt to transcend his/her geographical, historical and cultural limits.

This is not to say that postcolonial theory is free of problems. For many of us living in India, the moment of postcolonial theory, inaugurated by the work of Edward Said but also, in our context, by the work of Ashis Nandy and Subaltern Studies, constituted a crucial and liberating moment as indicated in Chapter 1. For the first time the enterprise of social sciences, of political and social theory and Marxism, began to be examined as specific knowledge formations that arose in specific historical contexts, in a specific part of the world. In other words, both the universalist claims of these knowledge formations as well as their intellectual and cultural hegemony came to be challenged over the subsequent decades. The effects of this recognition were dramatic, for it initiated a renewed engagement with our own intellectual traditions alongside serious scrutiny of the received wisdom of Western thought. But there was a serious difficulty here as well. The critique of Western knowledge and philosophy soon got inserted within a very unproductive discourse of 'indigenism' that thrives on the diet of high-pitched anti-West rhetoric. As an example, one might cite the case of the interrogation of modern Western science around the CSDS that involved scholars and scholar-activists like Vandana Shiva, J. Bandyopadhyay, J.K. Bajaj, Claude Alvares and others. This parallels the work of Gandhian scholar Dharampal, on science and technology in ancient India and the formation, in the 1980s, of the People's Patriotic Science and Technology (PPST) where even some left-wing people were involved. Important though the work emerging from these initiatives was, it also led to a number of scholars moving towards a right-wing indigenism.

Needless to say, this division unwittingly reinforced the old nationalist one of 'Indic tradition' *versus* the West, sometimes despite itself. Everything of Western and colonial provenance was considered worthy of being rejected. The long amnesia inaugurated by nationalist thought had enforced a certain territorial closure on a thought-tradition that had thrived on exchanges with Greek, Chinese, Arab and Persian traditions. There was no unadulterated 'Indic' tradition, for it had always been a tradition in dialogue with other traditions; furthermore, it had always been severely and seriously internally contested.[16]

It is for this reason that some of us based in South Asia prefer to speak of the 'postnational' condition, rather than the postcolonial.[17] The territorial closure imposed by nationalism and the long amnesia that followed can only be reversed by opening up our intellectual and cultural history for re-examination afresh. It is also clear that the internal conflicts within this so-called tradition had often been so violent that it required the presence of an 'outside'—sometimes in the form of Islam and sometimes in the form of colonial rule—as an enabling force for the assertions of the excluded and dispossessed. For instance, it is a well-documented and studied fact that the arrival of Islam provided the lower castes in particular, in different parts of the country with a possibility of an exit from the oppression they suffered within Hindu society (for example Richard Eaton 1993). No wonder then that numerous lower caste movements through the late nineteenth and early to mid-twentieth centuries, found in the colonial power an ally. It is the presumed unity of 'the nation' and its putative 'tradition' that becomes the object of investigation now, rather than the formations of colonial power—on which we now have a substantial body of very serious work.

A caveat is, however, necessary here. While it is true that many lower caste movements benefited from the presence of colonial rule, there were other oppressed sections, especially the tribal/indigenous people, the peasantry and the urban working class, who found themselves in serious opposition to colonial power. Their struggles often went beyond the confines of nationalism—a point that Subaltern Studies scholars have been at pains to underline. *The anti-colonial struggle is therefore not reducible to nationalism; nor can it be seen merely as the struggle of a middle-class elite.* This is a complex story—not at all amenable to Marder's oversimplified account of the colonial/postcolonial relationship.

As I said earlier, it is a bit puzzling to see Dabashi resort to the West *versus* non-West rhetoric, when his own work over the years has tended to warn against this false polarity. In his book on the Arab Spring, Dabashi had very forcefully put forward the argument that 'these revolutionary uprisings are post-ideological, meaning that they are no longer fighting according to terms dictated by their condition of coloniality, codenamed "postcolonial"' (Dabashi 2011: 11). In an interesting formulation, he had argued that these movements represent a new constellation where a *societal modernity* supersedes political modernity. Political modernity, he suggested, was ultimately a defeated project because it was predicated on a dichotomous frame that pitted it against European colonialism and American imperialism, where these direct contestations had produced 'three distinct (prototypical) ideological grand narratives: anticolonial nationalism, Third World socialism, and militant Islamism' (Ibid.: 13).

Clearly, 'postcolonialism', defined in this way, is an entirely different entity from what we identify as 'postcolonial theory' or 'postcolonial studies'. And yet, in terms of its defining binary, postcolonial theory does share a common ground with this 'political postcolonialism'—and Dabashi's call to move beyond it is important and needs to be taken seriously.

Žižek, Thought and the Non-European

Before we discuss what I see as the major challenge before non-European thought, let me turn to Žižek's thought insofar as it concerns us, non-Europeans, directly. Žižek here is only an instance of what I understand to be a more general problem of the Western philosopher/scholar. Another recent instance of this sort is the more pernicious but also more trivial book by the British Marxist Perry Anderson (2012) that takes to task almost all Indian intellectuals for partaking in what he calls 'Indian Ideology'—while drawing *all* the elements of his so-called 'critique' from the work done by Indian scholars—without any acknowledgement. Perry Anderson's book has been critiqued at great length by Partha Chatterjee, Sudipta Kaviraj and Nivedita Menon (Ruparelia et al. 2015) and I mention it here simply to underline that despite being of a very different genre, like Žižek, he too exhibits the same epistemic arrogance that sees the non-West as incapable of any thought.

I will confine my remarks here primarily to some sections of Žižek's book *Living in the End Times* (2011) as an exhaustive engagement with his thought does not interest me. Since Žižek is only the starkest symptom of a wider syndrome, what applies to him should apply with appropriate modifications to most Western thinkers.

At the very outset, he lays his philosophical cards on the table:

> Though one may be tempted to oppose these perspectives—the dogmatism of blind faith versus an openness towards the unexpected—one should nevertheless insist on the truth contained in the second version: *truth as opposed to knowledge is like a Badiouian Event, something that only an engaged gaze, the gaze of a subject who 'believes in it', is able to see*.... Lacking this engaged position, mere description of the state of things, no matter how accurate, fail to generate emancipatory effects—ultimately they only render the burden of the lie still more oppressive.... (Žižek 2011: xiv, emphasis added)

This is something a good believer too would say: You have to have faith in the word of God to be able to see Him and believe in His word. Structurally, both these claims are of the same order: 'Truth' is a priori, and the empirical world always a corruption, always 'Maya'—an ontological delusion—as a good Sankarite Advaitin would put it. Order resides in the idealized world of 'Theory' in such a Žižekian universe. I should, therefore, lay my own philosophical cards on the table: I begin from this messy, disorderly, empirical world. In this empirical world, one will always need to confront workers in flesh and blood, with all their caste and patriarchal prejudices: workers who participate in communal violence against minorities; workers who observe all the rituals of caste in their everyday lives; workers who live in blissful ignorance of the burden of the historical role placed on their shoulders by the 'philosopher/s of the epoch'! They constitute a living refutation of the 'true proletarian standpoint' that supposedly embodies 'true universality' that Žižek is so fond of invoking. However, this insistence on the empirical should not be understood in any naïve sense, for we have no direct access to it outside of our language and categories of thought. In a sense, the real challenge for thought is to confront *this* world, over and over again, each time the encounter with the empirical reveals the limits of our thought-categories.

Very early on in the book (Žižek 2011: x), we read about the underlying premise of the book (a simple one, he assures us): 'the global capitalist system is approaching *an apocalyptic zero-point*.' And we can easily see that this is the 'end time' referred to in the title of the book—the end of time, according to Christian theology—though many cultures across the world may find it impossible to understand this idea of a beginning and an end of Time. In many cultures, time *is* eternal—that is to say, without beginning or end: there is no sharp distinction between Eternity and 'historical Time', marked by the Fall.[18] But more interesting is the implication here that this end-time is not merely the end of 'global capitalism' but of Time as such. This is the corner that many Western Leftist philosophers have painted themselves into: *they have made capitalism integral to the ontology of the human condition. That is why Žižek often says that it is easier to imagine the end of the world rather than the end of capitalism.*[19]

Žižek explains this condition with reference to 'four riders of the apocalypse' (another Christian metaphor), namely, (a) the ecological crisis (b) the consequences of the biogenetic revolution (c) imbalances within the system itself (intellectual property, forthcoming struggles over raw materials, food and water) and (d) the explosive growth of social divisions and exclusions. We might just want to remind ourselves in passing that this is the very same Žižek who chuckled at Evo Morales' statement and claimed that the only good thing that capitalism has done is that 'Mother Earth no longer exists'. Points (a), (c) and (d) are today largely related precisely to the catastrophe that the European episteme has brought the world to, against which Evo Morales is revolting when he traces the current ills back to industrialization. Žižek, the product of the same epistemic machine that drives the European episteme cannot ignore the crisis and he also cannot imagine anything other than the end of the world—unlike Morales.

Tellingly, Žižek then 'takes up only the last point' for illustration for it signifies something very specific to him. Consider the following statement: 'nowhere are the new forms of apartheid more palpable than in the wealthy Middle Eastern oil states—Kuwait and Saudi Arabia.' He talks of how 'hidden on the outskirts of the cities, often literally behind walls, are tens of thousands of "invisible" immigrant workers doing all the dirty work.' (Žižek 2011: x).[20] 'A country like Saudi Arabia', he continues, 'is literally "beyond corruption": there is no need for corruption because the ruling gang (the royal family) is already in possession of all the wealth...' (Ibid.). That a handful of Western corporations own most of the world's wealth is, of course, an objective historical necessity but let that not detain us here. He goes on in this vein till we come to this gem of a passage:

> Should the situation persist, can we even imagine the change in the Western 'collective psyche' when (not *if* but precisely *when*) some 'rogue nation' or group obtains a nuclear device, powerful biological or chemical weapon and declares its 'irrational' readiness to risk all using it? The most basic coordinates of our awareness will have to change, insofar as, today, we live in a state of collective fetishistic disavowal: we know very well that this will happen at some point but, nevertheless cannot bring ourselves to really believe that it will. *The US attempt to prevent such an occurrence through continuous pre-emptive activity is a battle that has been lost in advance....* (Žižek 2011: x)

A number of things need to be noted. The 'we' who live in a 'collective fetishistic disavowal'—the addressees of this discourse—are the inhabitants of the 'West'. They live in a world that is peopled by rogues and irrational people, all but swamping the civilized, who try not to think about it—even though the US, their saviour, continuously tries to prevent something like a nuclear conflagration, even if inefficiently. That is precisely why this European philosopher can make the statements about nuclear, biological and chemical weapons that he does without a moment's pause. Is he really not aware that only once in history have nuclear weapons been used—not by 'Middle Eastern' lunatics but by the very USA, who he thinks is fighting a legitimate battle? And is it not true that western powers remain the ones to have used biological and chemical warfare most prolifically? Where then do Žižek's confident claims come from? It seems to me, they come from a continuing understanding that it is in the West alone that 'world-historical' agency lies—all others being 'irrational' savages.[21] That is how the apocalyptic crisis of capitalism is ultimately reduced to its Saudi Arabian and Kuwaitian avatar! That is where the end of time 'begins'.

As if this was not enough, Žižek performs another mind-boggling feat within the next few pages. This time he philosophizes on the Hindu tradition of 'Tantra'—all on the basis of having read one book! The book in question is *Sex, Politics and Power in the Study of Religion* by Hugh Urban (2003). Urban's work is generally very highly regarded in the field but can anybody from the non-West have the audacity to write about some spiritual practice in England or France or Germany on the basis of having read just one book? My point is the audacity of the assumption that all you need to know about India (or the non-West) are 'facts' which you can pick up from anywhere. After all, these are places where no intellection, thought or debate takes place. Dabashi's question, 'Can the non-European think' hits you with full force, when you encounter Žižek.

But what about the argument itself? What exactly is Žižek telling us here? Sample this:

> The gap between the official text of the Law and its obscene supplement is not limited to Western cultures; in Hindu culture, it occurs as the opposition between *vaidika* (the Vedic corpus) and *tantrika—tantra* being the obscene (secret) supplement to the Vedas, the unwritten (or secret, non-canonic) core of the public teaching of the Vedas, a publicly disavowed but necessary element. No wonder that tantra is so popular today in the West: it offers the ultimate 'spiritual logic of late capitalism' uniting spirituality and earthly pleasures, transcendence and material benefits, divine experience and unlimited shopping. (Žižek 2011: 7, emphasis added)

Now, for one thing, Tantra is something that pervades both Vedic and non-Vedic (nastika) faiths like Buddhism, Jainism and even Sikhism, according to some scholars, but this is by no means accepted by all. Many scholars believe its origins lie exclusively in the *sramanic,* that is non-Vedic, ascetic non-Brahmanical traditions, especially Buddhism. They will insist, with very sound reasons, that Tantra is fundamentally anti-Vedic and indeed incompatible with that tradition[22] (Chakrabarti 2001). It is not something that is simply reducible to a 'supplement'—obscene or otherwise—of the Vedas, as a disavowed but necessary element, as he tells us. In any case, what does it tell us about the relationship between the high Vedic and the Tantric world? At best this expression—the 'obscene supplement'—evades any proper specification or investigation of the relationship between the two worlds. However, Žižek's mode of theorizing should not surprise us, for this is simply the Western Left's theorization about capital(ism) projected backwards in time and sideways in space. Just as capital alone has agency and posits even its own 'outside', its heterogeneities, so here the philosopher sees the diverse practices of Tantra as mere appendages or outgrowths of 'Vedic teaching'—whatever that means.

More significantly, Tantra as it existed in India, from at least the fifth century CE onward, can only be read by the European philosopher 'retroactively'—through the experience of some twenty-first-century fad in the West (the 'spirit of late capitalism'!). Can one do any better in reducing the non-West to Europe's 'obscene supplement', for the non-West exists now, only to the extent that it is 'posited' by Europe/West?

It may be useful at this stage now, to contrast what Žižek says to what scholars in the field—both Western and Indian—who have spent decades studying the phenomenon, have to say about Tantra. Notice the huge diversity of meanings and practices that Tantra embodies, according to these scholars. In Paul E. Muller-Ortega's words, Abhinavagupta, the tenth-century Kashmiri Saivite philosopher, shows,

> (The) early Hindu Tantra rejects the dry vistas of traditional philosophical debate, which seek only representation of the Ultimate through conceptual truths. It rejects as well the self-enclosing renunciation of traditional Indian monasticism, which protectively seeks to isolate the monk from the imagined stain of worldliness. Transcending the dualities and distinctions of conventional thought and morality, the Tantra demonstrates an outward gesture of embracing delight in all of reality. (cited in 'Introduction', by Robert Brown 2002: 10–11)

Robert Brown (2002: 3) himself observes:

> The way for Tantric practitioners to reach dual goals, comes by connecting themselves to a power that flows through the world, including their own bodies, a power usually visualized as female. Tantrins identify the power, locate it, activate it, and use it for their own desires.

He sees Tantra as '*an accumulation of practices and ideas* from various sources distributed unevenly in different times, places and among individuals' (Brown 2002: 1, emphasis added).

Andre Padoux underlines:

> The use of sex is not found in all Tantric traditions. It is not prevalent but present nonetheless in the Saiva and Sakta groups that have a Kapalika origin or background and that have kept, if only symbolically, the Kapalika culture of the cremation ground with its cult of the Yoginis and its erotico-mystic rites and notions. (Padoux, 'What do we Mean by Tantrism?' in Brown 2002: 20)

These are just a few citations to illustrate the complex set of practices that constitute Tantra. Let me now turn to Žižek's philosophizing on Indian civilization and culture at large. Here is what Žižek has to say in one crisp and pregnant paragraph:

> What we find in the Veda is a brutal cosmology based on killing and eating: higher things kill and eat/consume lower ones, the stronger eat the weaker; that is life is a zero-sum game in which one's victory is another's defeat. *The 'great chain of being' appears here in the 'food chain', the great chain of eating*: gods eat mortal humans, humans eat mammals, mammals eat lesser animals who eat plants, plants 'eat' water and earth ... such is the eternal cycle of being. So why does the Veda claim that the top social stratum consists not of warrior-kings stronger than all other humans, 'eating' them all, but of the caste of priests? It is here that the code's ideological ingenuity becomes apparent: the function of the priests is to prevent the first, highest, level of cosmic eating, the eating of human mortals by gods. How? By way of performing sacrificial rituals. Gods must be appeased, their hunger for blood must be satisfied, and the trick of the priests is to offer the gods a substitute (symbolic) sacrifice: an animal or other prescribed food instead of human life. (Žižek 2011: 16–17, emphasis added)

Žižek begins this section with a prefatory sentence which says, linking to an earlier discussion on Confucianism,

> 'This same materialism is also clearly discernible in the Laws of Manu...',

where a footnote attached to 'Manu' gives the following reference: '*Laws of Manu*, trans. Wendy Doniger, New Delhi: Penguin Books 2000'. Two other references to this text follow two pages later, after a long discussion where Žižek seems to be talking as though he has full command of the original text. Doniger, it should be remembered, is not just the translator but a scholar of Hinduism of long-standing.

But let that pass. For the present, let us look closely at the quote mentioned earlier. His claim about the great chain of being becoming the 'great chain of eating' is not his at all, but a formulation of nineteenth- and twentieth-century scholars of Indology like Sylvain Levi and Francis Zimmerman whose work Wendy Doniger discusses at some length, all three uncited, of course, by Žižek. This is a specific reading and not just some 'Truth' about Indian civilization. It is an important and interesting formulation but one that is, like everything else, open to debate. Doniger herself does not present it as anything more than a much-discussed but plausible proposition. It is once again the Philosopher who steps in to transform this specific reading into a truth about an entire civilization. And then, most amazingly, the emergence of 'priesthood' and its special place in this culture is reduced to a simple matter of an expedient, a 'trick' to deceive the gods! This point too, with the added grandiose philosophical flourish, of course, is drawn straight from Doniger's work but presented as original insight.

'This', says Žižek with great flourish, 'was the first contract between ideologists (priests) and those in power (warrior-kings)', (Žižek 2011: 17) extending without any self-consciousness, the modern Western fiction of contract onto a civilization whose history and thought he has no clue about.

This breathtaking reduction of an entire civilization to a matter of trickery and contract is done entirely on the basis of the reading of a single text, in the English translation, by one scholar. For Žižek's information, we could mention that there are at least three other English translations of the same text (the *Manusmriti or Laws of Manu*), by different scholars (starting with William Jones in the eighteenth century), with their readings of the text—not to speak of entire libraries of books in Sanskrit, Persian, Pali and other regional languages that give a sense of the range of beliefs, practices and intellectual debates on the thing that comprises what we know as 'Indian civilization'. Scholars working in the field have long grappled with this ocean of material—but the Philosopher's engaged subjectivity gives him direct access to 'the truth', merely on the basis of a superficial reading of a single translation of a single text.[23]

If Žižek had even read a fraction of what serious scholars of Indian thought and politics have been writing for the past decades, he would have realized how ridiculous his 'theorization' sounds. It is not for me to give Žižek the reading list for these texts but he could profitably look up the vast oeuvre of Sheldon Pollock, especially Pollock (2009) that looks at the first moment of 'secularization' of Sanskrit around the beginning of the Common Era, for starters; he could read the work of David Shulman whose recent work (Shulman 2012) explores the relationship of imagination, thought and reality in South India or at the work of Johannes Bronkhorst (2011) or Lawrence McCrea (2009) that deals with complex debates in poetics and the question of rasa and meaning to just get a glimpse of the vast range of preoccupations of the civilization that he tries to sum up in one paragraph. There are literally libraries of books that he could profitably look at. He could read the works of twentieth-century Indian philosophers like K.C. Bhattacharya, J.L. Mehta, Bimal Matilal, J.N. Mohanty and more contemporary scholars of Indian philosophy like Jonardan Ganeri, Arindam Chakrabarti and others. I am not sure though that even all this will encourage the Philosopher to revise a word of what he has to say, or that he will start treating the non-West as anything more than a field of native informants—after all, his philosophy is *a priori* and other worlds are merely posited by what he believes to be the higher life-form. Remember, the anatomy of man is the key to the anatomy of the ape?[24]

Capital and 'Totality'

At the risk of partially anticipating an argument made at greater length in Chapter 6, let me now enter another aspect, another way in which the pre-capitalist forms are simply rendered, retrospectively, as moments in the history of capital's arising.

In an argument with Alain Badiou regarding the status of 'classes' in 'society', Žižek accuses Badiou of 'reducing classes to parts of a social body', apparently

> forgetting the lesson of Louis Althusser, namely that 'class struggle' paradoxically *precedes* classes as determinate social groups, that is that every class position and determination is already an effect of the 'class struggle.' This is why 'class struggle' is another name for the fact that 'society does not exist'—it does not exist as a positive order of being.' (Žižek 2011: 198)

So far so good, and one could perhaps agree with the latter part of the statement (society does not exist as a positive order of being) without necessarily agreeing that something called 'class struggle' is what accounts for it. Anybody who has read Ernesto Laclau and Chantal Mouffe's *Hegemony and Socialist Strategy (2001/1985)* would be familiar with the idea of the 'impossibility of society' and the difficulties of taking the 'positivity of the social' for granted, which one might recall, drew heavily on their reading of the Althusserian notion of *overdetermination* as an expression of the fact that 'the social constitutes itself as a symbolic order', which implies that social relations lack an ultimate literality that would reduce them to necessary moments of an immanent law' (Laclau and Mouffe 2001: 97–98). One may agree or disagree with the details of their exposition, but it is nevertheless true that this point is not really altogether new.

My problem with Žižek's claim, however, lies elsewhere—in the following explication of this proposition and the specific theoretical instance he uses for the purpose:

> In other words, one should always bear in mind that for a true Marxist, 'classes' are *not* categories of positive social reality, parts of the social body, but categories of the real of a political struggle which cuts across the entire social body, *preventing its 'totalization'. True, there is no outside to capitalism today, but this should not be used to hide the fact that capitalism itself is 'antagonistic', relying on contradictory measures to remain viable*—and these immanent antagonisms open up the space for radical action. (Žižek 2011: 198–199, all emphasis added)

Žižek, like most Western Marxists, finds himself in a bind here. Having once proclaimed 'capitalism' to be a 'totality' with its own internal logic and then having proclaimed—on the basis of their own narrow experience—that 'there is no outside to capital', how is he to understand dissonances and 'radical political action', especially from sectors that are no longer outside in his view? How then do you understand practices that do not quite fit the notion of an immanent 'logic of capital'? Here we are presented with a subterfuge: capitalism is self-antagonistic—that is to say, *in order to remain viable, it also posits its own potential negations.* As an instance of this process, Žižek says: 'If, say a cooperative movement of poor farmers in a Third World country succeeds in establishing a thriving alternative network, this should be celebrated as a genuine *political event*' (Žižek 2011: 199, emphasis original). Why the cooperative movement of poor farmers in a Third World country should be a consequence of capital trying to remain viable is not very clear to many of us on this side of the divide but we shall come to that question later.

Also notice that this claim by Žižek is very different from Marx's that capitalism brings with it its own grave-digger in the form of the proletariat—which in his scheme of things was the necessary consequence of the uprooting of 'precapitalist' life-forms, on which alone the edifice of capitalism could be erected. Marx's idea of the proletarian grave-digger of capital arose from the historical optimism of a certain Hegelian rendering of history. In that understanding, the appearance of the exploited proletariat was but a moment in the unfolding of the drama of human emancipation. But the empirical-historical thinker in Marx could not do away with social forms that are destroyed through large-scale dispossession or what he calls 'primitive accumulation'—they have to be accounted for even if they are destroyed. In Žižek's case, on the other hand, every antagonistic element is capital's own creation for 'there is really no outside to capitalism'. The situation is now one of despair and not just for historical reasons but for reasons entirely theoretical. For it is clear from his example that between Marx's time and his, the 'poor farmers in the third world' have not obliged the philosopher by disappearing into the pages of history; they are alive and kicking, fighting *and* forming cooperatives. They have also not allowed therefore, the 'logic of capital' to play itself out. But the Hegelian philosopher cannot believe that this can be anything but a situation *posited by capital itself*! And yet, if it is posited by capital itself, how can one read resistance into it? Thus his despair and thus his need to believe that capitalism *can* be challenged in *some* fashion. If it is not an insurrection, let it be the formation of a poor farmers' cooperative! He is now even prepared to celebrate that as a *political* event.

The problem here with Žižek as with most Western Marxists is that they have no way of seeing dissonances and life forms other than capital as anything but the effects of capital, just as in some other variants, they are seen as the effects of modernity: there is no such thing as 'tradition' (even reconstituted tradition), but something that is already an effect of modernity. If one were to trace the philosophical genealogy of this idea, one would have to go back to the Hegelian/Marxist (but also the Enlightenment) moment where all these societies outside the 'modern', capitalist west, were seen as societies/peoples without history, without change or the capacity for change. They were inert masses brought into the orbit of history and civilization by the West. Anything that produced a change in them could only have been introduced from outside.

The world looks very different, however, when seen from this side of the divide. That is why the 1960s debate on capitalist development in the 'peripheries', referred to earlier, was marked precisely by this anxiety among Marxists as to why capitalism was *not* developing in the non-West. That is why, Kalyan Sanyal's work (2007) turns to address precisely this question—but freed of Marxist anxieties. Sanyal sees 'postcolonial capitalism' as a formation where the effects of primitive accumulation are continuously reversed through governmental intervention, where the so-called 'informal sector' functions on a logic that is completely at variance with the logic of accumulation. Sanyal sees large sectors of this economy that he refers to as those of non-capital, as functioning on the basis of an implicit understanding of need.

That is why, when Subaltern Studies scholars began to engage with the history of peasant revolts and the working-class movement, they had to inevitably confront the history of capital in India. They came to the conclusion that the 'universal history of capital' had failed to play itself out in these societies. Thus, Dipesh Chakrabarty (2000) refers to 'two histories of capital' (H1 and H2), where the latter refers to life-worlds that are in some sense external to capital's universal history. Žižek enters into a debate with Chakrabarty and follows the latter's argument through parts where Žižek seems to be conceding that co-existence of non-capitalist life-worlds, gods and spirits and so on, with capital, may actually be a more general condition (Žižek 2011: 280–285). But this agreement is only apparent and Žižek's theoretical response is not unexpected:

> Such co-existence holds not only for India, but is present everywhere, including in the most developed societies. It is here that one should apply the properly dialectical notion of totality: capitalism functions as a 'totality', *in other words, elements of pre-existing life-worlds and economies (including money) are gradually re-articulated as its own moments, 'exapted' with a different function*. What this means is that the line separating H1 and H2 is by definition blurred: parts of H2 'found' by capitalism to be external to it, become permanently re-articulated as its integral elements. (Žižek 2011: 284, emphasis added)

So thinks the philosopher for whom capitalism as a coherent totality is an a priori assumption (though he has forgotten his own subterfuge by now—that 'class struggle prevents totalization'). Needless to say, such an *a priori* assumes a highly problematic form from the perspective of those who are not only challenging, resisting or fighting their integration into 'the totality' but also from the standpoint of those who continue to engage in practices that capital/ism cannot really always deal with or articulate within itself. This certainly needs to be demonstrated at length—a task that is not possible within the confines of this chapter but which I have undertaken elsewhere (Nigam 2014). As an *a priori* assumption, however, it makes more sense for us to see these opposing forces as forces arrayed in battle, none really able to contain, appropriate and reproduce the other as its own moment in the fashion of a Hegelian totality. That is to say, it makes more sense for us to see them in terms of what Laclau would say is the 'failure of the structure to be'—a structure that is always threatened, indeed, *constituted by its 'outside'*. In such an understanding, the 'structure' has no existence except as what its conditions of existence allow it to be. It is a structure that is, therefore, never in control of itself—things always escaping it, if one were to get Deleuzian.

There is also a powerful tradition in the Mahayana current of Buddhism and the great third century Madhyamika philosopher, Nagarjuna, that revolves around the idea of *Sunyata*, which can be translated into modern philosophical language as 'nothingness' but perhaps more correctly, as 'emptiness'.[25] This term in Buddhism and in Nagarjuna's words refers to the claim of the lack of independent existence, or of the essence of things—at the level of 'ultimate truth'. Thus Nagarjuna 'relentlessly analyzes phenomena or processes that appear to exist independently and argues that they cannot so exist' (Garfield 1994: 219).

This idea of things not having independent existence is a way of making the following claim: That things/processes do not exist *independently* of other things. That is to say, Nagarjuna does not deny their truth; what he denies is the idea of some sort of an internal essence. This is so because to Nagarjuna, this idea is tied closely to his key concept—*pratitya sammutpada*, or dependent arising. 'This term denotes the nexus between phenomena in virtue of which events depend on other events, composites depend on their parts and so forth' (Garfield 1994: 221). That is to say, if we are to understand anything—and Nagarjuna is not saying that you cannot, except that it is always at one remove—we must first recognize that they make sense only in the larger order of things. A more contemporary philosophical way of saying this would be to claim that there are no self-enclosed structures or totalities that have their own internal logic; that structures, to the extent that they exist, are always constituted by their larger field composed of other entities, other structures—*even their own dissonant parts*. The different elements of a 'structure' are what they are, then, not simply because they exist within a set of relations within the structure but because the structure is itself an element that acquires meaning in its relationship with other 'structures'. Thus, 'capitalism' too cannot be understood as a self-enclosed sovereign totality for its 'structure' too is dependent—on other 'structures'—the environmental eco-systems, where peasant communities or indigenous peoples' communities themselves may be part of the eco-systems; industrial labour, which too is not simply part of the 'capitalist economy' but always also part of larger or local urban eco-systems.

Seen thus, the empirical instances that Žižek marshals in order to demonstrate that capitalism can appropriate all dissonant elements and reproduce them as its own moments, will now appear in a very different light. Capital, at the end of the twentieth century, before the onset of neo-liberalism, was not a totality in command of the universe but was seriously threatened by the combined power of labour and environmental movements (high wages, labour regulations and the growing ecological movements). The victory of neo-liberalism and the collapse of the Soviet bloc gave it a shot in the arm that was certainly not immanent to capital's inner logic. Indeed, the debate around the social clause in the mid-1990s, during the final stages of the Uruguay Round of the GATT negotiations, when the WTO was being put in place, showed serious fissures and divisions between capital in the west and Western governments and also between capital in the west and capital in the 'third world'—so much so that western governments were willing to demand union rights and other important labour and environmental standards of their rivals in the third world. They were prepared to go so far as to link these standards to 'fair trade', not because they represented the 'enlightened bourgeoisie' of the 'advanced West' but because these standards would help undercut the trade advantage that the lack of them gave their third world rivals. There was no immanent logic of capital in evidence here—only various components of 'capital' in confrontation with each other. We could go on but let these instances suffice for now. Before we end, however, I want to delve a bit more into Žižek's relationship to Marxism as it will also help me further clarify my own methodological points of departure, coming as I do from within the history of Marxism—a different Marxism certainly but Marxism nevertheless.

Žižek, the Theologian and Marxism

In a well-known couplet, Mirza Ghalib, one of Urdu's finest poets says,

imaaN mujhe roke hai jo khiNche hai mujhe kufr
ka'aba mere peeche hai kaleesa mere aage

[Faith holds me back when infidelity beckons/
The Kaaba lies behind me; before me, the Church] — Mirza Ghalib

It is difficult to miss the immense subversiveness of the dilemma encapsulated in Ghalib's couplet quoted here. This dilemma of the believer is produced by the constant threat of corruption—the Kaaba behind the believing Muslim holds him back from indulging in, or falling prey to, the infidelities and temptations that always lie in wait.

Substitute Marxism for Kaaba and 'postmodernism' for Church, and you have the perfect Žižekian incarnation of this classic Ghalibian dilemma: Not quite at home in the Faith (Lacan, *jouissance*, surplus-enjoyment, the Real…) and yet, not able to leave it either, for the fear of what might befall one deserting the Order. Faith is the anchor that holds one back from committing all kinds of blasphemies. Nevertheless, the seductions of infidelity force our philosopher to turn for sustenance precisely to the philosophers and ideas he mistrusts: unlike most members of the Marxist faith, he repeatedly returns to Nietzsche and Heidegger, to Derrida, Foucault, Laclau and Deleuze. He takes over their language and makes himself at home in it. Is there a hidden jouissance in thus frequenting this forbidden territory?

Thus, he can in one breath defend the entire heritage of Marxism (from the 1917 October revolution to 'revolutionary terror') and at the same time claim that the attempts to trace the moment of the Fall (the Late Engels, Lenin's deviation from the classical path, Stalin's perversities and so on) must be rejected: 'the Fall is to be inscribed in the very origins', says he (Žižek 2008: 175).

Some years ago, Slavoj Žižek wrote a series of essays advocating a passionate 'return to Lenin' and a 'reassertion of the politics of Truth' (Slavoj Žižek 2002) and 'Can Lenin Tell Us about Freedom

Today?' (Žižek 2001). He set up his argument in opposition to those who 'dismiss the politics of Truth' as 'totalitarian' and argued for the need to 'break out of the deadlock' created by the post-Marxist and postmodernist endeavour to 'relegate politics to the domain of doxa'. The breaking out of this deadlock, he argued, must involve the reassertion of the 'politics of Truth' and must take the form of a return to Lenin (Žižek 2001: 1). He has since then, continued his journey along this path with ever-growing zeal, defending 'totalitarianism' or what is just another name for it, 'revolutionary terror', often with its proper name—the 'dictatorship of the proletariat'. In a more recent work (Žižek 2008) he moves his defence of these themes into the sublime:

> anti-totalitarian thought appears in all its misery as what it really is, a worthless sophistic exercise, a pseudo-theorization of the lowest opportunist survivalist fears and instincts, a way of thinking that is not only reactionary but also reactive in Nietzsche's sense of the term. (Žižek 2008: 4)

And in case anyone misses the 'true meaning' of this claim, let me underline that the reference to 'lowest opportunist fears' and reactive politics is a direct reference to so-called 'identity politics'—race, caste religion and so on. Thus, he says:

> In contrast to this approach, Badiou and others insist [and Žižek wholeheartedly endorses] on the fidelity to the One which emerges and is constituted through the very political struggle of/for naming and, as such, cannot be grounded in any particular determinate content (such as ethnic or religious roots). (Žižek 2008: 5)

Any careful reader of Žižek's can see that the insistence on 'fidelity to the One' is an insistence on the Universal but more so, it is a direct import from theology. A 'One' that 'cannot be grounded in any particular determinate content' is like Brahman, untouched by the 'particular determinate content' that is analogous to Maya. The fidelity to that One/Brahman can never be affected by the Maya of identity. At another level, his argument espouses that global, overdetermining struggle that subsumes every other struggle, namely the struggle against

Capital but the structural relation between the theological and the anti-Capital levels remains unshaken. Thus, he claims that

> This book [2008] is unashamedly committed to the 'Messianic' standpoint of universal emancipation. No wonder then, that to the partisans of the 'postmodern' doxa the list of lost Causes defended here must appear as a horror show of their worst nightmares…' among which he includes 'the revolutionary terror from Robespierre to Mao; Stalinism; the dictatorship of the proletariat…. (Žižek 2008: 6)

I am aware that this issue of 'Truth' (with a capital T), against which Žižek pits 'postmodern doxa', has been a very touchy issue for many well-meaning people but I do not wish to go into that question here. However, this much should be clear by now that this 'Truth' that Žižek defends has nothing to do with empirical reality or what really exists—however, we may want to understand that reality. Rather, it is an *a priori*, entirely metaphysical entity in his way of seeing things. What I do want to underline here is that there is neither anything particularly shocking nor particularly postmodern about this insistence either on the non-availability of Truth (epistemically) or on the position that there simply is no Ultimate Truth (ontologically). In our own sub-continental tradition, we have both, a radical epistemic denial of the access to Truth in Jaina philosophy's notions of *anekantavaad* and *syadvaad*; and an equally radical rejection of the ontological possibility of Ultimate Truth or *paramartha satya* in Nagarjuna and certain important currents of Buddhist philosophy that I have discussed earlier (Tripathi 2016: 83–87; also see note 23). Nagarjuna distinguishes between two orders of 'Truth' as many other Indian philosophers do—the *vyavaharika* or *samvritti satya*, that is practical or conventional truth on the one hand, and *paramartha satya* or ultimate truth, on the other, and insists that paramartha satya simply does not exist. Hence, his crucial notions of *sunyata* or emptiness and *anatma/anatta*—the ontological void or nothingness, and the 'non-self' as the true reality of the Self, in a manner of speaking (Garfield 2015; Nishitani 1983).

Žižek's stance is one of a new Messiah who has descended to destroy all the pagan worshipers of particularity and lead the world on to the One transcendent Truth. It is worth pointing out that Žižek openly gives specific content to this 'One' as in the Christian ideal. Let us look at the following two quotes from him

> Yes, there is a direct lineage from Christianity to Marxism; yes, Christianity and Marxism should fight on the same side of the barricade against the onslaught of new spiritualisms—the authentic Christian legacy is much too precious to be left to the fundamentalist freaks. (Žižek 2000: 2)

If this were a programme Žižek was outlining for the European or American Left, one would really have no quarrel with him. A deeper and more respectful engagement with all religious/spiritual traditions is certainly important today and as the reader will see, it forms an important part of the argument of this book. But as I indicated, that is precisely what he is not advocating: he *is* the monotheistic messiah who is out to destroy the pagan worshippers of particularity and what is more, he will not tolerate even its residues within Marxism. Lest I be accused of putting words in his mouth, here is Žižek himself, talking about Mao Zedong.

> One should be very precise in diagnosing, at the very abstract level of theory, where Mao was right and where he was wrong. Mao was right in rejecting the standard notion of 'dialectical synthesis' as the 'reconciliation' of the opposites, as a higher unity which encompasses their struggle; he was wrong in formulating this rejection, this insistence on the priority of struggle, of division, over every synthesis or unity, in terms of general cosmology—the ontology of the 'eternal struggle of opposites'—this is why he got caught up in the simplistic, properly *non-dialectical*, notion of the 'bad infinity' of struggle. *Mao clearly regresses here to primitive pagan 'wisdoms' on how every creature, every determinate form of life, sooner or later meets its end*... (Žižek 2008: 185, emphasis added).

What is left in this Marxism then, for those pagans who populate large parts of the Afro-Asian world or Latin America, is not a matter of concern to our philosopher.

To Žižek, the significance of Lenin lies in his 'unconditional will to intervene in the situation', not—as he puts it—in the pragmatic sense of 'adjusting theory' to reality but by 'adopting *the unequivocal radical position*' (note the use of the definite article) from which alone, he argues, it is 'possible to intervene in a way that it changes the coordinates of the situation' itself (Žižek 2001: 2). Žižek, in fact, claims that 'freedom is "actual" precisely and only as the capacity to "transcend" the coordinates of a given situation…that is, to redefine the very situation within which one is active' (ibid.: 3).

Žižek's insistence on the 'revolutionary' will to intervene and the will to change the coordinates of a given situation may seem to provide a much-needed corrective in today's world, where radical politics has been gripped by a fatalistic frame of mind, always having to choose the 'lesser evil' in any given situation, or simply acting in a pragmatic way. But that is not what Žižek means when he uses the term 'pragmatic'; for him, *any attempt* to rethink the practice of theory and its conceptual paraphernalia is tantamount to 'adjusting theory' [his term] to reality and is, therefore, pragmatic. His idea of 'transcending the coordinates of a given situation' simply amounts to an assertion that Theory (with a capital T) is prior to all empirical-historical reality and actually quite far removed from Lenin's sense of politics that is deeply cognizant of its contingent and conjunctural nature, which is why Lenin always insisted on what he called the 'concrete analysis of the concrete situation'.

However, my interest here is not in a re-examination of Leninist theory and practice, important as this task might be in order to come to terms with the legacy of twentieth-century socialism.[26] Here, I am only interested in making clear my own methodological points of departure via this discussion of Žižek.

One of the important things that happened in the aftermath of the collapse of Soviet socialism, was that haltingly and hesitatingly, an attempt started being made to cast a fresh look at the entire history of Marxism and communism. Even within the most hidebound sections of the Left, there was some attempt to acknowledge the immense diversity of Marxist theory and practice with a relatively greater degree of openness—though not always to the extent one would have liked to see. The sum and substance of Žižek's intervention have been to institute what can only be called a counter-revolution in Marxist thinking that was in the process of a renewal of the radical emancipatory project.

The Žižekian intervention seeks to put an end to all questioning and doubts and institute in their place a metaphysical messianism that directs all its critique outwards. But why should that surprise us? After all, his declared model is the Church and St Paul. This is a point that Žižek makes repeatedly: his understanding of Marxism's history is modelled on his reading of the history of Christianity where Lenin is to Marx what St Paul was to Christ, for it was they who gave institutional form to their Prophets' ideas. His open and unabashed 'defense of the Christian ideal' and his self-professed Eurocentrism, go hand in hand with his defence of Lenin. Lenin, in Žižek's hands, is truly a banner of regression that seeks to put a stop to all attempts to re-examine the history of Marxism on the one hand, and to clamp down on whatever postcolonial theory since Edward Said has managed to achieve by way of disturbing/challenging the hegemony of Western/European thought. Indeed, he has also lately been working to rid the white European Left of all 'guilt' by vigorously arguing that s/he should 'unashamedly' swear by Marx's early writings on India ('British Rule in India' and 'Future Results of British Rule in India' 1853) where Marx notoriously described colonialism as the 'unconscious tool of history'. This he does by completely disregarding that other episode in Marx's engagement with the East—his study of the peasant communes in Russia and his *Ethnological Notebooks*. That last chapter of Marx's life constitutes a fascinating moment in history when he not only started obsessively studying the Russian peasant communes but undertook a detailed study of India as well. His knowledge of India in the 1850s was quite superficial in comparison to the detailed study he made during this time. In the course of these studies, Marx began seriously rethinking the necessity of capitalism and considering the possibility of communal property being the basis of a transition to socialism. Žižek wants us to steer clear of that 'Late Marx' and espouse the European and Eurocentric theorist of revolution of the 1850s and 1860s. In other words, even in relation to Marx's own intellectual development, Žižek intervenes in a regressive fashion, restoring to Marx his earlier Eurocentric self, ironing out all the ambiguities, doubts, confusions and quests and replacing them by one single, self-serving narrative that is meant to salvage the European male Leftist's bad conscience.

Thinking Otherwise

With this, we come now to our final question. If even our most basic engagement with the empirical must take some a priori assumptions as our starting points, we will do well to reject the totalizing metaphysics of the Hegelian-Marxist kind and look for other metaphors. My own preference, as I have indicated earlier, is for the idea of a 'structure' that is constituted by its 'outside', always threatened by its dissonant internal other; it is therefore always incomplete, always threatened by what lies beyond its 'control'. In my discussion of Nagarjuna's idea of 'emptiness' and 'dependent arising', I have tried to indicate that from that point of view, the category of a structure or a totality is itself problematic. If the idea of dependent arising is essentially one that understands 'being' itself as empty (*anatta* or non-self), as an effect of a contingent encounter between different elements and constellations, then the concept of a structure will prove to be simply unworkable. The crucial distinction here will be between a methodological approach that prioritizes the totality or structure and one that argues that structures themselves are the consequence of contingent encounters between different elements and constellations.[27] We can see the encounter of these different forces in terms of other metaphors—such as that of 'confluence', as used for instance, by Ranjit Hoskote and Ilija Trojanow (2011)—which are not simple flows merging together but complex processes involving conflict as well. The idea of confluence works especially in the case of ideas in the pre-colonial context where it was not the power of the barrel of the gun that settled the superiority of ideas. Indeed, superiority and inferiority were not even terms in which these exchanges took place. One thinks of the great centres of learning in medieval Baghdad or Cordoba, where scholars from all over the world were invited, where translations and transmissions of different texts and ideas from China and India among others took place. One thinks likewise of the influence of Arab philosophers like Al Farabi, Ibn Sina and Ibn Rushd in the early European institutions of learning—especially from the thirteenth century on. Colonial domination and capitalism transformed even this terrain of intellectual and cultural transactions—the battle of ideas, never an easy or simple affair, now became akin to a real battle across cultural divides where political power determined the 'superiority' or otherwise of ideas. One could also think of these confrontations of capital with pre-capital/non-capital as 'encounters'—contingent and unpredictable in their outcomes.

I take Dabashi's injunction mentioned earlier—that of the need to transcend the West versus non-West binary instituted by the colonial condition and continued through the postcolonial, seriously. In so doing, I also want to raise some questions about the challenges for the non-European thinker today, though we will return to this issue at greater length in the final, concluding chapter.

One way of taking Dabashi's injunction seriously is to move beyond this need to say that 'we also have philosophy' or 'we also have thought'—to the same white man whom he described as a chimera. For some of us grappling with the issues of what it is to think in India/South Asia today, it is becoming increasingly clear that this task is impossible to accomplish—indeed even to begin meaningfully—without challenging the canon itself. The canon of *philosophy* in particular. For there is a certain self-referentiality within which philosophy circulates—its universalism is always already established, *a priori*—such that it can talk to itself, in endless circular exegeses. Plato, Aristotle, Kant, Descartes, Spinoza, Hegel, Heidegger, Deleuze, Badiou, Žižek, Ranciere...the circle sometimes expands a bit to induct a Spinoza, a Heidegger or a Nietzsche—but never an Al Farabi, Ibn Sina, Ibn Rushd or Ibn Khaldun. The charmed circle is impossible to break into—unless, of course, you decide to reconcile yourself to the terms laid out and leave your skin behind—which is to say, the history that makes you.

In the list of philosophers that I have mentioned earlier, there are some easily recognizable absences—Marx, Foucault and lately Latour. All considered to be lesser philosophers but perhaps precisely for that reason, closer to our notion of what philosophy or thought might be or can be today. For neither Marx nor Foucault nor Latour demand that before you start reading them you must first bow before the great canonical figures of philosophy. On the contrary, they invite you to read and engage with them from your own vantage point. If you want to understand capital or power, the modern institutions of discipline and labour, human relationship with the non-human, then the door is wide open for you to enter. In a manner of speaking, bringing up Marx and Foucault, in particular, also brings up another important issue: that of the relationship between philosophy and history that allows us to steer clear of the kind of metaphysics espoused by Žižek but also to move beyond the purely self-referential, exegetic mode.

Note that what I am talking about here is the style and mode of 'doing philosophy' by bringing it down from its metaphysical heights into the messy world of the social and the historical. It is not that Marx or Foucault are exempt from Eurocentric assumptions but the point is that they engage with their times in ways that are open—and in so far as such processes, institutions and disciplines exist outside the West, these 'philosophers' might have something to say to thinkers in other contexts as well. In a sense, the challenge of doing philosophy in the non-West too involves a similar move—of bringing thought down from its assumed universalist pedestal to speak to different histories and be alert to historical difference—in other words, *to become historical.* Indeed, in a manner of speaking, we will often need to reverse the relationship and bring in diverse historical trajectories and experiences (as for example of 'capital' discussed previously) to interrogate philosophy itself.

Thus, instead of claiming that 'we too had/have philosophy', it is important, it seems to me, to underline that we have today the responsibility to think differently. *To think in ways that are at once historical and philosophical.* Or to put it somewhat differently, *the challenge is to think at the borders of history and philosophy.* We do not have the luxury of indulging in the universalist mode of self-referential philosophizing that philosophers in the West have. For them, everything has always been already thought in its essentials from the narrow ground of their experience, and every new philosopher has to prove himself or herself to first be an exegete—whose only point of reference is the canonical Western text. For us, on the other hand, thinking involves challenging the given-ness of that universality of thought; it involves challenging the canon itself. And for this reason, more importantly, thinking for us involves a withdrawal, a stepping back, from entering into 'a dialogue' with Western philosophers, the terms for which are always-already set for us.

The challenge before non-Western thought, then, is that of reconstituting the paraphernalia of philosophy itself. And in order to be able to accomplish this, it must enter into another territory as well—that of an exploration of conceptual resources from different intellectual traditions. How have people in the three continents (Asia, Africa and Latin America) thought about their lives and times—through different ages? Writing these histories, reading and re-reading texts produced by them, entering into a critical dialogue with them—all these become necessary so that we can make them part of our own contemporary thought apparatus. This is easier said than done. For we cannot simply lay our hands on some ready-made material and mould it to our purposes; nor can we simply enter these traditions to seek answers to our contemporary problems in some instrumental fashion. Rather, we need to perform theoretical and philosophical labour on those materials in order that they may once again start speaking to us.

This may be the reason why the names that Dabashi cites as 'philosophers' are not easily recognizable as philosophers. Perhaps these thinkers have already made some of these moves in the manner stated by Mignolo, from pure, speculative philosophy to thinking at the borders. This, however, constitutes only the first step of a long journey. A critique of Eurocentrism must eventually lead to new concepts, new theoretical frameworks; it must lead to a reconstitution of thought and with it, of the human sciences.

Notes

1. I suppose such criticism must have come from other quarters as well, for some years down the line, the third Idea of Communism conference was held in Seoul, Korea. That, however, is another issue and cannot be discussed here.
2. It should be stated clearly here that what is at stake in this exchange is not the tragedy that 9/11 was, but rather the perception across large parts of the world—the Global South—that it was the USA in fact that represented Evil, if at all we could think of the episode in those terms. There is no

doubt, however, that it is once again, not the reality of 9/11 but the way it was perceived across the world that was at the centre of the controversy.

3. Hamid Dabashi, 'Can Non-Europeans Think?', *Aljazeera*, 15 January 2013. http://www.aljazeera.com/indepth/opinion/2013/01/20131141426387975 42.html (last accessed on 8 September 2019). Dabashi's more considered, systematic response to and reflections on the theme appeared subsequently as a book. See Dabashi (2015).
4. Santiago Zabala, 'Slavoj Žižek and the Role of the Philosopher', *Aljazeera*, 25 December 2012, http://www.aljazeera.com/indepth/opinion/2012/12/201212241222154069 39.html (last accessed on 28 February 2020).
5. Walter Mignolo, 'Yes, We Can: Non-Western Thinkers and Philosophers', *Aljazeera*, 19 February 2013, http://www.aljazeera.com/indepth/opinion/2013/02/20132672747320891.html (last accessed on 28 February 2020).
6. Clearly this was not the case with Marx's 'working class', which was no less historical-empirical than it was a theoretical category. He spoke of actual class struggles, even when he entered the realm of abstract theorizing.
7. Here Mignolo is citing Francis Bacon, where Bacon talks of the 'three faculties of the rational soul', namely, Memory (History), Imagination (Poetry) and Reason (Philosophy) as though they exhaust all forms of thinking—'there can be no others'.
8. 'Retarded' capitalism was one of the widely prevalent terms in the debate on capitalist development/underdevelopment in the 'peripheries' in the 1960s, 1970s and 1980s.
9. There is something quite interesting here, for most Indian Marxists had till recently held a completely contrary view. They all celebrated Lenin's genius in 'making revolution' in a backward country and in realizing that the imperialist chain can be broken at its weakest link. Most communist parties, therefore, saw their task in India along Leninist lines, as ushering in some form of 'democratic revolution'—people's democracy, national democracy or new democracy, etc. In the aftermath of the collapse of the Soviet Union, however, their 'analyses' took immediately to the more familiar, older idea that socialism can only be based on a firm capitalist foundation. This is the idea that underlies, for instance, the CPI(M)'s stand on industrialization in West Bengal that led to the unfortunate situation in Singur and Nandigram.
10. Here I am referring to institutional, party-Marxism. As distinct from this, Marxism as an intellectual tendency and as a discourse on modernity and politics has had a far more interesting and complex history. An

exploration of that is not possible within the limits of this chapter but certainly needs to be undertaken in all seriousness.

11. This is a stance explicitly adopted by Žižek (1998) himself though and I will return to this essay briefly, later in the chapter.
12. Admittedly, the landscape of nineteenth-century thought is far more variegated and the initial concerns are largely geared towards social and religious reform within Hindu as well as Muslim societies in different ways. I am grateful to P.K. Datta for pointing this out. In a sense, the discussion in Chapter 4, on the difference between the social reformers and the 'politicals', shows a continuation of the concern with the social question right through the anti-colonial struggle. However, it is still important to underline that from the late nineteenth century, that is to say, with the emergence of nationalist discourse, politics increasingly starts coming to the centre stage. However, in relation to thought more generally, the point is that reflection on abstract metaphysical questions largely recedes, making way, even in religious thought, for a reconstitution that is 'politically' inflected in the broader sense of the term.
13. In a sense, this can be said of liberalism as well but in a very different way. Nationalists did have a liberal critique of colonial rule—about it not following its own liberal principles in the colony. The crucial difference, it seems, had to do with the fact that Marxism allowed for a robust critique of empire, alongside a critique of class exploitation—thereby presenting before nationalism itself a serious problem. For nationalists 'internal critique' became anathema and ever so often, the interests of the landed and urban capitalist sections acquired predominance over the interests of the peasants for instance.
14. In extreme cases, this political imperative manifests itself in particularly crude ways, reducing every intellectual question to a matter of justice and power.
15. Michael Marder, 'A Post-colonial Comedy of Errors', *Aljazeera*, 13 April 2013, http://www.aljazeera.com/indepth/opinion/2013/03/201331411225576 1369.html (last accessed on 28 February 2020).
16. For a sophisticated recent exploration of the impact of one aspect of this pre-colonial philosophical confluence in India, see Jonardon Ganeri (2011).
17. See the set of essays in 'The Postnational Condition', *Economic and Political Weekly*, 7 March 2009. The group of South Asian scholars involved in the conversation included Malathi de Alwis and Pradeep Jeganathan from

Sri Lanka, S. Akbar Zaidi from Pakistan, the late M.S.S. Pandian, Satish Deshpande, Mary John, Nivedita Menon and myself from India.

18. There is an interesting discussion in Sanjay Palshikar (2014: 40–45) where the question of the *asuric* or the demonic tendencies is discussed, drawing largely on the *Puranas*. Repeatedly, Palshikar puzzles over the fact that there are references to decline or degeneration setting in without any ostensible reason:

> At the end of the Krta Yuga, the mental perfections are gradually lost. No reason for the loss is given (*Vayu Purana* 1.8.71). The wish yielding tree of the *Treta Yuga* perish because lust and greed 'possess' people suddenly, while at 8.80, the *Vayu Purana* blames the people ('due to their own perversity'), a little later (8.84) it says: 'On account of their perversity and *due to what was destined to happen in the course of time*, (emphasis mine) all the trees... perished.' People meditated and the trees materialized again, but after some time 'they [that is, the people] were overcome with greed once again (8.89). After the trees perished, people took to agriculture. Once again there was greed and unpleasant consequences followed. But the wording is significant: 'Then again all of them were overwhelmed with lust and greed and *as a result of unavoidable fate or due to the Treta age* (emphasis Palshikar's) (1.8.130). In the *Bhagavata Purana* narration, everything is fine till Vishnu 'retires to his region'. As soon as he does that, *Kali* enters the world and people begin to take delight in sinful ways. (*Bhagavata Purana*, 12.2.29). (Palshikar 2014: 43)

Palshikar's surmise is that 'the phase of degeneration, even though human beings cannot be held responsible for it, is not senseless. It is part of the ontological necessity. Its role is to pave the way for the divided totality to close in on itself and become Unity again' (Ibid.: 44). While this does help us make narrative sense of decline or degeneration, it still does not explain why decline repeatedly sets in, even when they were once in an ideal state. My sense is that the key ontological assumption here is that Time itself is the cause, no other cause is needed to justify why things change or change in the way they do—hence Mahakaal or Time as the great destroyer or Annihilator. This is not exactly a timeless, changeless Eternity but a Time that is always the cause of change but itself has no beginning or end.

19. Sometimes this is said in a part serious and part ironical way but like most of Žižek's writings, there is always a 'zone of indistinction' so to speak, where his jokes seem to express his own fears and his secret beliefs.
20. The irony seems to completely escape him that this description could fit most Western cities.
21. For a discussion of his recent Eurocentrism, see Nivedita Menon (2010), written as a response to Žižek during his visit to Delhi.
22. Also see the discussion on the Puranic mode in Chapter 5.
23. I discuss these points at greater length further in the chapter.
24. Readers will recognize this as the opening of the famous passage from Marx's *Grundrisse*, where the idea was to claim that it is only with the appearance of the higher social form that the secret of the lower is revealed.
25. Most scholars seem to agree that this doctrine or idea is central to Buddhism as such but also that it is in Nagarjuna that it is given its fullest exposition. I am also aware that in the huge body of scholarship on Buddhism and Nagarjuna, there are pretty divergent interpretations of various issues connected with the key concepts involved. Starting with the concept of *sunyata* itself, we get a range of differing interpretations on the related concepts of *svabhava* (inherent nature), *samvrtti satya* and *paramartha satya* (conventional truth and ultimate truth) and so on. It is not within my competence to judge as to which among these different positions is closest to Nagarjuna's intent but it does seem to me that there is a fairly wide agreement that interdependent existence is so crucial as to throw the question of the 'existence' of any entity into doubt. The point being that if one insists on interdependent existence or dependent arising, then every self or entity is what it is, *only* in that relationality. To that extent, ideas like those of a bounded self, an autonomous subject or a bounded existence (of inanimate objects) too become seriously problematic and unthinkable—though some scholars argue that Nagarjuna was discussing dharma-like entities, rather than phenomenal objects, while some others believe he refers to 'concepts' and to the impossibility of metaphysics when he talked of ultimate reality and sunyata. At the moment, I am only interested in drawing out some implications from this key philosophical issue raised by Nagarjuna's thought for thinking our own predicament/s. For some other important works, see Gowans (2003), Nayak (1979, 2000), Jayatilleke (1963), Chinn (2001), Loy (1993), Garfield and Priest (2003).

26. As a matter of fact, Žižek really misses the whole point of the Leninist 'will to intervene' itself: Lenin repeatedly points out that revolutionaries cannot simply call a revolutionary situation into existence or create it out of nothing; *they must always act upon a given situation.* We need only recall Lenin's assertion in the context of the collapse of the Second International that 'to the Marxist it is indisputable that a revolution is impossible without a revolutionary situation' and that not every revolutionary situation leads to a revolution ('The Collapse of the Second International', *Collected Works*, Vol. 21, Progress Publishers, Moscow, 1977, p. 213). One of the critical conditions for a revolutionary situation to arise, in Lenin's view, is that of a 'considerable increase in the activity of the masses' as a consequence of which they are drawn into 'independent historical action' (Ibid.: 214). Lenin implicitly makes a distinction here, between a revolutionary situation and a non-revolutionary situation. And we know that a Leninist intervention is predicated upon a certain specific kind of configuration of forces and antagonisms, called 'overdetermination' by Althusser, where different conflicts coalesce into an explosive unity. We also know that Lenin's own response after the defeat of the 1905 revolution and especially after 1908, was to wait for the 'new revolutionary upsurge'. Further, more fundamentally, Lenin's legacy itself needs to be considered afresh today—both in terms of its relevance for the present and in relation to the fate of 'actually existing socialist' societies. Žižek confronts neither. Surely the political practice of the communist movement has revealed sufficient reason for the understanding that the 'politics of Truth' that he identifies with Lenin, led to totalitarianism. The ontological and epistemological privilege—in relation to access to the Truth—granted to the 'working class' in the Marxist tradition, and its transference to the 'vanguard' in the Leninist schema, has been discussed often enough. It has been convincingly shown to lead to an authoritarian, if not totalitarian mindset. Within the history of Marxism, there is clearly a larger body of work—and other political currents—that make a strong critique of the vanguardism of the Leninist framework. These range from Rosa Luxembourg to council communism. Lenin and Leninism constituted only one tendency within the history of Marxism and the radical Left. It was a tendency that was responsible, eventually, for destroying all heresies and heterodox voices critical of the 'Church'.
27. For a more detailed discussion of this question of a contingent 'structure', see Chapter 6.

4

Theorizing the Political

Mandala and the Social Polity[1]

> Cosmological schemes of various sorts in Tantric Hinduism and Buddhism have been referred to as mandala—for example, the cosmos as constituted of Mount Meru in the center surrounded by oceans and mountain ranges. At a philosophical and doctrinal level, the Buddhist *Sarvastivadin* school represented the relation between consciousness (*citta*) and its associated mental phenomena (*caitta*) in terms of the law of satellites, wherein consciousness placed in the center is surrounded by ten *caitta*, each of which again is surrounded by four *laksana*, or satellites...
>
> At quite a different level, Kautilya in his *Arthashastra,* used mandala as a geo-political concept to discuss the spatial configuration of friendly and enemy states from the perspective of a particular kingdom. (Tambiah 1973/2013: 503–504)

All discussions of politics and 'the political' tend to go back to ancient Athens and the idea of the *polis* where free men periodically assembled in the public square to decide on matters of public importance. There is an underlying assumption that whatever the histories of the political—or of the state—in other parts of the world, they are really irrelevant now, for the story of modernity and the modern state is an entirely different one. After all, who can dispute that modernity, especially in colonial contexts, instituted a fundamental rupture in the traditional ways of knowing and doing and instituted altogether new ways upon which our modern institutions are built. Athens however, escapes this fate despite its antiquity, because it is now an assumed modernity's common past. The assumption that thereby, everything else of that past and of all other pasts is erased without residue, is unsustainable and can lead to fundamentally wrong analyses and understandings of both past and present. Methodologically, therefore, it is important to recognize that: (a) the appearance of the modern state is an entirely new, indeed ruptural phenomenon, even in the history of Europe and the advent of the colonial state in the colonies is even more so, at many different levels, including the epistemological; (b) even though this newness needs to be given due weight, it also needs to be recognized that the old traditional forms, and the practices associated with those forms, do not simply exit the stage obediently, just because the modern demands it.

There are myriad ways in which those ways of knowing and being, long thought to have been erased, continue to animate and write our present in ways we may not even be aware of. One of the purposes of this chapter is to suggest some possible lines of connection that may help understand some practices better. In doing so, this chapter also attempts to gesture towards other histories of the political.

The epigraph to this chapter from the Sri Lankan anthropologist Stanley Tambiah draws attention to one widely extant cosmology that also found its material analogues in what Tambiah calls the 'galactic polity'—the idea of the galaxy being used by him here to underline the form that he identifies with the *mandala*. The context of Tambiah's discussion is Thailand—and Southeast Asia more generally—but the cosmology that he refers to has a much larger resonance across South Asia, and through his reference to Kautilya's *Arthashastra*, he wants to alert us to the pervasiveness of the mandala. One thing that is evident about this form, politically speaking, is that there is no notion in it of centralized power of the sovereign. Tambiah (2013: 514) says

> At a surface level the cosmological account gives a magnificent picture of the exemplary center pulling together and holding in balance the surrounding polity' but, it is possible to properly appreciate its sense 'only after we have properly understood the decentralized locational propensity of the traditional polity and its replication of like entities on a decreasing scale....[2]

Among historians, the character of 'the state' in India and its different forms in the pre-colonial era, have long been a matter of dispute, centring especially on the idea of the 'segmentary state' (Kimura and

Tanabe 2006; Kulke 1995). The point of dispute in this debate is the idea of the modern sovereign centralized state with its fixed territory that is often anachronistically projected on to pre-colonial India, as Burton Stein, one of the key proponents of the 'segmentary state' idea argues (Stein 1995: 135). We will return to some of these themes later but for the moment, it would be worthwhile noting that in different ways, many political thinkers of modern India point us towards a notion of a state in pre-colonial times that stands in relative marginality to the social order. Scholars like Rajni Kothari (1970), D.L. Sheth (1984) and Ashis Nandy (2003) have long argued that a distinctive feature of Indian society traditionally was the relative marginality of the political order. While Nandy claims this was part of a larger civilizational understanding, Kothari reads in it a repeated failure to build a political centre. These scholars also suggest that this feature continues to structure the way politics is practiced in modern times, in the life of post-independence Indian democracy.

The argument in this chapter is about theorizing the political *from* non-European contexts, not necessarily only *about* them. In other words, even though the specific discussion here will rely largely on the Indian experience, the implicit claim is that it will have a bearing on how we think about the political as such. The point is not to underline the fact that 'we are different' or that categories of Western thought 'do not work in our contexts', for that has been done for far too long and is ultimately a way of avoiding the task of theorizing our own historical formation. Nor will it be my claim that whatever the West has or had, 'we too had' in some remote past. That kind of exercise too has been done often enough in the past, especially say, in the way scholars tried to find parallels to Western concepts in Indian thought or to find ancient roots of democracy in India on the basis of scant evidence. Certainly, there is evidence that there were elaborate procedures of deliberation, holding of meetings and voting on resolutions, especially in the *gana-sanghas* but much more historical and theoretical work needs to be done to enable a better understanding of the ancient polity. Mere gestures to such deliberative practices or to some instances of representation and immoderate claims about modern democracy based on them serve no knowledge purpose—even if it might rhetorically suit the purposes of certain kinds of politics.[3]

It is important while recognizing that all thought, including political thought, did not come to the world from classical Greece, that just as notions of *polis* and democracy were retrospectively recovered and imbued with certain meanings in the context of the rise of the modern West, it is the work of contemporizing that makes that ancient legacy meaningful in a new way. In a sense, many nationalist scholars did do that, claiming a democratic inheritance by drawing especially on a passage from the *Mahaparinibbana-sutta* in the context of the Buddhist sangha, where Buddha says that the *sangha* 'will survive as long as, among other things, it has frequent assemblies, maintains concord, acts in accordance with the *Vinaya* (the discipline ordained for the monk), and honours the elders' (*Digga Nikaya* cited in Thapar 1984: 82).[4] Where these scholars erred was in trying to read their own traditions in the light of the new knowledge from the West, attempting to show that they too had all that the West claims it had rather than trying to understand their own history on its own terms. Take for instance the very ancient concept of *matsya nyaya* (the 'logic of the fish' where big fish eat small fish) that is routinely interpreted as our ancient version of the Hobbesian 'state of nature'. The fact is that there is no one account or imagination of the birth of the state or political power in the ancient texts. In the Santi Parva in the *Mahabharata*, we have the powerful claim that, 'Once there was no ruling authority, no king, no coercion and no coercer, for people took care of each other out of a sense of righteousness.' With the decline of righteousness, people became covetous, lustful and wrathful—that's when you have the emergence of the 'state'. This is the context of Bhishma's exposition of the idea of *rajadharma* and *danda* or punishment. The Santi Parva then talks of *matsyanyaya*, not as part of the theory of origin of 'state' or kingship but as the chaos and anarchy that results in extraordinary situations like droughts. A Buddhist story of the emergence of the state 'begins with the pristine utopia where food was not required since the physical body was luminescent. People were not divided into families, there were no individual or group possessions and consequently, there was no need for social laws. But some among the people tasted earth, found it delicious and greed and craving entered the being of man' (Thapar 1984: 120). Everything started going wrong thereafter. People now started requiring food and they started hoarding it, lust and passion emerged, and with them families. All kinds of ills started emerging, necessitating the emergence of the *Maha-sammata*—the one chosen consensually for ruling over them. Given such a wide range of different accounts including the Buddhist one where the very name *Maha-sammata* suggests chosen by common consent, it is strange that *matsya-nyaya* should become *the* account of the emergence of the state among nationalists.

This stance of attempting to find the roots of every modern idea in ancient India is an expression of a continuing colonial hangover. This attitude is so widespread that we have seen even the most sophisticated contemporary scholars trying to disprove that 'we' were in any sense different from the West. We can, at best, accept that we might have had different histories (a trifle difficult, it would seem, not to concede that) but it is as if to accept that we might not have had say, a concept of 'history' and 'historical consciousness' is to concede that we were barbarians—though if that were the case, surely, that too must be acknowledged.

The point, therefore, that I am trying to make here, is that referring to our specific histories and our specific cultural formations (which are always also encoded relations of power and domination), does not simply imply a celebration of those cultural-historical contexts. On the contrary, it can only mean a critical engagement with those contexts—not flinching from the most 'ruthless criticism of all that existed', at least where necessary. Mere celebration of our great Vedic and Upanishadic heritage is not decolonization, in my sense of the term. Moreover, the field of what we can generically call 'Indian philosophy', as we know, is neither exclusively Vedic or Upanishadic, nor without serious and severe contentions between different philosophical schools.[5]

Political Power: Mandala and Segmentarity

'The Indian state is barely visible to comparative sociology', says Nicholas Dirks as he begins the exposition of his justly acclaimed study of the 'little kingdom' of Pudukottai, *The Hollow Crown*. When this state appears, it does so, he argues, 'as a weak form of Oriental Despotism, destined to disappear as suddenly...as it emerged' (Dirks 1987: 3). He continues to then take 'Weber, Marx, Maine, and more recently Dumont' to task for having held, that in contrast to China, 'the state [in India] was epiphenomenal (Ibid.: 3). Describing Marx's view as typical of this genre, Dirks cites him thus:

> Just as Italy has, from time to time, been compressed by the conqueror's sword into different national masses, so do we find Hindustan, when not under the pressure of the Mohammedan, or the Mogul, or the Briton, dissolved into as many independent and conflicting States as it numbered towns, or even villages. (Dirks 1987)

Thus, he says, 'states came and went', but 'village communities endured' (Ibid.: 3). Dirks' discomfort with Marx (and all others mentioned earlier) is clear, even though there is a slippage here between Marx's 'independent and conflicting States' and Dirks' reduction of them to 'village communities'. But the more relevant point follows. Dirks claims that after all, 'for sociology, caste and not the state, held these village communities together.' And further, as a true dissident of the discipline, Dirks goes on to make a larger point about the discipline that it sees caste, more generally, as 'the foundation and core of Indian civilization' (Ibid.: 3). Dirks' key point is:

> It is my contention in this book that until the emergence of British colonial rule in southern India the crown was not so hollow as it has been generally made out to be. Kings were not inferior to Brahmans; the political domain was not encompassed by a religious domain. *State forms, while not fully assimilable to western categories of the state, were powerful components in Indian civilization.* (Dirks 1987: 4–5, emphasis added)

I want to underline here Dirks' claim that 'state forms' even though they weren't fully graspable through western categories of the state, were nevertheless powerful components in Indian civilization. My concern here is that this is an internal debate within the Western sociological context, the terms of which are entirely set between Western scholars as to whether it is the state or the caste order that held village communities together. For the dissident and revisionist Dirks, it was a radical gesture, within his context, of repudiating the great founding fathers—Weber, Marx and Maine—for their Orientalism and rescuing India from the taint of caste and even the suggestion that the political domain might be swamped by the religious. Caste and religion are all signs of backwardness while the state, even if it does not fully fit into the western definitions, is a sign of universality (or perhaps modernity and secularity) in some sense. Having thus set the stage, Dirks then goes on to say that his book 'is about the relation between the Indian state and Indian society in the old regime', and the transformation of that relationship 'under British colonialism, when the crown did finally become hollow' (Ibid.: 5). Notice the use of the expression 'Indian state' in the singular, which is remarkable because he is actually looking at and studying in-depth, only one of the hundreds of what he himself calls, after Bernard Cohn, 'little kingdoms'.

The point here is that Dirks' huge investment in the caste/religion versus the political/state dichotomy (and his clear preference for the latter) comes out of a particular 'worldview' and makes sense in a particular way, precisely because that distinction has become unquestioned common sense in that theoretical context. In itself, Dirks' key claim in the book is unexceptionable and he shows very convincingly, through a detailed combination of the ethnographical and the historical materials, that far from being a rigid structure, 'caste was embedded in a political context of kingship', which implied that it had to do, not so much with 'purity and pollution, but rather with royal authority and honour, and associated notions of power, dominance and order' (Dirks 1987: 7).

As distinct from Dirks' work, which is primarily interested in demolishing the Dumontian framework that sees caste primarily in terms of purity and pollution, I draw on Bhupendranath Datta's *Studies in Indian Social Polity* (Datta 1983), mainly in order to underline that for Datta too caste was centrally about power—not always reducible to *political* power, hence *social* polity. Datta's own study is based on his doctoral thesis and is a kind of *longue duree* take on the caste question. He sees caste fundamentally as a formation of power where there are and have been various ups and downs in the fortunes of the lower castes in the long struggles between the Sudras and the forces of Brahminism. On that score, there does not seem to be any incompatibility between his reading of the relationship between the caste and political power and that of Dirks but because Datta is not constrained by the need to demolish or affirm either a Marx or a Dumont—despite his clearly Marxist commitments—he has no difficulty in acknowledging the centrality of the 'caste system' as a formidable structure of power.[6]

We will return to the question of caste and caste power later but for the present, I want to underline another aspect of the nature of political power in India. It is not just that the social polity operates at one level, at a distance from political power proper, but also that the very structure of political power here is dispersed rather than unitary and centralized. A lot of historiographical ink—and blood—has been spilt over the decades in trying to settle this matter, and once again, the problem has been precisely that despite dealing with Indian or Asian material, there seems to have been a lot of investment in exorcising certain Western ghosts and therefore reading these materials in some very specific ways.

I want to return to the notion of polity referred to by Tambiah in the context of Southeast Asia. That this is not a specifically Southeast Asian formation but arises in tandem with a larger cosmology is underlined by Tambiah himself. It is a matter that historians of ancient and medieval India have long grappled with, even if political theorists have not really deigned to venture there. However, for a non-historian, especially a political theorist, entering this highly charged field, where battle-lines among contending schools are very sharply drawn, often the differences appear quite insubstantial, mainly concerning nomenclature. This may also be because times have changed and so has our vocabulary of research, and it may be that many of the protagonists might today read their own interventions differently.

Let me begin with an outspoken opponent of the 'segmentary state' argument. Brajadulal Chattopadhyaya, has argued that:

> Temporal domain was defined by the extent of royal power but Kingdom was not defined in concrete territorial terms; even the *janapada* or *rashtra*, one of the constituent limbs of the state in the *Saptanga* formulation, was not 'internally coherent and closed

> towards the outside' (Heesterman). The state was thus not a static unit but one that was naturally dynamic.... The territorial composition of the Mauryan empire in Asoka's period can be characterized as a combination of several nodes such as Pataliputra, Ujjayini, Taksasila, Tosali and Suvarnagiri as well as areas of such peoples as Bhojas, Rathikas, Pulindas, Nabhhakas and that of the *atavikas* or forest people. (Chattopadhyaya 1995: 212–213)

The *Saptanga* notion refers to the traditional idea of political power as constituted by seven elements, namely *svamin* (lord/king), *amatya* (minister), *janapada* (countryside), *durg* (fort or the fortified city), *kosh* (treasury), *danda* (army/ force) and *mitra* (ally). Chattopadhyaya here is referring to this notion in a general way but it also appears, with minor variations, in the *Manusmriti* and the *Arthashastra*. The order mentioned is as it appears in Book Six of the *Arthashastra*, 'Mandala Yoni' ('Basis of Circle', in Olivelle's translation 2013) but it also appears in *Manusmriti* with *durg* as the fourth element and *rashtra* or *janapada* as the third (Yamazaki 2006: 37–38). Chattopadhyaya quotes J.C. Heesterman to the effect that this notion of the territory was neither internally coherent not closed to the outside. It is worth noticing that the concept of the mandala is quite central here; what is more, *mitra* or ally is not incidental but is considered as a constituent part of the configuration of power that to my mind only makes sense in this mandala form. Chattopadhyaya goes on to make a direct reference here to the mandala form:

> Such fluid situations...are schematized in the *mandala* concept of the political theorists who locate the *vijigishu* at the core of the *mandala*, and the royal mystique, represented by the Chakravartin model of kingship, is a logical follow-up of this formulation. *It has been a bane of writings on the political history of early and early-medieval India to search for approximations of the Chakravarti among the kings of big-sized states; the ideal is only a recognition of the existence of disparate polities and of military success as a precondition of the Chakravarti status which was superior to the status represented by the heads of other polities....* (Chattopadhyaya 1995: 213, emphasis added)

The burden of Chattopadhyaya's argument, however, is that ongoing political processes involve a move away from lineage-based polities to what he calls 'state-societies'—a trend towards aggregation and indeed a qualitative transformation. These changes, says Chattopadhyaya, need to be seen alongside the changes occurring in the economic, social and religious domains. The significant correlative changes he identifies are, at the economic level, horizontal spread of rural agrarian settlements and at the social level, the process of caste formation, based primarily on the horizontal spread of the *varna* ideology, drawing in 'widely dispersed and originally outlying groups into a structure which allowed them in large measure to retain their original character except that this character was now defined with reference to the structure' (Chattopadhyaya 1995: 13–15). 'State-societies' then involved the integration of local polities into supra-local polities. From Chattopadhyaya's general stance against the segmentary state argument, it would appear that we will now emerge into a regime of a unitary or quasi-unitary state. But that is far from being the case. For as he says a little later, the empirical evidence from Rajasthan, on which he himself has worked, suggests that 'the distribution of political authority could be organized by a network of lineages within the framework of the monarchical form of polity, retaining at the same time areas of bureaucratic functioning' (Chattopadhyaya 1995: 218).

Chattopadhyaya, in fact, continues to talk of the 'dispersed foci of political power' and claims that it was present 'even in traditional historiography' (implying that the 'segmentary state' argument is nothing new). In traditional historiography, this notion had appeared within the formulation of 'feudal tendencies' and was 'applied generally to a pattern of polity which was considered not sufficiently large in terms of its approximation to an all-India empire and which could not, therefore, be considered centralized.' Recent perspectives related to early medieval India, he says, have shifted from acceptance of 'centralization' and 'bureaucracy' as essential characteristics of a large state structure '*to detailed analyses of dispersed foci of power within such structures.*' And this concern, he says, 'is common both to those who characterize these structures in terms of "feudal polity" and their critics to whom the "feudal" model is either "outworn" or is an exclusively European formation which hinders a proper understanding of the uniqueness of the Indian political system' (Chattopadhyaya 1995: 223). In a sense, the ideological imperative is already neatly laid out here but just in case, we missed the point, Chattopadhyaya tells us that despite this commonality there is a difference between the two positions—it is between their respective notions of 'parcellized sovereignty' and 'shared sovereignty': 'Opposition to the "feudal" model is best articulated in the model of the "segmentary state" which is currently bandied about, at least in the circle of Western Indologists, as a major breakthrough in our understanding of the traditional Indian political system' (Ibid.: 223). So here we have, on the one hand, a Marxist or Marxism-friendly argument that sees the Indian formation as 'feudal' and is invested in asserting its commonness rather than difference with the European formation, and the other, 'Western Indologists' looking for India's uniqueness. At least so Chattopadhyaya renders the difference but his choice of words ('bandied about') reveals his own preferences and alignments quite clearly. In fact, in a footnote, he goes on to say that 'this particular brand of criticism in respect of Indian polity has emanated, curiously, from American institutions', that once again aligns his criticism with that of Marxists. As I suggested in the very beginning, this is the choice we are always faced with: Are we like them? Are we different? Which of these two claims is more liberatory?

From the point of view of my argument, it is not really necessary to either defend or criticize scholars like Burton Stein or Aidan Southall who first made the segmentary state argument in the East African context, for the simple reason that whether one uses the language of segmentarity or not, the phenomenon of the 'dispersed foci of power' is not really in question. Thus, Chattopadhyaya himself goes on to argue that this phenomenon (of the dispersed foci of power) cuts 'across all major political structures of the early medieval period'. He uses the traditional name for it, namely the *samanta* system which is present in some form or the other in all major [Indian] polities. Further:

> *Samanta* is of course, a broad spectrum category and encompasses a proliferating range of designations in use in the early medieval period. Not all these designations emerge simultaneously, but by the twelfth-thirteenth centuries such terms as *mahasamanta*, *samanta*, *mahamandaleswara*, *mandaleswara*, *ranaka*, *rauta*, *thakkura* and so on came to indicate a political order which was non-bureaucratic and in the context of which, in the overall structure of polity, the

> *rajapurusas* constituting the bureaucracy had only a limited part to play. (Chattopadhyaya 1995: 227)

Chattopadhyaya is at pains to explain that while 'the *samanta* in its trans-political connotation corresponded to the "landed aristocracy" of the period', its presence along with other phenomena associated with it, seems to have 'weakened...the hold of the state over both the polity and the revenue potential of its constituent territorial units' (Ibid.: 227–228).

Little wonder then that Burton Stein can respond to the critiques of Chattopadhyaya and Hermann Kulke (1995, Introduction) claiming 'that a reconciliation of the views of Kulke and Chattopadhyaya with my own are possible as well as meaningful'. Stein's point here is that all three of them are actually 'dealing with evolving structures within a single broad form' and in their own ways, 'are privileging some and neglecting others' (Stein 1995: 146). It is not necessary here to follow Stein's argument in any detail, but it is interesting to note that towards the end of the essay cited earlier, he also responds to Nicholas Dirks' critical comments in his work on Pudukottai discussed earlier. Stein's point is that once again, there is no real incompatibility between his argument and that made by Dirks, who in his reconstruction of the pre-colonial 'old-regime' of the Pudukottai realm, 'shows how, in texts and in social contexts, the territorially segmented system of authority and social organization of the Kallars was constituted by the royal enactments of gifting and privileging. Lesser Kallar lords were linked to their king by ties of service and kinship while Brahmans and other non-Kallars were bound by gifts' (Ibid.: 156).

It seems, therefore, that the differences with respect to the point that I am interested in pursuing here, are quite inconsequential and at the end of the day, really about ideological stances and nomenclature. The key issue is put quite succinctly by Hermann Kulke, who is by no means a supporter of the 'segmentary state' view but has developed his own 'integrative model' of state formation. In his words:

> The politically most persistently competitive institution of the central royal power was, of course, feudatory or samanta chiefs. In the 'conventional model' of the unitary state, they played only an

> insignificant role, usually as 'vassals' of their royal overlords. For supporters of the Indian feudalism school, they were the unavoidable products of the process of 'feudal fragmentation' of central authority. In the segmentary state concept, they represented the autonomous segmentary local or trans-local political holders of 'actual political control' over their own nuclear area.... The integrative model so far has primarily focused on modes of integration which originated from the centre or at least strengthened the central position. *But the recent studies on the 'little kings' in the intermediate zone or on the 'jungle kings' in the periphery clearly demonstrated that we have to concede more space to them and their various modes of competition and negotiation in the concept of state formation.* (Kulke 2006: 73–74, emphasis added)

In his overview of the study of the state in pre-modern India, Kulke suggests that perhaps Indian history could provide 'emic' models and institutions, such as the *mandala* concept of the *Arthashastra*, castes, *samantas* and *jagirs*, which could form the basis of a future Indian model (Kulke 1995, Introduction, pp. 1–47).

From our point of view, certainly categories like *mandala*, castes, *samantas* need to be taken seriously but not only because they will explain Indian historical formation/s better but also because, in doing so, they can tell us something about the political in general, something that always enriches our overall understanding of political power and the (premodern) state.

It is also perhaps pertinent to our concerns and the discussion so far that when Clifford Geertz (1980) discusses the Balinese *negara* (a version of the Sanskrit *nagar*, *nagari*), he finds political forms not very different from the ones we have been discussing so far. He tells us that in the Indonesian languages, the term means 'more or less simultaneously and interchangeably, "palace", "capital", "state", "realm" and again "town"' and is the general category used to refer to 'the classical state of precolonial Indonesia' (Geertz 1980: 4). But once again this is not *an* Indonesian state, for like the 'little kingdoms' that we have been discussing, Geertz also tells us that there is practically no record of how many *negaras* there were in Indonesia, that they definitely run into hundreds, perhaps even thousands (Ibid.: 4). He observes that the 'political development of precolonial Indonesia does not consist of a relentless unfoldment of a monolithic "Oriental Despotism," *but of an expanding cloud of localized, fragile, loosely interrelated petty principalities*' (Ibid.: 4, emphasis added). This is not the place to discuss Geertz's notion of the 'theatre state' in nineteenth-century Bali but it is important to note the interesting paradox that he underlines in relation to the 'classical state in Tabanan': despite being organized top-down in terms of cultural hierarchy, as a political 'system of domination' it looked very different. The relevant passage is worth quoting at length:

> Rather than flowing down from a pinnacle of authority or spreading out from a generative center, power seems instead pulled up towards such a pinnacle or to be drawn towards such a center. The right to command was not delegated from the king to lord, lord to lordling, and lordling to subject; rather it was surrendered from subject to lordling, lordling to lord and lord to king. Power was not allocated from the top, it cumulated from the bottom. This is not to say that the system was democratic, which it certainly was not; nor that it was libertarian, which it was even less. It is to say that it was—radically, pervasively, inveterately—confederate. (Geertz 1980: 62–63)

The point of referring to Geertz's *negara* is not to say that it replicates what we have been discussing so far, but to draw attention to definite resonances between this confederate form and the mandala form, where the political centre is not quite the 'state' of the Western political tradition.

More importantly, the point of the earlier discussion is not to say that all the characterizations mentioned—the galactic polity, the segmentary state or the negara—are essentially the same; it is rather to underline that despite variations, there is a common thread in them that is worth taking seriously. This common thread pertains to the 'dispersed foci of political power', where there is perhaps an unstable dynamic between the little kings and rajas and the larger central forces of empires. The idea of the mandala certainly suggests something stronger—a normative vision or in Tambiah's words, a 'cosmological vision' around which such polities may take shape. In practice, though, these may be differently inflected by the logic of relative power between the different nodes. Indeed, in Tambiah's argument, the galactic polity is no pristine *dharmic* formation, for at the level of the 'political process', 'politics' itself operates:

> The foregoing is intimately connected with the major paradox of divine kingship and perennial rebellions that was the hallmark of the galactic polities. Any of the traditional chronicles such as the Sinhalese *Mahavamsa* or the Burmese, Thai, or Javanese counterparts will reveal the pattern of brief reigns, frequent rebellions, usurpations, and assassinations that characterize court politics. It is well known that there were no settled succession rules, and that the princes procreated in profusion in harems, formed a multitude of contestants, whose propensity for hatching intrigues was matched by the reigning king's own tendency to kill off his rivals. (Tambiah 2013: 516)

In fact, what is significant for someone who is primarily interested in the trajectory of the modern and the contemporary state is the dispersed nature of political power in all these cases. In a slightly different but related sense, Rudolph and Rudolph had recently made an argument that linked the federal impulse in India with the problem of state formation itself and argued against the largely European story of absolutism and indivisible sovereignty by proposing a theory of 'negotiated and shared sovereignty' (Rudolph and Rudolph 2010).

I will try to argue in what follows that much of that dispersed form of power continues into the modern period and can be seen to be active not just in the existence of the six hundred-odd 'princely states' during the colonial era, but also the peculiar afterlives of such states as of smaller landed entities, in the way politics is conducted through the colonial period and in the post-independence era of democratic politics. This politics is 'inveterately confederate' and most often its key figure is the regional satrap.

The Constitution of the Modern Political in India

In the early to mid-1960s, Rajni Kothari published a series of essays in different journals that constituted a novel attempt to conceptualize the form and substance of Indian politics. Among the most significant and enduring ideas that emerged from there was that of the Congress 'system' (Kothari 1964). The significant part of the essay on the Congress 'system', despite its being heavily couched in the language and vocabulary of the then-dominant behaviourialist political science, was that it was able to see Indian politics in Independent India as a competitive multi-party system that was nevertheless dominated by a single party—the Congress that functioned as the 'system' as it were. Kothari's focus there was on describing the way this Congress 'system' functioned, the centrepiece of which was the 'party of consensus', namely the Congress. It functioned through 'an elaborate network of factions', through which political change takes place as through it, not only 'new men come to power but new kinds of men' bringing in new orientations to power and new ideological predilections (Kothari 1964: 1163). This system got 'aggregated at the State level where individuals who had risen to power within the Congress organization sometimes constituted a chief opposition to government, provided an alternative leadership' and in many instances overthrew those in power (Ibid.: 1163–1164). Government, dissent, opposition—everything was contained within this larger structure. At the time Kothari wrote this he was not keen to go into an explanation of why such a political form might have emerged; he merely saw the post-independence Congress as a continuation of the movement that it had been during the days of the anti-colonial struggle. By the time he wrote his *Politics in India* (1970), he was ready to undertake an exploration of that question. There was in his explication now, a reference to the pre-colonial, civilizational Hindu past that had 'contributed considerably to the unity of a new India, and imparted to its modernist design depth, flexibility, and manoeuvrability' (Kothari 1970: 81–83). The new elite that emerged, says Kothari, 'was essentially a "national" elite for the first time in India'.

> In place of either local notables resolving local disputes which was a characteristic of traditional society, or of enlightened individuals scattered at various places...there now emerged a body of men who thought in national terms, talked of a national consciousness, and of India's future as a nation. (Ibid.: 87)

The reference to the past remains in Kothari, somewhat of an uninterrogated gesture to a benign pluralism and diversity of Hindu civilization. The point that I want to underline here is that his deep understanding of contemporary politics and of the Congress, in particular, led him to imply that the Congress itself was an analogue of the *mandala* form—with a central power tied in so many ways to the regional satraps who controlled the organization and who despite swearing formal loyalty to the central leadership, also constituted the main centres of opposition and political efficacy. In an earlier time, the Congress had the power to even allow independent party organizations like those of the Labour Swaraj Party or the Congress Socialist Party to function within it.

Mere gestures to the plurality and diversity of Indian society or to the marginality of political power do not really tell us much if we simply leave them at the level of gestures. Kothari as well as his colleagues, Ashis Nandy (2003) and D.L. Sheth (2018), suggest a relative marginality of political power in traditional Indian conceptions of political authority, but the actual forms and meanings are never really explicated. For Nandy, it remains a normative horizon, for South Asian cultures are *normatively* anti-state because they privilege culture over the state. Kothari, on the other hand, sees it as the repeated failure of Indian society to build a political centre that to him and to Sheth, would happen for the first time when the Congress emerged as the embodiment of nationalism.

Nonetheless, there are important hints in the writings of these scholars that point us towards a possible different way of conceptualizing the place of political authority in traditional India and it is important to hold on to the idea of dispersed foci of power for the moment—without necessarily having to pronounce on whether it was adopted as normatively superior ideal or whether it was simply a consequence of the social formation—the caste order for instance—that made political authority relatively marginal.

Whatever be the case, it is interesting to see the ways in which some of the effects of this dispersed power inflect power and politics even in colonial and postcolonial times. For instance, a study by Howard Spodek (1973) on urban politics in the local kingdoms of the Saurashtra (Kathiawar) peninsula, in the period just before the British arrival in 1807–1808, found not only internal tensions between landowning town rulers and merchants but also tensions and warfare between neighbouring towns which were headquarters of hostile rajas. He found more than 200 little kingdoms in that area alone, and they were so often at war that trade between them was minimal (Spodek 1973: 255). The three big kingdoms among these comprised anything between 600 to 900 villages, whereas five others held something between 100 to 200 villages.[7]

It seems that often when nineteenth-century Indian intellectuals wondered how a small trading company could colonize an entire subcontinent like India and reached the conclusion that it was because of 'internal disunity', it wasn't just caste divisions they were thinking of. Here was a subcontinent of literally hundreds of little principalities and kingdoms that, apart from a very general cultural connection, had little sense of being one political entity.

William Richter's study (1971) looks at the involvement of Indian princes in politics, especially in the wake of changed relations with Indira Gandhi's Congress as it abolished their privy purses. His study shows that between the integration of princely states into the Indian union and 1967, most of the erstwhile princes and their heirs were actively involved in Congress politics. These ranged from the princely kingdoms of Odisha, Chhattisgarh, parts of Madhya Pradesh, especially Gwalior, Rajasthan and Gujarat, Punjab, Haryana, Himachal Pradesh, Jammu and Kashmir, Tripura, Manipur, Mysore, Maharashtra and Madras. Only in the late-1960s did some of them in Madhya Pradesh, like the Rajmata of Gwalior and others in Rajasthan and Uttar Pradesh, start supporting the Jan Sangh (Spodek 1971: 537).

This sits quite neatly with Kothari's formulation regarding the hold over the state-level Congress organizations, of powerful individuals—though Kothari sees them entirely as ideologically motivated nation-builders rather than erstwhile princes seeking a new way of wielding power within the electoral-democratic set up that is being put in place. It is possible to speculate here that not only do these princes and rajas not turn into democrats and nation-builders overnight, they also bring with them their own sense of entitlement and power, and styles which may be completely at odds with the democratic ethos.

An important part of the story of the modern 'democratic' state lies in the transmutation of the old networks of dispersed power into nodes of power in such domains of mobilizational politics. At this level, the 'political' and landed power of the satrap and the 'social' power of caste seem to become indistinguishable. This story is perhaps best told in the following account by Chinnaiah Jangam of the Reddys of Rayalseema, written in the wake of the arrest of Y.S. Jaganmohan Reddy of the YSR Congress for involvement in multiple financial scams.

Chinnaiah draws a straight connection between the pre-colonial legacy of the Poligars, who were administrative and military governors appointed by the Nayaka rulers of South India (among them the Vijayanagar Empire and the Kakatiya dynasty) and local power and its relation with modern politics. In Chinnaiah's telling this is the story of the 'feudal roots of democratic politics' in Andhra Pradesh:

> As landholding administrative functionaries with military and revenue powers, the Poligars—ancestors of the current day faction leaders in the Rayalseema region of Andhra Pradesh—ruled and controlled not only the material resources but also the lives of millions in their sphere.
>
> In the course of history, the Vijayanagar empire collapsed and its glory ceased but the landlords (Poligars) who were its backbone survived and remained a formidable caste group. They took complete control over the villages under their influence by organizing armed gangs. (Chinnaiah 2013: 11)

The initial story is well known. The Poligars revolted against the British in the early days of colonial rule as they saw their independence threatened. Even though the East India Company sought to violently suppress the Poligar revolt, they eventually only managed to subdue 'this formidable feudal class by turning them into allies.' Their becoming allies of the British facilitated smooth revenue collection and ensured law and order, underlines Chinnaiah (2013: 11). The Poligars divided the fertile land and the attached/dependent lower caste labourers among themselves. Their sway over the villages was total although there were personal rivalries and violent conflicts among different landlords. Nothing moved or entered into the villages without their permission, including proselytizing activities of Christian missionaries. They even converted to Christianity to get closer to colonial rulers, while retaining their caste Hindu identity. And then came the anticolonial movement and soon the 'feudal factionist elites who were successors of the Poligars in Rayalseema jumped on to the bandwagon of nationalist organizations like the Congress to organize and mobilize rural folk under their leadership' (Ibid.: 12). After Independence, the same kind of caste rivalries and personal feuds formed the basis of electoral mobilization (Ibid.: 12). In the rest of the article, Chinnaiah shows how the political career of Y.S. Reddy and his son, closely followed the patterns of doing politics as the landed Poligars had always done.

It is also important to underline at this point that princely states and smaller *jagirdaris* of all sorts continued to flourish and with a fair degree of autonomy with respect to organizing their religious *sampradyas* and orders, and their ordering of caste practices (including caste-based segregation), even during different phases of Muslim rule (Bahuguna 2013; Khan 2015). In fact, many of the regional chiefs became chiefs due to their close relationship with the Mughal rulers from whose land grants they established themselves (Sreenivasan 2014). Many of the princely states were ruled by Muslim rulers and even though the Mughal state, for instance, was fairly centralizing in many respects, the social polity was left largely untouched by them. Partly this may have been pragmatic as in the case of Shams al-Din Iltutmish who warded off the influence of the theologians by arguing that Muslims, despite being rulers 'were still like salt in a dish', too small in numbers to be able to wage war against the infidels; or others like Ghiyas al-Din Balban who more forthrightly kept theologians like Zia al-Din Barani at bay 'by dismissing them as mere seekers after narrow worldly gain' (Alam 2004: 42). But the stance among the later rulers influenced by the *Akhlaq* tradition was quite clearly normative. 'The goal in the discourse on political organization in *akhlaq* literature is [thus] 'cooperation', to be achieved through justice (*adl*) administered in accordance with a law which is protected and promoted by a king whose principal instrument of control should be affection and favours (*rafat-o-itminan*), not command and obedience (*amr-o-imtisal*)' (Alam 2004: 55). The emphasis on justice, Muzaffar Alam tells us, is throughout argued from the point of view of a secular ethic' (Ibid.: 58).

Given all this, it makes no sense to think that once colonialism came and initiated the process of setting up a modern state governed by modern law, everything of the past was simply erased. Colonialism did not start writing its script on a clean slate and it is interesting to map how much of what came to be written as modern was actually still deeply inflected by the power relations and the conceptual universe of the pre-colonial world.

Contrary then, to what we have come to regard as the story of the political in India—by which I mean something more than the independent Indian state *per se*—it seems to make more sense to see it as the coming together of three different processes and currents. The overriding factor is, of course, that of the institution of colonial power, in two phases as it were, to follow an important distinction made by Sudipta Kaviraj. The first phase is that of the rule of the East India Company when stealthily but surely, colonial power entrenched itself. In this period, we have colonial rule without a colonial state. The second, after the Great Revolt of 1857, when India was put directly under the rule of the British state and there was a colonial state proper in place after that. The second element comprised the various princely states with whom the colonial power entered into treaties and worked out the framework of their relative autonomy under British paramountcy. Between them, they constituted 'two-fifths of the area and one-third of the population' of the Indian Empire, excluding Burma (Copland 1999: 8). To be sure these 600 odd princely states did not exhaust the entire range of small principalities and samantas that dotted the map of India. Nevertheless, even the range of kingdoms within these 600 was huge—in Copland's words, 'the biggest ones were comparable to the countries of Europe; but the smallest ones could have fitted into some suburban backyards' (Ibid.: 8).

The third element of the emergent political is the nation-to-be that pits itself decisively against the colonial state, identifying it as an alien element, which it, therefore, seeks to replace. The abiding antagonism between the first and the third elements—the colonial state and emergent nationalism—is what Partha Chatterjee has identified as nationalism's demarcation of the 'outer' domain of colonial enslavement and the 'inner' domain of the nation's cultural/spiritual sovereignty. By and large, the significance of this distinction has been missed. The coupling of the 'nation-state', carried over from Western experience, made it difficult to see that this was not just a rhetorical distinction for many. On the one hand, there was Hindu nationalism, whose ideologues continued to maintain a very sharp division between the alien/ated entity called the state, constituted in essence through Western intervention and the 'authentic' being of the Nation. The reason that the Rashtriya Swayamsevak Sangh (RSS) stayed away from the state for most of its history should be sought partly in this understanding of the modern state as an alien imposition. At another level, it also ties up with what has been understood as a specificity of the Indian formation, where power was always dispersed rather than situated in any central institution. On the other hand, almost an inversion of this approach was the position articulated by someone like Ambedkar, whose investment was in the State and Law, which he wanted to use, if need be, against the emergent Nation. The story of emergent nationalism, therefore, is not a simple story given its hugely contested nature. There are different levels of contestation within, in terms of the challenges nationalism has to face from the non-Brahmin and lower caste movements on the one hand, and the Muslims on the other, and one of the prime expressions of this conflict occurs around the question of power, posed starkly as a choice between political power and social reform.

Ambedkar, the Political and the Social

It is well known that one of the key issues that divided the anticolonial struggle in its early decades was the issue of social reform. The division is between the social reformers and those whom Ambedkar refers to as 'the political school of the intelligentsia', 'political Hindus' (Ambedkar 2007: 3) or sometimes simply as 'the politicals' (Ambedkar in Rodrigues 2002: 121). In *Annihilation of Caste*, Ambedkar offers a synoptic view of the struggle between the latter, represented by the Congress, and the former mainly gathered under the banner of the Indian National Social Conference, founded by Mahadev Govind Ranade, not long after the formation of the Indian National Congress. As Ambedkar puts it, 'While the Congress was concerned with defining the weak points in the political organization of the country, the Social Conference was engaged in removing weak points in the social organization of Hindu society' (Ambedkar 2007: 4). For a while they functioned as 'two wings of one common activity', holding their annual sessions within the same *pandal* (Ibid.: 4). 'But soon the two wings developed into two parties, a 'political reform party' and a 'social reform party' between whom there raged a fierce controversy.... The Political Reform Party supported the Congress and the Social Reform Party supported the Social Conference' (Ibid.: 4). Ambedkar records that Tilak was instrumental in 'withdrawing the courtesy' that had till then been extended to the Social Conference by allowing it to hold its sessions within the same pandal as the Congress (Ibid.: 5). The struggle between the two wings, as is well known, reached its high point with Tilak's followers threatening to burn down the *pandal* if the Social Conference was held.

Ambedkar's analysis of the failure of the Social Reform Party focused basically on the limited nature of its reform agenda. The fact that the social reformers associated with the Social Reform Conference were mostly 'enlightened high caste Hindus who did not feel the necessity for agitating for the abolition of caste' and concerned themselves only 'with the reform of the high caste Hindu Family' was what lay at the root of its failure (Ibid.: 8). It is Ambedkar's view that the reformists would not have had to face defeat, had they also taken up questions of caste reform involving lower caste populations: by confining themselves to the narrow agenda of the reform of the Hindu family, they reduced themselves also to the position of a small minority, whereas they could have found enthusiastic support among the lower caste populations had they expanded the agenda of social reforms. Though the 'politicals' won the day, Ambedkar's point is that it was 'a very limited victory' (Ibid.: 8) because *politics and 'political constitutions' can only be meaningful and effective in terms of transformation or 'reconstruction of society'* (ibid.), if they adequately recognize 'social organization'. Two points can be deduced from this discussion. In the first place, the question of micropower in society at large, or what we can call the 'social polity' after Datta, lay at the heart of the question of transformation. This alone could make political transformation and even constitutions meaningful, for changes merely at the political level would always remain shallow and meaningless as far as the larger social body was concerned. There is something in this disjunction that is of much wider relevance across historical contexts and cultures, but there is also something profoundly contextual, insofar as it is deeply embedded in a sense of the structure of power in colonial India that draws in turn from the way the relationship between the 'society' and political power was structured traditionally in Indian history. Secondly, following from the first, the initiatives towards social transformation had to have the backing of large numbers of people and could not rely merely on intervention at the level of the political.

However, the crucial point worth recognizing here is that in Ambedkar's understanding 'the political' (or what we might call by that name today) was not a given, self-existing entity. And it was not simply reducible to the colonial state. The political was an entity in the making—an emergent instance that had to be shaped through active intervention in the here and now. A large number of his interventions and his entire political-intellectual energy from the beginning are therefore tied to the question of representation and 'safeguards'. From his depositions before the Southborough Commission to his participation in the Round Table Conferences and his response to the Communal Award—in all these instances this is what seems to me to be centrally at stake. Thus, when he claims that 'the Communal Award is, so to say, the nemesis following upon the indifference and neglect of social reform' (Ibid.: 9), he is underlining this tangled relationship of the social and political, but also underlining the moment of the shaping of the emergent political. After all, what is at stake here is the negotiated nature of the political that follows from the fact that many of the backward and lower caste representatives and those of minorities had actually cooperated with the colonial government, participated in the Round Table Conferences and thus ensured that they too had fair representation in the new arrangements of political power that were being put in place. That is why he can claim that the Communal Award is a victory of the social reform party (Ibid.: 9) for in the shape of the political that will thus emerge, the question of social reform will acquire a very different resonance.

Ambedkar is aware of the power of the appeal that the position of the 'politicals' has, especially in the colonial context, where it is evident that the priority of the political question would mean, above all, political independence. This thesis—that political reform was to have precedence over social reform—caught the imagination of the people, according to him. As he put it, if there was one single cause to which the blocking of the Social Reform movement could be attributed, it was this cry of political reform (Ambedkar in Rodrigues 2002: 120).

Ambedkar considers a number of possible versions of arguments that could be made in defense of this thesis, each interesting and powerful in its own right. However, his response to one of these is particularly important and merits greater attention—the one which holds that it is necessary to have political power to ensure that each individual member is to be conferred certain fundamental rights by law (Ambedkar in Rodrigues 2002: 122). Ambedkar's response here veers towards the question of the efficacy of rights and how they are to be ensured. Despite the very laudable objective that this argument seeks to achieve, he says, it is misguided to assume that once such rights are instituted by the law, they will thereby be also preserved. 'As experience proves, rights are protected not by law but by the social and moral conscience of society' (Ibid.: 122). This basically means that if such laws and the fundamental rights instituted by them are opposed by the community, 'no Law, no Parliament, no Judiciary can guarantee them in the real sense of the word' (Ibid.: 122). He cites Burke in order to buttress his claim that 'there is no method found for punishing the multitude. Law can punish a single solitary recalcitrant criminal. It can never operate against a whole body of people who are determined to defy it' (Ibid.: 122). This argument, in a sense, flows directly from his understanding of the social polity that he sees as distinct from the macro-political domain of lawmaking and parliamentary intervention. But once again, his focus is on the viability of such laws if they cannot have the backing of large numbers of people in society. And yet, it is interesting that Ambedkar hardly ever talks of 'the masses' or 'the people' as either a homogeneous entity or in any positive sense. The idea of an undifferentiated mass carries an ominous ring to it—something he has witnessed ever so often in nationalist mobilizations, especially as it is staged under the leadership of Tilak. This 'mass' was seen in action in the mobilizations against the Age of Consent Bill and again soon thereafter in the threats to burn down the pandal of the Social Conference. Mass mobilizations are therefore always fraught with danger, especially for those most vulnerable.

This is where his understanding of democracy also comes in, for democracy was at once something larger than the state as well as a way of containing the problem of the unrestrained mass. His fundamental thesis is that democracy and democratic government are not possible in an anti-democratic society. 'The politicals never realized that democracy was not a form of government: it was essentially a form of society' (Ambedkar in Rodrigues 2002: 123). A democratic society does not have to be marked by unity or community of purpose but it must conform to two conditions: it must exhibit an attitude of respect and equality towards others and it must have a social organization free of rigid social barriers (Ibid.: 123).

The law, in his understanding, is necessary to ensure this while simultaneously placing limits upon social practices that were demeaning to the dignity of the Dalits but it cannot ensure compliance purely on the basis of force. That is where the agenda of social reform comes in. Social reform, in this sense, is not simply about enacting laws to prohibit or allow social practices but rather, about the transformation of social practices themselves. Democracy or social democracy, here, is the name of that project of social reform that will ensure a proper institution of the social for the social too in another sense, is not something that already exists. 'Society' is not something that pre-exists modernity. As we know, in his discussion of Hindu 'society', Ambedkar makes his well-known observation that '*Hindu society as such does not exist. It is only a collection of castes*' (Ambedkar 2007: 17, emphasis added).

Society, he goes on to argue, is constituted by people possessing things in common—it is not just about having similar habits and customs. 'And the only way by which men can come to possess things in common with one another is by being in communication', society exists 'by communication, indeed in communication' (Ibid.: 18). One might argue that indeed, the greatest danger that Ambedkar saw in nationalism was precisely that a new sense of a being-in-common was coming into view that was recreating the place of pre-eminence of the upper castes in the new political. The new nationalist political, in this sense, aimed at subsuming the social, the new being-in-common. And that was the danger, the real threat to the future emancipation of the Dalits and other lower castes. The challenge, therefore, had to be met at both levels—the state and society.

This brings us to an important aspect of the relationship between the political and the social. For what Ambedkar seems to be arguing, quite relentlessly, is also that the political is not, and cannot, be autonomous of the social. The structure of social power determines the nature and limits of political power. But this does not mean that the political should be seen as subordinate to the social. After all, his life-long battle was all about staking a share of the Dalits in the new power structure that would come into being after independence as this alone would provide them the ground to stand upon and fight back against their oppression.

These ruminations of Ambedkar reveal an underlying idea that visualizes a complex relationship between the social and the political—one which cannot be specified in terms of one determining the other or one having absolute priority over the other. The relationship between the two is an unstable one where the former can easily overwhelm the latter if the task of social reform is not undertaken on an urgent basis.

I suggest that in Ambedkar's thought there is a sense *of a profound disjuncture between two different histories, two different domains with different chronologies*. Society and politics in the India of his time do not constitute, to him, a single and undifferentiated totality or structure where all its parts are related in some coherent fashion. For, on the one hand, there is 'the social' that tells the story of a long and virtually uninterrupted history of caste oppression from ancient times; on the other, there is the relatively new element of 'the political' that following the advent of colonialism is still in the process of being put in place. A new colonial state is in operation but clearly, that does not exhaust the emergent political. The contours of this domain are still unclear but there is no teleology here in the way it will shape up. It requires active intervention and shaping on part of the oppressed castes for that alone will determine the shape of things to come. The two entities, to be sure, are marked by very different temporalities, punctuated by very different rhythms. The time of the 'social' is a slow, 'everyday' time tied to the rhythms of Hindu society's existence in the *longue duree*, whereas the time of the 'political' belongs to the rapidly changing present, embodying rapid movement and exhibiting a sense of urgency precisely because it is the arena of acute contestations for power among different communities and social groups. Its different temporality is also accounted for by virtue of its being instituted by a modern colonial power that has its own global coordinates.

Even if this is not spelt out by Ambedkar in so many words, it is evident from the body of writings and lectures he authored that they address these two temporalities throughout his career. It is equally evident that he sees in them a serious disjunction or dislocation between two different histories of two different entities that do not quite tie up into a whole. As mentioned earlier, this is the other side of the same recognition that is implicitly present in practically most leaders and thinkers of the colonial era and in a sense, underlies the distinction between the 'inner' domain of culture (where the nation is supposedly sovereign) and the 'outer' domain of politics (and of enslavement).

Ambedkar saw the political domain as the domain of the modern—the state, constitutionalism, law, rights and citizenship—but within the specific structure of nationalism that he saw materialize before him, this promise seemed to stand threatened. Nationalism illuminated to him an essential difficulty with some of the modern concepts and their practical forms as they emerged in the West. His critiques, therefore, of actually existing democracies as well as of the idea of constitutional government, went way beyond simply saying that there is something wrong with the Congress or nationalist idea of democracy and constitutional government: they moved to take on the form of a critique of these concepts themselves. His critiques were directed at the liberal illusions regarding the law, citizenship and adult universal suffrage that elided the question of continued, rampant inequalities in society. Thus:

> I have no hesitation in saying that both these notions [representation and universal suffrage] are false and misleading. If democracy and

> self-government have failed everywhere, it is largely due to these wrong notions. Habits of constitutional morality may be essential for the maintenance of a constitutional *form* [emphasis original] of government. But the maintenance of *a constitutional form of government is not the same thing as self-government by the people.* (Ambedkar in Rodrigues 2002: 133; emphasis added)

Ambedkar's critiques centre on the broad class division in society, on the one hand and abstract notions of representation and citizenship on the other. In the first, they find some kind of resonance in Marxist critiques which too pronounce democracy as bourgeois or sham because of its inability to take on the question of class domination in society. Ambedkar however, does not take his critique to the extreme that would lead him to reject democracy altogether. Rather, he proposes measures that will split the political from within. In other words, he refuses to accept the largely universalist conception of the political and of the state as a moment external to the social. His critiques, in fact, seek to inscribe the very heterogeneity of the social at the heart of the political.

Conceptualizing the 'Social Polity'

I want to conclude with a brief discussion on the nature of the postcolonial political, especially the idea of the 'social polity' that we haven't yet attempted to properly conceptualize. As mentioned earlier, the author of the term, Bhupendranath Datta, used it almost coterminously with the 'caste system'. The term, however, requires much greater elaboration if it has to mean anything more than what can already be signified by the use of the term 'caste system'. With all the work that has become available since Datta wrote his tract, we might find it difficult to sustain the idea of the 'caste system', especially in the context of modern mobilizational 'democratic' politics. For, as Rajni Kothari (1994) put it long ago, 'casteism in politics is no more and no less than the politicization of caste,' and this actually leads to a transformation of the caste system. This transformation took place, in his view, at both structural and ideological levels. Within the social structure of caste, 'a whole variety of new alignments took place that undermined the rigidity of the system', thanks to both 'the splitting and federating of caste along secular political lines', which enabled them to bargain with political parties. Ideologically, there took place a shift, Kothari had argued, 'from hierarchy to plurality and ordained status to negotiated positions of power, from ritual definitions of roles to civic and political definitions of the same' (Kothari 1994: 1590). While Kothari is absolutely correct on this and the important work of the Rudolphs in the 1960s, too had underlined the role played by caste associations in the democratic process, it is by no means certain that the 'system' ever operated with the rigidity that the normative scheme of *varnashramadharma* or the *Manusmriti* sought to impose on society. We discussed earlier the enormous power wielded by the Reddys of Rayalseema that they had acquired as officials in the Vijayanagar Empire. But as Sambiah Gundimeda points out, the Reddys were not high up on the scale of ritual hierarchy but rather belonged to the 'sat-Sudra category in the traditional Hindu social structure' (Gundimeda 2009: 52). We have also seen in Dirks' study of Pudukottai kingdom that the Kallars were able to rule despite being from a lower caste background because very often it was relations of power rather than the hierarchy of ritual status that was critical in determining the degree of power wielded by any social group. There are, after all, any number of Sudra kingdoms and principalities all through history. We can certainly talk of caste *practices* that operated in the social domain, where matters of purity and pollution were important; we can also see that in relation to *atishudra* or *panchama* or Dalit populations, all the other caste groups were equal offenders. But the intermediate structures of 'political power' that we have earlier encountered, perhaps largely because of the dispersed nature of such power, exhibited a fairly high degree of heterogeneity. This was possible also because many of the local chieftains acquired power through land grants by the monarchs in recognition of various services rendered, rather than through ritual superiority.

The idea of dispersal of power or of its relative marginality appears in the works of various thinkers and scholars who have attempted to grapple with these particular tendencies in Indian politics. Kothari, in his classic *Politics in India* (1970), while mapping the historical antecedents of politics in India, noted that the 'Indian system was a loose accommodation between a remarkably stable social order and a transient and unstable political order' (Kothari 1970: 25). This 'remarkably stable order' in Kothari's understanding, *was* the caste system but was 'limited for the most part to the village or a network of villages'; there is certainly no sense thereof an invariant stable social order that is either pan-Indian (whatever that could have meant in earlier times) or even spread over a large region. Thus, to Kothari,

> India's great failure in the past has been its inability to erect a political authority, a coherent and persistent center. Looked at in this sense, the traditional Indian community can be characterized as largely apolitical in its organization. (Kothari 1970: 25)

Strictly speaking, when I use the term 'social polity', I am not referring only to these formations that supposedly exist only at the level of villages or network of villages—what Ambedkar had called a 'conglomeration of castes'. Rather, I am also referring to those formations that acquire, alongside 'splitting and federating', a new lease of life in modern mobilizational politics. These caste associations, or say khap panchayats, begin to play roles that are far from benign and often are ways of organizing against the lower, Dalit Bahujan castes.

In the Indian context, we need to bear in mind the fact that not only does the 'social' actually have a much longer history that is autonomous of the colonial political, it stands indeed, in a very different relationship to the pre-colonial political as well—a history that stretches back into antiquity. It is a relationship widely remarked upon by many an important thinker of the colonial era ranging from Bhudeb Mukhopadhyay to Rabindranath Tagore and Gandhi, where 'samaj' is seen to have long existed quite autonomously of the king/the ruler/political power. This is the train of thought that Sudipta Kaviraj takes up for sustained reflection over a number of essays, but with one difference—he takes away the positive, almost romantic, charge that attaches to this idea of the 'autonomy of the social' in Mukhopadhyay and Tagore. The autonomy of the social, in Kaviraj's reading is now recognized for what it is—the caste order that is kept in place through a series of rigid rules sanctioned by religion. What he calls the 'social constitution', in fact, keeps political power in its place—in relative marginality.

In Ambedkar's terminology, it would be dubbed the system of 'graded inequality' where any number of castes exist in a vertical hierarchy that is maintained through a rigorous system of prohibitions and allowances. The system is kept in place primarily through the grid of social power rather than through the direct intervention of political power, which is why, as we saw, he is centrally concerned with the social question. That is why Ambedkar insists that the caste order does not merely embody a particular division of labour but rather of labourers—that is to say, it fixes the social position of specific groups of labouring populations with little possibility of movement across occupations.

It is this domain of micropower of the social polity that Kaviraj and Ranajit Guha take up in their explorations of the political. Kaviraj too insists that:

> The rules of the caste order as a system of social relations are [thus] impervious to the constant fluctuations of royal power. The constant ebb and flow of power from dynasties or kingdoms or individual rulers constitutes a stratum of events that occur at the insignificant surface of deep social life, affecting the lives of a very small number of individuals who are born, by their caste fate, to endure the impermanence and aggravations of a life of political power. (Kaviraj 2010a: 48)

Notice once again the distinction between the level of political and royal power that operates at this superficial level and what Kaviraj calls 'deep social life'. It may sound strange in a tradition that produced the *Arthashastra*—the text attributed to Kautilya as well as the long arthashastra tradition of political theorizing that preceded it—that political power remained relatively marginal. It would seem from the range of texts on government, political power was quite central to Hindu tradition as well. We should, therefore, remember two things here. First, many of these texts are prescriptive and do not necessarily 'reflect' the actual empirical situation on the ground. Second, it is entirely possible that because of the existence of a large number of kingdoms within the *mandala* form, the need for a whole tradition of such prescriptive texts was felt more acutely. Some scholars of the *Arthashastra* actually believe that the Kautilyan text of that name was written precisely for the little kingdoms and not the rulers of big empires. Scholars of *Arthashastra,* like Olivelle, also believe that the sections on the preservation of the varna order that appear at the end of each chapter are actually later interpolations, since the main body of the text and the chapters do not seem to really display much concern with the varna order. This argument resonates with the now accepted understanding that the text was originally called *Dandaniti* and was not a *shastric* text at all and also does not seem to contradict the idea that the preservation of the varna order was really not dependent on political and royal power or that there may have been tensions between the actual situation of relative fluidity and the desire to enforce varna order.[8]

The colonial state marks a major rupture insofar as the grammar of political power is concerned. It is a modern governmental state whose tentacles penetrate into the deepest corners of society, vis-à-vis which it has a transformative agenda. That this transformative agenda is not always successful is a sign of its alien-ness and therefore, of its need for alliance/s with the locally powerful elements, as Guha argues. These locally powerful elements, we might recall from our earlier discussion, could be the local samantas or the small kings and rajas—and their world operates within a religious idiom. Guha dwells at length on the constitution of local power under the colonial rule which is crucial to our understanding of the idea of social polity. At another level, in another essay, he takes up precisely these formations of local power in the context of emerging nationalism, where again, we can see the same dynamic play out.

The colonial state, Guha argues, stands in a relation of 'absolute externality' to the society it rules, 'with no mediating depths, no space provided for transactions between the will of the rulers and that of the ruled…' (Guha 1998: 65). Given this absence of any mediation, says Guha, its own dominance as well as the central role of the colonial state in the construction of the political domain, required that it rely on an alliance with traditional structures of power. Guha looks at the way in which despite different histories and constituting two very different languages, colonial power and traditional forms of micropower mesh together to produce a distinctive configuration of *local* power.

In a series of sustained reflections on the nature of colonial power, Guha focuses on what he calls the 'organic composition of power', which he says comprises two aspects, namely dominance (D) and subordination (S). Dominance, according to him, is characterized by a mix of coercion and persuasion (C and P respectively), and subordination by a mix of collaboration and resistance (C* and R respectively). He recognizes that two different idioms are at work within each of the four constituents of D and S—one of which derives from the metropolitan political culture of the colonizers, the other from the pre-colonial political traditions of the colonized—in short, from two distinct paradigms (Ibid.: 24).

At least at the level of the operations of power, Guha does not see any incommensurability between these two paradigms. Thus, for instance, alongside the colonial idioms of Order and Improvement, Guha sees the simultaneous operation of the idioms of Danda (Order *and* Danda) and Dharma (Improvement *and* Dharma), that go on to produce the new configuration of power. Thus,

> Order as an idiom of state violence constituted a distinctive feature of colonialism.... But the idiom of Order did not function all by itself. It interacted with another idiom to make C (coercion) what it was under colonial conditions. That was an *Indian* idiom—the idiom of Danda, which was central to all indigenous notions of dominance. (Guha 1998: 28)

And then, the most crucial point for our purposes:

> The private feudal armies and levies, caste and territorial *panchayats* governed by local elite authority, caste sanctions imposed by the elite and religious sanctions by the priesthood, bonded labor and *begar*, the partial entitlement of landlords to the civilian and criminal jurisdiction over the tenantry, punitive measures taken against women for disobeying patriarchal moral codes, elite violence organized on sectarian, ethnic and caste lines, and so on are all instances of C framed in the idiom of Danda. (Guha 1998: 28–29)

The configuration of the political field then, marked by the logic of dominance and subordination, was a complex one where colonial power at the apex, maintained itself through a whole range of local and intermediate operations of power whose moral justifications came largely from an indigenous paradigm. Equally important, as can be seen from the passage quoted previously, the area of operation of the paradigm of *danda*, was in Guha's reading, applicable to the large domain of what we would recognize as *the social*, as distinct from the political.

In one of his reflections on power and the political, Guha turns his attention to nationalist mobilizations and offers a rare and perceptive critique of the operations of such micropower within them. Coercion as an element in mobilization draws Guha's attention to something that Ambedkar would certainly have appreciated, given the latter's mistrust of nationalist mobilizations. Apart from physical coercion in the destruction of foreign goods, coercion came precisely in the form of caste sanction and Guha gleans a dossier compiled by the Intelligence department, in 1909 in the wake of the Swadeshi movement for evidence. According to it, these sanctions included 'withdrawal of ritual services, refusal of inter-dining, boycott of wedding receptions and funeral services, and other pressures amounting to partial or total ostracism of those considered guilty of deviation from Swadeshi norms' (Guha 1998: 110).

Since deployment of caste sanctions is 'basic to Hindu orthodoxy' and since it was clear that the Swadeshi movement relied on them 'to no mean extent', says Guha, 'it should help us grasp the character of Indian nationalism itself as a tissue of contradictions with its emancipatory and unifying urge resisted and modified significantly by the disciplinary and divisive forces of social conservatism' (Guha 1998: 111). What is most interesting from our point of view once again, is the fact that 'the incidence of sanction as documented in the intelligence reports' is 'quite striking in its geographical distribution' for it revealed that most cases were 'reported from small sleepy villages located far in the outback'. This to Guha, clearly showed the 'grassroots character of the movement', and the religiosity that was obviously a function of its rural character. The fact that the sanctions were more numerous in the more politically active districts suggested to him 'a fairly high correlation between nationalism and casteism' (Ibid.: 111).

Between caste sanctions and the nature of social boycotts, Guha's conclusion regarding the early nationalist mobilizations during the Swadeshi movement is scathing:

> The manner in which offenders... were disciplined shows how deeply casteism had penetrated Swadeshi mobilization. The name by which that discipline came to be known was 'social boycott'. It linked itself by this name to the central strategy of the campaign, that is, boycott of foreign goods, and sought its justification in the authority of a nationalism poised to challenge the hegemonic pretensions of the raj. At the same time, by a play on the word *samaj*, Bangla for 'society', the designation made that discipline into a concern of the micro-society of jati or caste which...had a samaj or caste council to deal with those of its members who violated its code...*Social boycott set out to serve the interests of the big society that was the nation by insisting on procedures used by the little society of castes to resist innovation and change.* (Guha 1998: 114, emphasis added)

What is even more fascinating for us is that Guha records that in the politically most active districts, it wasn't just the unlettered rustics who were imposing sanctions and boycotts, but rather groups like the lawyers. 'They often operated as a well-knit nationalist force, with the local Bar Association assuming some of the functions of caste councils', advising priests, barbers and washermen not to serve those considered guilty of deviation from the Swadeshi code (Ibid.: 119).

We can now roughly indicate what we mean by the idea of social polity. One of the major difficulties with our theorizations of politics in the Indian context is that because they have drawn on categories and concepts derived from the very specific experience of Western modernity, they largely miss out on what is specific and in fact, quite central to the making of the political in India. Here obviously, the caste/varna/jati has a centrality to the emergence of the modern political, of which again, it should be clear by now, there are layers. The context of our discussion here is caste but it should also be apparent that there are larger resonances of this form of power with the way religious communities also function. All the instances that I have discussed earlier might give the impression that the social polity has only negative features that are essentially anti-democratic in character. One of the reasons for my stressing this aspect is that most of the discussions on the modernity of caste associations (the Rudolphs), or of the politicization of caste (Kothari), only underline the positive aspects of associational life and secular mobilization that are enabled through them. In my understanding, both aspects are important for an understanding of how the social polity functions but since the darker aspects have been generally left out altogether by scholars, the need to underline this negative side becomes more important.

The significance of grasping this complex relationship between the way in which the modern form of macro—that is state—power is shaped and structured by the micropowers of caste, should be evident by now. Especially if we take Ambedkar's thought on this matter seriously, we should be able to appreciate that his insistence had to do with the very viability of any meaningful project of social transformation. Mere transformations at the formal-political level do not and cannot count for much unless the project takes the bull by the horns where it matters most—in the domain of the social that is also the domain of micropower.

It may be useful to wind up this discussion of the social polity in the light of our earlier discussion on the dispersed foci of power that the *mandala* form possibly mutates into in modern times. If that is the case, as I have tried to suggest earlier, then the 'social polity' may involve another tier of power lodged between the micropowers of caste and the macro-power of the state, which is what provides it a sort of 'relative autonomy' vis-à-vis the state and submerges the central state, often accounting for its inefficacy in many crucial matters.

Notes

1. The term 'social polity' is taken from the title of an important book by Bhupendranath Datta, *Studies in Indian Social Polity*, originally published in 1944. Datta, younger brother of Swami Vivekananda, was perhaps one of the most erudite Marxists of his time and one who also seriously engaged with the history and caste and caste power in India. He does not explain the term

social polity anywhere in the book but in the very first sentence, we read: 'In studying about the origin of the *Indian social polity known as the caste system* we will have to go into the roots of its genesis, growth and condition in different epochs of Indian history' (Datta 1983: 1; emphasis added).

2. The idea of 'sovereignty' when it comes to a discussion of politics, and the overpowering desire to make oneself legible and understood to the West, however, is so powerful in the early twentieth century that we often keep forgetting what the terms used for such descriptions traditionally were. Thus, tellingly, the translation of the Arthashastra by none other than R. Shamashastry (n.d.: 362–369) renders the title of Book 6 as 'The Source of Sovereign States' where the title in the Sanskrit original is simply 'Mandalayoni'! [Udaiveer Shastri (1925: 204–214). R.P. Kangle's translation (1972: 314–320) however, translates it more correctly as 'The Circle of Kings as the Basis'. I use the expression 'more correctly' because it is not quite clear what the enigmatic expression 'Mandalayoni' really means. Patrick Olivelle (2013: 271–276) in his translation stays close to Kangle's rendering, calling Book 6 'The Basis of the Circle'.
3. Romila Thapar (1984) for instance, discusses the Vrjji assembly at length, which met in the assembly hall (*santhagara*):

   > The figure is nominal and exaggerated but the Vrjji assembly would in any case have been large since it was a confederacy of eight clans. The assembly elected one person among them to preside. The *gana-raja* or *pramukha* was assisted by an *upa-raja*. Regularly assigned seats suggest a ranking within the *gana*. A quorum was necessary and voting by proxy was permitted. The resolution before the *gana* was moved, discussed, had three readings and was finally put to vote. (1984: 81)

   Vrjji was among the sixteen *Mahajanapadas* of ancient North India, from about 1000–600 BCE. The gana-sanghas were tribal 'states' of a range of different kinds, some of them exhibiting interesting features. For instance, one such *gana-sangha* 'state', that of the Licchavis, was ruled collectively by 7707 influential persons who referred to themselves as *rajas* collectively (See Yamazaki 2006: 47).
4. Among early twentieth-century nationalist scholars, see especially Jayaswal (1943) and Ghoshal (1959).
5. It should also be clarified here that I will continue to use the term 'philosophy' for what were known as the *darsanas*, without getting

oversensitive about the delicate differences between the two categories. In a manner of speaking, this is a way of bracketing questions about Western categories and knowledge, as well as questions of translatability that will otherwise keep distracting us. The baggage of Western knowledge is formidable, and it is virtually impossible to utter a single word today that has not already been used, reused and discussed many times over by different scholars and it is well-nigh impossible to keep referring back to their debates.

6. It is interesting of course, that this is the title Datta chose for the English version of his book, while the Bengali version simply refers to it as *bharatiya samaj paddhati*. Partha Chatterjee has drawn my attention to the fact that the term 'social polity' probably comes from the German language with which Datta was familiar, having done his doctorate from Germany. But the fact that Datta chose this term, which recurs on a few occasions in the text, is significant in my view, precisely because it points to a domain of social power that I want to return to later in this chapter.
7. Spodek's study deals with the changes that started occurring in the area with the advent of the British and how the rajas took to modern ways—an interesting set of developments in themselves but do not concern us here.
8. Most of the points here about the *Arthashastra* are based on detailed discussions with Patrick Olivelle, with whom we had many sessions of intensive reading of the text.

5

Secularism and Subalternity

The Paramodern and the Puranic

After Secularism

The crisis of secularism is not news any longer, given that in India the first salvoes against the secular creed were fired in the mid-1980s, with two very significant interventions by T.N. Madan (1987) and Ashis Nandy (1995), inaugurating a debate that went on for almost two decades.[1] Nonetheless, its crisis, and the range of issues it raises, still continues to dog 'us' today. By 'us', I mean the partisans of the 'secular', people who still believe that there might be something that we need to salvage here, and not throw the baby out with the bathwater. Though, increasingly, I have come to believe, if there is anything to be salvaged in it, it is ironically 'spiritual'—if we can talk of the spirit of secularism in any meaningful sense. Theoretically speaking, we could think of two possible ways of responding to secularism's ongoing crisis. We could abandon the very term—or at least bracket it—and contemplate other possible ways of thinking of religious 'tolerance' or accommodation. Alternatively, we could radically redefine the term, investing it with our own desired meanings ranging from different notions of co-living and coexistence between religious communities to 'state secularism' of different kinds. In general, I prefer to hold on to the signs called 'secularism' and the 'secular' in order to see what kinds of practices are articulated around them, though that is not what I intend to do in this chapter.

In this chapter, I will take secularism's crisis as my starting point in order to explore one critical question raised by its failure, namely that of premodern or non-modern ways of being (and thinking) that the secular sought to transform, often quite thoughtlessly. Thoughtlessly, because these modes of being were assumed to be passive modes that could simply be transformed into modern ways—to which, it was believed, they would surrender simply because of modernity's superior knowledge. Thoughtlessly, also because it failed to—and continues to fail to—appreciate the meaning of the 'spiritual' in ordinary everyday lives of people. In the Indian context, I call these modes of being the 'Puranic' mode, which continues to be widely prevalent in the larger domain that I call the 'paramodern'. I introduced these terms at the beginning of this book and will elaborate their possible contours at greater length throughout this chapter. For the moment, I want to underline that these modes have displayed great resilience; they have survived continued assaults of the secular-modern to 'eradicate' what the latter considered outmoded or archaic ways of 'thinking' (as if the former modes resided in some autonomous domain of subjectivity that could be disentangled from ways of being). Indeed, not only have they survived, they have in their own way actively resisted the attempts of the secular-modern to transform them.

The explorations undertaken in this chapter are not meant to be an exercise in what secular-moderns often derisively label 'romanticizing the past', for it must be recognized straight away that these are not 'past' modes of being but 'non-synchronous synchronicities'—very much part of our contemporary existence which have to be dealt with.[2] The secular-modern confidence about the eradication of 'mistaken' or 'outmoded' beliefs or ways of thinking arose directly out of their faith in the ideology of Progress that simply consigned these life forms to the past. If, on the other hand, we recognize them not as remnants of past forms but as active and important aspects of our contemporary existence, then we clearly need to think of them differently. To try and understand these modes of being, rather than simply decry them as remnants of the past and repositories of superstition, requires a different approach from the one we have become used to adopting. Expressions like 'romanticizing the past' only betray continuing, unreconstructed modernist prejudice. This chapter seeks, with all modesty, to undertake the task of trying to understand what the Puranic mode means.

If we try to think about the presence of these ways of being in our contemporary as non-synchronous synchronicities (or non-synchronisms for short), we will have to deal with them differently and the very project of secularism will need to be thought afresh. Such a rethink can hopefully, open out new possibilities for revisiting some of the fundamentals of the project itself—towards something like a post-secular secularism. I do not use this term to simply refer to the idea of religious toleration, accommodation or co-living but try to understand the logic of secularism's crisis by delineating its relationship with the society—in this case, India—it seeks to transform. As would be clear already, my interest here does not lie with the doctrinal aspects of secularism or the secular—or 'secularity' to use Charles Taylor's term. As a matter of fact, Charles Taylor's retelling (Taylor 2007) of the story of the 'secular age' in Europe is important to bear in mind as we go along, primarily because it tells us something that we do not normally keep in mind: that the phenomenon of 'disenchantment' in Europe was not an undertaking spearheaded by self-proclaimed secularists but as Taylor is at pains to underline, occurred in the long process initiated by the Reformation. The Reformation was not simply a banner of revolt against the Catholic Church but equally against the old spiritualism of 'natural religion'. Taylor does not dwell on this point at length, theoretically speaking, but it seems to me to be of central importance for our discussion of what I call the 'Puranic life'. At one level, a similar role is played by Islamic monotheism in Arabia, where it overcame the older spiritualism of the pagan world through a long and protracted struggle. Here too, that struggle was conducted in the name of Allah and a higher and rational spirituality. The crucial fact that that struggle was carried out in the name of God or Allah, in the name of a higher spirituality and not by a largely rootless secular elite in the name of scientific thinking and scientific temper, makes all the difference in our understanding of how in a completely different context, in India, the secular modern comes to deal with the Puranic world. But this element of monotheism also introduces another dimension of complexity into the issue for it is not quite certain that it succeeded in eliminating—despite the tremendous cost—the older spirituality without residue. Here it may be apposite to cite Mohammed Arkoun's observation that:

> Despite this official, written, 'learned' Islam, *a popular Islamic culture* developed under the leadership of many local saints who were able to

> share the dialects, the beliefs and customs of the various ethnic groups which the remote government [of the great Islamic empires] was unable to control politically. An ethno-sociological account is needed of this neglected but exuberant Islam, so often *condemned as 'superstitious' and illiterate* by the 'orthodox' Islam concentrated in the urban social classes. *It is true that popular belief was based on the invisible beings such as those called* jinnis (genies or *djinns*) in the Quran, the cosmic forces. (Arkoun 2002: 159, emphasis added)

Arkoun further underlines this aspect from his personal experience of what was being taught in Kabyle society in Algeria in the 1930s and 1940s: 'The most significant, noticeable fact was that everywhere, popular Islam was taught as an animist, naïve, ritualistic system of belief, overlaid with superficial elements of the Islamic creed' (Ibid.: 159).

I consider this point to be significant, not because it tells us of something that a society like India's lacks, but simply to underline that this a society with a very different history where monotheism as such never really struck deep roots—relatively small pockets of Islamic and Christian influence apart. In fact, more importantly, it raises the more difficult question of whether such projects of transformation of entire ways of being are not fundamentally misplaced. For a secular state and a secular elite to undertake that task with no alternative notion of spirituality to offer makes it even more complicated.

In his explorations of the genealogies of the secular, Talal Asad makes a distinction between the 'secular' as an ontological and epistemological condition and 'secularism' as a political doctrine. The 'secular' in Asad's reading is a concept 'that brings together certain behaviours, knowledges, and sensibilities in modern life' (Asad 2003: 25). In other words, it is a condition that is expressed in a certain reconstitution of ways of knowing and being specific to modernity. However, Asad cautions us, this 'secular' should neither be seen as 'continuous with the religious that supposedly preceded it' nor as a 'simple break from it', that is, not the opposite, 'an essence that excludes the sacred' (Ibid.: 25). It is radically new but acquires a specific form and content in different contexts, having thus, *neither a singular origin nor a stable historical identity* (Ibid.: 25). Thus, if we are to follow

Asad's argument, it is not only the political doctrine of secularism that is plural and multiple in origin/s but *the secular itself*, acquiring as it does, different lines of connection between the religious/sacred that preceded it.

I largely agree with this proposition and therefore, follow Asad in distinguishing 'the secular' as an ontological and epistemological condition from the concrete and complex historical trajectories of both 'the secular' and of 'secularism'. However, I depart somewhat from Asad's injunction and take seriously secularism's *self-representation* as marking a radical break with the pre-secular or the non-secular, the religious and the sacred. Thus, even while acknowledging that the 'actually existing' secular or historical secularisms do not or may not really conform to this self-perception of a radical break, I want to underline that *it is this perception of a radical break that determines the conduct of states and the secular elites*, even in countries like India in the aftermath of the state's attainment of independence from colonial rule. What I call the Puranic mode and the paramodern world can only be understood if we recognize this aspect of the modern state's investment in the secular. And it is only this recognition that allows us to see the critical significance of the point made earlier with reference to Taylor's narrative of disenchantment and secularity.

The Indian debate on secularism produced a range of insights that helped to clarify issues pertaining to the relationship/s between secularism, religion, communalism, nation-state and modernity. In retrospect, however, it seems that many of the insights produced in the course of the debate have now become a new set of self-evident truths, beyond any further inquiry and interrogation. Thus, for instance, it was a very important and useful intervention made by Ashis Nandy, that emphasized that 'communalism' was not really about religion; that what we 'knew' as religious-strife and religious conflict was, in fact, a new and modern phenomenon. To quickly recall the fundamental point made by Nandy, communalism is a modern and therefore 'secular' (in Talal Asad's sense) phenomenon about recasting and often welding together political communities in the image of the nation-state. In Nandy's terms, it is predicated on the emergence of a *new kind of religion—religion-as-ideology*—that is less about the way people live (and their spiritual needs) and more about affairs of the secular political world. This religion-as-ideology, he argues, stands opposed to the 'inchoate character of lived religions' where dividing lines between communities are always quite unclear and fuzzy. It is also worth underlining here that in Nandy's reading this radically secular task of welding together a modern political community in the place of relatively inchoate lived religions itself calls into being a political elite that does not owe allegiance to any particular sect but can actually rise above all of them.

Those familiar with the contours of Nandy's argument will also recognize that in his rendering, the resources of religious toleration are to be found in the latter, non-secular domain of lived religions, while the domain of state and politics breeds intolerance, forcing communities to recast themselves in the image of the nation-state and assume a singular identity. To be sure, this important insight in Nandy was not a claim to the effect that *because* communalism is a secular-modern phenomenon, *therefore* it has nothing to do with religion. On the contrary, by calling it 'religion-as-ideology', Nandy underlined the fact that in it, religion in some fashion, continued to play a significant, if reconstituted role. However, in the heat of the debate that followed and the rhetoric and acrimony that began dominating the debate, this insight seems to have been thrown to the winds. So, where most secularists continued to reiterate the binary distinction of the religious *versus* the secular and thus argued for strict separation, the anti-secularist argument also lapsed into the very same binary.[3] The only difference was that the latter insisted that communalism belonged, purely and simply, to the domain of the secular-modern, rather than to the religious. The crucially important question, from my point of view, is precisely that the phenomenon of communalism *problematizes the neat binary opposition between the religious and the secular*. Indeed, this is the complexity of this new discursive formation where the secular mediates the re-signification of religion—rewriting it into the emergent story of nationhood. With the emergence of nationalism, rather of contending nationalisms, the Hindu-Muslim question was no longer about religion alone but also about the nation—the so-called 'two-nation theory' being its constant reference point. In a way, we see a wide prevalence of this kind of 'religion' in our contemporary world where religious identities become handmaidens of the state—interested less in piety and more in the aggressive pursuit of identity in politics. Understandably, therefore, there is always a question about how religious such religiosity can be. This kind of religion-as-ideology is very different from the monotheistic religions of earlier times referred to above for they were not secular in Nandy's sense. This is obviously a question that calls for much more investigation and study but we can certainly say, whatever critiques of monotheism one might have, is that they concerned themselves centrally with spiritual matters and weren't instrumental in the sense in which modern secular religion-as-ideology is. Nandy's championing of such inchoate popular religiosity is pitted against such modern religions-as-ideology formations as well as the secular state and secular elite, neither of whom actually have either the resources or the wherewithal to provide the spiritual sustenance that lived 'natural' religions provide.

In the Indian context, it has often been argued that 'secular'/'secularism' are not the opposites of 'religious/sacred' but of 'communal'. Thus, positing the 'secular *versus* communal' is a very common way of addressing some of the major issues in Indian politics and society today. Now if communalism is at once traditional *and* modern, religious *and* secular, what about its antithesis? Can 'secularism' simply be 'secular'? If secularism defines itself in relation to communalism, then surely, its secularity too must exceed itself and stretch out beyond the purely secular.

As a matter of fact, in contexts such as India's, this is precisely what happens. Secularism comes to live a secret life as it were and the fundamental secular idea of the formal equality of individuals gets easily inserted within the discourse of Hindutva. While many secularists argue in favour of cultural and religious rights of minorities, strictly speaking this position is incompatible with the secularist creed: cultural rights or religious rights can often be very closely tied to highly discriminatory and oppressive practices within religious communities and these do not allow for a direct relationship between the individual and the state. That is really the democratic challenge for our times—of defending the cultural rights of minorities but also holding the communities to account in some fashion. A defense of cultural or religious rights is necessary but it cannot be based on the secularist position; such a defense can only be mounted on the basis of the idea of substantive equality and can be articulated as a multiculturalist position that does not sit easy with a secularist one (Mahajan 2014). It is the secular insistence on the abstract, unmarked individual as the bearer of rights that Hindutva, in its earlier phases, had rhetorically deployed against all those who sought to protect the cultural rights of minorities, especially their personal laws.[4] The demand for a Uniform Civil Code was a major plank in Hindutva mobilization and the formal argument for it always was that a single law for the entire country would allow for equality between individuals, irrespective of community allegiances. Needless to say, a single law is always likely to be normed by the practices and beliefs of the dominant, majority culture and therefore becomes an easy disguise for a majoritarian position.

Incarnations of the 'Individual'

However, there is something beyond the manifest level that also needs to be taken into account. While it is evident that this discursive strategy of Hindutva draws very heavily on the liberal idea of individual rights, the individual that emerges within Hindutva discourse is very different from the one in liberal discourse. Read through Golwalkar's writings, especially Golwalkar (1966), and it will be evident that it is precisely the liberal notion of individual rights that is his greatest enemy (along with communism) that in his view, is responsible for breeding self-centredness and sapping the National spirit.[5] Thus we must not be misled by the mere appearance of the word 'individual', for the individual here is simply an extension of the National Self or the *Virat Purusha.* To put it in Golwalkar's own words: 'The highest scope for the development of the individual was secured in the process of his best service to the *Virat Purusha* (Corporate Person) of society' (Golwalkar 1966: 100).

This is not the disembedded, unencumbered individual who is the bearer of rights in liberal legal discourse—upon whose formal equality is premised the discourse of modernity as a matter of fact.

This individual, as the quote suggests, is thickly bound with the national community through a range of *duties and obligations*. It is, in fact, very interesting to see how in Hindutva discourse in general, but in Golwalkar's in particular, the very idea of equality is undercut and indeed, disavowed via a resort to a particular Advaitic spin on the idea of diversity. Thus, quoting a statement of Yajnavalkya's, addressed to his wife Maitreyi, where he tells her that 'man is not loved (by wife) because he is the husband, but that there is Atma in him', Golwalkar says:

> It is in this sense, i.e. the same spirit being immanent in all, that all men are equal. *Equality is applicable only on the plane of the Supreme Spirit. But on the physical plane the same Spirit manifests itself in a wondrous variety of diversities and disparities.* (Golwalkar 1966: 18, emphasis added)

What we find here is an idea of the individual who is not only an extension of the National Self, for then at least at that level, she would be equal to all others; the individual here is equally marked by that ultimate marker of internal inequality—of caste—as the insistence on the centrality of *varnashramadharma* by Golwalkar amply shows.[6]

This idea of what we might unsatisfactorily call the 'embedded individual' is another important strand within Hindutva discourse that must be seen as simultaneously accounting for its infinite malleability, as also a source of potential internal tensions. At one level, it allows for a reasonable degree of flexibility in terms of its modernist-liberal self-presentation; at another level, it provides the space of imaginations of an organic nationhood—a collective national personality. In the writings of both Savarkar and Golwalkar, these imaginations acquire almost delirious dimensions as they go about trying to define the Nation as Hindu and as existing from time immemorial but that is not something that we can go into here.

At the first level, then the idea of 'formal equality' of individuals is deployed by Hindutva ideology to trump minority rights, in much the same way as 'classic secularism' might. But it does not do so to uphold individual rights or equality. Even so, its reference to the idea of the individual does, quite misleadingly, open out a pathway through which a sort of 'liberal' notion of citizenship is articulated within Hindutva discourse, whenever required. At another level, this discourse draws on the more explicitly fascistic notions articulated for example, in Golwalkar's (2015) tract *'We', or Our Nationhood Defined.* Here, minority rights are trumped not just by invoking the idea of formal equality; rather, there is an explicit demand that the minorities must either fully assimilate themselves into the Hindu nation, or live completely at the mercy of the Hindu Race—*without citizenship rights* (Golwalkar 2015: 47–48). Much of this strand derives its nourishment from the experience of Nazism and the way it dealt with its minorities, especially the Jews. This tract, withdrawn by the RSS because of the embarrassing glorification of Nazi Germany (Ibid.: 35), displays an obsessive concern with this question and the threat posed to any nation by 'unabsorbed minorities'.

Both levels exist simultaneously in Hindutva discourse—the 'individual' and its 'embeddedness'. Yet, it is worth emphasizing that some of these revealing references to Nazi Germany apart, most of Golwalkar's discussion of nationalism and the minority question *revolves around the more 'normal' cases of nationalism in the West.* This is the most significant aspect. In a symptomatic discussion, he blames the League of Nations for foisting a dispensation on Czechoslovakia that led to the freezing of unabsorbed minorities within it. In his reading, it is the presence of such minorities with extra-territorial loyalties, such as the Sudeten Germans, which is eventually responsible for the nation's downfall. Recall that Hitler used the so-called 'persecution of Sudeten Germans' in Czechoslovakia as the final pretext for aggression, aided ably by the local Nazis. Written a year after the Sudetenland Crisis, this tract sees distinct parallels with the presence of Muslims in India.

A closer reading of the history of fascism of various shades and of the Hindu right in particular, suggests then a chilling possibility: that fascism is an always-present possibility within the structure of all nationalisms.[7] This possibility derives from the very fact that all nationalisms, in fact, *produce* the problem of 'minorities' in their quest for a homogenous national culture. Given the fact that in earlier times, communities lived in large swathes of areas across territories from which nation-states came to be carved out and given the inability of nationalisms to deal with the problem of 'unabsorbed minorities', this possibility always remains potentially explosive. As scholars have pointed out in recent times, for all their despotism, Empires like the Ottoman or the Mughal could deal with immense cultural diversity without great difficulty; *minority cultures began to be perceived as a problem at the precise historical moment of transition from empires to modern nation-states, with their search for a homogeneous national culture.*

This question of the always-present possibility of the fascist element in all nationalisms actually points towards the problem with our modern condition that we began this chapter with. But it is not just nationalism that is at issue here for the raw material from which nationalism forges its cultural identity is drawn from the field I designate as the Puranic—precisely the one that the rationalist secular moderns have drawn away from. While one must be careful not to draw direct causal connections between these different phenomena, the fact that the fascist imagination breeds on such a ground has also been noticed elsewhere. I have referred earlier to non-synchronisms or the co-presence of different modes of being, drawing on Ernst Bloch. It may not be out of place therefore to mention here that in his works of the early 1930s, during the rise of Hitler, Bloch directly connects such non-synchronisms to the growth of Nazism. Bloch observes that 'this sort of patriotism, this foam at the mouth and dimming eye with which people honour Germany in Germany' actually recalls a 'primitive-atavistic participation mystique', the ties of primitive man to the soil which contains his ancestral spirits' (Bloch 1977/1935: 26). Needless to say, notions like 'primitive' and 'atavistic' bespeak of Bloch's continuing modernist commitments and we can safely set them aside. In any case, Bloch does not make any simplistic connection between past modes of being and fascism for he is equally aware that if the 'peasants sometimes still believe in witches and exorcists', 'a large class of urbanites believe in ghostly Jews' and 'in Elders of the Zion' (Ibid.: 26). In other words, it is a far more complex configuration that makes possible the success of the fascist imagination. What is clear to Bloch and which is of immediate interest to me in this chapter, is that the 'irrational' and the 'fantastic' are not to be shunned because they represent something primitive, on the contrary, there is something to be learned by Marxists (Bloch's addressees) about why they fail to connect where fascists do.

The Paramodern and the Puranic

This is the question of what I will call the 'paramodern' and it has to do with that which modernity seeks to expunge and expel but which actually accompanies it throughout its life as its inseparable shadow. The paramodern, populated by humans, spirits, jinns and demons of all kinds, constitutes perhaps the biggest challenge even today, in conceptual terms, for the modernist project of enlightenment. As the discussion further will try to show, the paramodern is not just about a world where humans cohabit with spirits and demons, they also constitute a world that the moderns have little sense of. Banishing such modes of being (and modes of thinking and knowing constitutively tied to them) to the netherworlds, out of sight of the moderns, is hardly of any help, even from the point of view of the larger project of social transformation that even a more modest and reconstructed modern project might be invested in.

What is worse is that the only way moderns can deal with them is by bringing the force of law to 'eradicate' what they believe are superstitions and backward ideas. It is important to underline that here I am not talking of tackling specific, degrading practices like untouchability or human sacrifice for that matter, to take two stark instances, where a combination of interventions may be necessary and justified. We cannot have a single and simple undifferentiated argument and method of dealing with practices that are deemed 'non-modern'. The point rather, is that by forcing a secular order on entire populations whose lifeworld is populated by ancestors and spirits who make their this-worldly journey more bearable and liveable, modernity leaves them bereft in the face of impersonal forces like the Law and the State. This situation is always disempowering and diminishing in more ways than one—stripping life of its richness for which modernity has no substitute. The tired discourse of modernity, scientific temper and secularism over the decades has simply imposed a certain modernist common sense without any discernment and discrimination between different modes of being. Thus, an argument against untouchability—a reprehensible non-modern practice for sure—is invoked in order to decry and destroy Adivasi lifeworlds (another form of the non-modern) for instance. As a matter of fact, what our contemporary experience demonstrates is that it is from this ground of the culturally and epistemically dispossessed, so to speak, that the main challenge to the secular-modern project of enlightenment emerges. The fascist element in many modern or modernizing societies, I will suggest, actually breeds on the sense of disempowerment and ridicule that is the lot of these segments of the population in the new world that is thrust upon them. For a fascist or right-wing project, defence of a 'tradition' facing obliteration at the hands of a new class of people, namely the intellectuals—the oracles of the secular modern—and other sundry scapegoats becomes possible in a context like this. It finds its fertile soil in the paramodern, in a context of large-scale cultural and epistemic dispossession.

This is the space where, what Pradip Datta (2010), in his reflections on the Hindutva conceptions of the past, has called 'myhstory' operates. Datta's 'myhstory' is a peculiar hybrid of the mythic and the historical that emerges in different combinations in the political discourse of Hindutva. In fact, in an early attempt to come to terms with this 'myhstory', we could usefully refer to Neeladri Bhattacharya's (1991) reading of Hindutva discourse on the eve of the Babri Masjid demolition that Datta also refers to. Bhattacharya's intervention at that time, coming from within the universe of the secular-modern, clearly saw the problem with secular history and historiography, insofar as it operated with a simple binary of history as the bearer of truth and myth as a repository of the fantastic and the false. Bhattacharya was able to see this problem of secular discourse precisely because his attention was focused on the *popular*: 'Popular conceptions of the past' he argued, are often structured by myths, which they see as true histories, in contradistinction to desacralized and demythicized 'scientific histories', which are considered false (Bhattacharya 1991: 122). Datta's discussion, however, focuses more specifically on the operation of Hindutva discourse, where he sees 'Hindutva's myhstory as using the past for present political practice. Here the past, he says, 'does not simply inspire and explain' but is the very grammar of action (Datta 2010: 105). What is important from the point of view of the discussion in this chapter, however, is that even in Datta's discussion the space of Hindutva discourse and the space of the popular inextricably get tied up. This hybrid genre of 'myhstory' or mythic history, argues Datta, is not a Hindutva invention but is already in evidence in Bengal in the nineteenth century as one can see in the work of Partha Chatterjee and Sumit Sarkar (Ibid.: 107). In other words, I would suggest, we see them as, in some fashion, integral to the world of the paramodern or what I will call, more specifically, the Puranic mode of being. Datta's reference to Romila Thapar's work to underline that such early mythic histories 'can be seen to follow the narrative trajectory of puranic stories', where they 'make an easy narrative transition from cosmological origins to the more historically identifiable world of lineages' is significant in this respect from the point of view of the argument that I want to develop further (Ibid.: 107–108). For puranic narrative modes, I want to suggest, should not be seen simply as narrative strategies but as ways in which—or through which—lives are lived.

If the paramodern is the space produced by the modern across different societies, I want to suggest that in the Indian—and perhaps the larger South Asian context, this space is inhabited by what I will call the *Puranic* mode of being. Though there is hardly any agreement among scholars about the precise nature of relationship between the high texts (the Vedas and the Upanishads) and the Puranas, one of the influential ways in which it has been understood is with reference to the fact that while the high texts are hardly read except by specialists, it is the Puranas that are more widely known and determine conduct in this world. If modern Hindu reformers like Devendranath Tagore of the Brahmo Samaj and Dayanand Saraswati, the founder of the Arya Samaj, were utterly dismissive of the Puranas, it was not simply because of their espousal of idolatry and their reliance on the fantastic alone but also because of the fact that they represented a move away from the high tradition of the Vedas and the Upanishads (Rocher 1986: 9–10). On the other hand, we do have important figures like Rajendralal Mitra who saw the Puranas as the 'great store-house of ancient Indian knowledge' and Madan Mohan Malaviya who similarly considered them as 'encyclopaedias of ancient and medieval Hindu culture and religion' (cited in Ibid.: 12–13). In the sense that I use the term Puranic here, I am not really interested in the significance of these texts for 'Hindu religion' so to speak: whether they are central to the tradition as Mitra and Malaviya believe, or marginal and/or undesirable accretions as Devendranath Tagore and Dayanand Saraswati think it is, are irrelevant to my concerns here.

For my interest here is not so much in the 'texts' called the Puranas but to particular modes of being that these texts were trying to domesticate by drawing them into the Brahmanical fold. It is clear, after all, from the way a stalwart of modern Hinduism, Rajendralal Mitra explicates it, that the very strength of the Puranas is that they are able to communicate with 'the lowest capacity':

> They [Puranas] are records of everything that in ancient times interested people from the highest to the lowest. They treat alike of philosophy and theology, cosmogony and chronology, history and fables, science and art. Nothing comes amiss to them; and *every subject is treated in an easy colloquial style suited to the lowest capacity.* (cited in Rocher 1986: 12, emphasis added)

I am broadly persuaded by Kunal Chakrabarti's argument, made in the context of the Bengal *Puranas*, that the texts themselves are attempts by the Brahmins to reach out to sections of the population that lay outside the Vedic fold and to appropriate their traditions within the Vedic-Brahmanical fold (Chakrabarti 2001). For this purpose, they devised a minimalist strategy of insisting on only some preconditions, so to speak: acceptance of 'the infallibility of the Vedas, the ritual prerogative of the *brahmanas* [Brahmins], maintenance of *varnashrama dharma*, and the rejection of Buddhism' on which, says Chakrabarti, 'the *Puranas* display an absolute unanimity of opinion' (Chakrabarti 2001: 25). On all other matters, the Puranas are open to incorporating local customs, including the cults of innumerable indigenous goddesses—not always benign and demanding of animal and human sacrifice as well. The readiness on the part of the Bengal Puranic authors to accept this trade-off, so to speak, leads to these texts becoming an eclectic mix of traditions. Chakrabarti's reading here agrees with that of R.C. Hazra, who sees the development of Puranic rites and customs as a response to the wide prevalence of a range of religious movements ranging from the anti-Vedic (Buddhism, Jainism, Ajivikism), semi-Vedic (consisting mainly of Vaisnavism, Saivism, and Brahmaism) and non-Vedic (Saktaism). Hazra actually argues that 'the original character of Vaisnavism and Saivism was also most probably non-Brahmanical as both the Pancharatras and the Pasupatas were irreverent to the *varnashramdharma*' (cited in Chakrabarti 2001: 45–46). So widespread was the threat perceived, to the Brahmanical social order, that we can see 'an obsessive fear of the Kali age [Kaliyuga] in all the early Puranas' (Ibid.: 46).

Having said this, Chakrabarti tells us that the Bengal Puranas are 'highly persuasive'; 'they seldom engage in "rational argument", they do not issue commands without providing what they consider suitable justification.... Justification is usually provided in the form of an anecdote describing an incident in the life of a mythical character.... Thus descriptive rhetoric is the principal mode of enunciation in the Bengal Puranas (Chakrabarti 2001: 24). As a result, says Chakrabarti, the texts are invariably prolix, endlessly repetitive, and in certain respects manifestly self-contradictory. 'They disproportionately exaggerate one possibility often only to contradict it later' (Ibid.: 24). This mode of argumentation and persuasion is accompanied by anecdotes that obviously are not anecdotes in our modern sense but have all the qualities of myths and the fantastic about them. That these are 'highly persuasive' is, in no small measure, a consequence of the fact that, at some level, they partake of the same ontological universe to which the addressees of the Puranas belong.

But who are the addressees of this Puranic discourse? It is interesting perhaps that one of the Puranas, the *Devibhagavata*, states in so many words that since 'women, *sudras* and unworthy *brahmanas* are debarred from listening to the Vedas...it is for their benefit that the Puranas have been written' (cited in Chakrabarti 2001: 57). It is worth bearing in mind, however, that this description ('women', 'sudras' and 'unworthy brahmanas') is actually the official description by the Brahmins who wrote the Puranas. These are categories of people who are perhaps to be identified not simply as women and lower castes but more importantly, as the inhabitants of a world that is often difficult to assimilate within the Vedic universe—given that goddess-worship also had its almost inevitable corollary in Tantricism which not only rejected the infallibility of the Vedas and the authority of the Brahmins but believed in equal opportunity of worship for women and sudras as well (Chakrabarti 2001: 47, 69). More importantly, it was the association of left-handed or *vamachari* Tantricism with practices that were anathema to Vedic Brahmins, such as the consumption/practice of five 'M's for instance (mangsa or meat, madira or wine, matsya – fish, mudra – parched grain and maithun – sex) that made it a taboo. Nevertheless, the pervasiveness of Tantra in both the Buddhist and Hindu universes was to eventually lead to some kind of accommodation even of Tantricism—albeit the right-hand variety—within the Vedic universe (Ibid.: 69).

In the world in which the Puranic texts emerge and attempt to assimilate non-Vedic indigenous populations within the Vedic order, there are all these 'dark' and 'uncontrolled' forces and a range of esoteric practices meant to deal with or control them that may or may not have been eventually fully integrated within the dominant order. Undoubtedly, the degree of integration and assimilation varies greatly across regions. In relation to Tamil Nadu, Geoffrey Samuel (2009) cites a study by George Hart where the latter has argued that 'the South Indian king was surrounded by a number of ritual specialists from low-status castes (drummers, bards, spirit-mediums, funeral priests, perhaps also priests of Tamil deity Murugan) who played a crucial role in relation to his power' because

> the role of groups 'of low birth' in ancient Tamilnad was to control, or order, dangerous power…[they] had an inborn ability to deal with dangerous power, whether in the form of dead spirits or just dangerous power… (cited in Samuel 2009: 236)

These 'dangerous' demonic powers obviously did not threaten only the king's existence; equally, they impacted the lives of ordinary folk and therefore needed to be controlled or propitiated.

In a more contemporary account, Priyadarshini Vijaisri (2015) takes us to a world very different from that of medieval Bengal that forms the context of the Bengal Puranas that we have discussed earlier via Chakrabarti's account. Vijaisri's account is of a Dalit (Madiga) goddess from contemporary Andhra Pradesh. While all the major Puranas and the Bengal Puranas that Chakrabarti discusses are, without doubt, brahmnical texts, Vijaisri takes us to the world of outcaste Puranas like the Jambuvapurana or the Yadavapurana, which follow a similar structure as the other Puranas, but more importantly inhabit the same universe. She tells us that what began as a research project on the study of modernity and its relationship to the identity of women and the goddess in the post-colonial context 'eventually led me to the actual tumultuous ritual space—the village goddess festival.... I found myself at the threshold of a dynamic space where outcaste ritual specialists were awe-inspiring, feared, and at the same time revered as representatives of the goddess' (Vijaisri 2015: xiii). Her fieldwork was conducted in Karnataka and Andhra Pradesh between 2004 and 2009, though mainly in villages around Tirupati, where she witnessed 'the annual *kolupu* celebrations associated with the Goddess Matangi, also known as Matamma' (Ibid.: xiv). This is the Puranic world seen not through Brahmin eyes but through the Madiga narratives like the Jambava Purana—a clan narrative of the Madigas—and Kataamaraju Katha and many others. It is impossible to do justice to Vijaisri's complex narrative of the Matangi/Matamma figure but some points do need to be underlined. So to put it in her own words:

> It is necessary, in this context, to understand the conception of the Matangi/Matamma as the Primordial Mother in mythological narratives to deduce corresponding cultural imagination/s of dangerous and sacred femininity. It needs to be noted that goddesses like Ankamma, Gangamma and Poleramma are associated with an analogous tradition where the priests belong to the other predominant outcaste community, the Malas. While the Madigas and the Malas are culturally opposed, with no intercaste relations, their conception of the goddess indicates a basic unity. Thus, most outcaste clan goddesses are popular village goddesses and generally referred to as Sakti, suggesting a primal source of energy.... Here, two distinct and interconnected traditions can be discerned; one the Brahmanical upper-caste mythology and the other, Sakta associated with outcastes and the cluster of powerful peasant, pastoral and artisanal castes.

> The genesis myths across [outcaste] tradition hint at the sexual tension, with allusions to the creator—the male Brahma and the female Adishakti—as incestuous. While there is not much speculation about the incestuous male creator, the folk, the Puranic and Hindu texts exhibit anxiety about the primordial Mother. (Vijaisri 2015: 83)

That these legends and narratives are living traditions, believed in and lived by communities today is the crucial point—and we can clearly see from the passage cited above that the *Puranic* world remains, in a slightly different way from the Bengal narrative, a site of serious struggle and contestation. What is really critical in this particular narrative of Vijaisri's is that the outcaste goddess is equally revered by the upper castes. The source of this power of the outcaste goddess over the upper castes is as much linked to elements that are central to the Puranic universe. Consider for example, the fear that the destructive powers of the not-so-benign goddess can inspire among the upper castes: 'In the legend of Gonekatava Reddy [that is narrated and dramatized several times, on several ritual occasions through the week], the goddess Matangi with a chain of 106 carts, loaded with deadly disease causing spirits, is on the march to exterminate those who denigrate her as a sorceress and a corpse-eating demoness' (Vijaisri 2015: 95). Eventually, according to the legend, 'she unleashes dreadful diseases into the city. The city is engulfed in chaos and flames rage by the afternoon' (Ibid.: 98). And so despite the immense power of the upper castes, there are all these ritual occasions when they must show their reverence to the goddess—after all, as we saw above, her representatives protect even the kings from 'dangerous powers'.

Apart from the dangerous powers, there is, of course, any number of friendly or benign spirits too that inhabit this same space. And these are not just stories of our remote past. This mode of being is not separable from the domain of everyday life of literally millions of ordinary people who, even in contemporary India, live with deities, jinns and spirits of all kinds. The paramodern covers a complex and vast space of popular existence that secular moderns have literally no purchase over. One more point needs to be underlined. Though I am using the term 'Puranic' mode of being, this should not be understood as a purely 'Hindu' phenomenon. Indeed, precisely because the population groups in question are those who were traditionally outside the Vedic Hindu fold, they are quite diverse in their formal religious affiliations.

In fact, Shahid Amin's study of the myth and history—or mythical history—of Ghazi Mian (Amin 2015), supposedly a nephew of Mahmud of Ghazni according to hagiographies (though he actually had no nephew, according to historical evidence) also gives us a sense of what I am calling the 'Puranic universe'. In this work, Amin is more interested in the challenge that the legend and afterlife of Ghazi Miyan throws to notions of 'syncretism' as well as historical certitude but it is difficult to miss the larger imaginative universe within which the cult of Ghazi Miyan takes shape. Ghazi Miyan, in Islamic hagiographies, is the warrior who destroyed infidels to establish the rule of Islam. It is therefore doubly interesting to see how he becomes a figure of worship and reverence among non-Muslim, Ahir/Gujar women in particular, in parts of northern India. The key moment of the emergence of the cult, according to ballads popular even now, is the story of a '*banjhin*'—an infertile woman called Jashoda (Jaswa in the ballads)—who is the wife of the chief of the cowherds, Nand. Jaswa, turned out by her husband's family for not being able to produce a son, roams about in the wilderness and with her wails, the jungle itself begins to wilt. All the beasts then go to the Goddess of the Forest saying they are being forced to leave the forest of their birth as everything is wilting and even lake Anarkali is drying up. As Jaswa's tears dry up, so does the forest that then catches fire. At this point the Goddess, Banaspati Mai leads Jaswa to the grave of Hazrat Syed Salar in the seventh wilderness—a person of great *barkat* (powers), whose fame is yet to reverberate through Hindustan. Jaswa does as told and soon the tables are turned. After some ups and downs which obviously demonstrate the powers of Ghazi Miyan, Jaswa is taken back into the family and 'with Ghazi Miyan's intercession, Allah ensures that Jaswa's womb is fructified'. In the ninth month 'baby Kanhaya or Krishna is born to Jashoda alias Jaswa but as Amin remarks: 'This is, of course, contrary to both the epics and to medieval Krishnite devotional poetry: Yashoda (Jaswa of the ballads) is childless; she is not Krishna's biological mother…' (Amin 2015: 60–63). Amin's point in the book and in narrating ballads like these is not to show their syncretic character but instead to underline the sectarian histories of both conflicts and their recollections through which a space of encounter is created in which syncretisms may be born. My interest in citing this story here has nothing to do with any of these issues; it lies rather in pointing to this space and this particular mode of being where humans live with all kinds of other spirits, benign as well as malign, which does not recognize any notion of causality in the way we moderns seek to explain events. My claim is not that this mode is specifically Indian, but I do want to resist the temptation to immediately reduce it to some generic explanation drawn from other times and places, or to read it through theorizations already available from other contexts, into which this mode of the Puranic may or may not fit.

The Paramodern—A Historian's Perplexity

In the following two sections, I will discuss this space of the paramodern with reference to a historian's quandary in dealing with narratives relating to the early twentieth century and then with some instances from our own times in the twenty-first century.

On 4 February 1922, there occurred an 'anti-police riot' of the peasants in Chauri Chaura, 'a small market town of north India'. At the height of the Non-Cooperation movement, the villagers of Chauri Chaura surrounded a police station and set fire to it. Many policemen died. Many decades later, historian Shahid Amin tracked the event, its official memorialization and the local memories around it (Amin 1995). Amin wrote about the riot 'as an event fixed in time (early 1922), and also as a metaphor gathering significance outside this time-frame' (Amin 1995: 3). It is well-known that the event, even though it was inspired by Gandhi's call for non-cooperation, so 'pained' the Mahatma because of its resort to violence that he withdrew the movement. The colonial state predictably responded to the incident with arrests, repression and punishment. Amin tracks down relatives and surviving members of the families of participants. At one point in the narrative, Amin tells us of his conversations with Naujadi, the widow of Rameshar Pasi, one of the participants who served an eight-year prison term as a result of his role in the incident.

Amin, the historian, tells us that '(I)n Dumri [one of the villages] the end of the event is remembered for its immediate result, not for its national consequences. Repression, punishment, survival—these are the themes with which Naujadi, Sita and others close their accounts of Chauri Chaura' (Amin 1995: 161). None of the relatives of the rioters framed their stories, he tells us, in terms of what Chauri Chaura meant to an ongoing freedom struggle or to Mahatma Gandhi for that matter. But this does not mean that they did not remember 'Gandhi Maharaj'. On the contrary, 'Gandhi's presence in Dumri is, in fact, so dominant that it has the effect of displacing every other nationalist actor, apart from the local volunteers, from the recollections of the event' (Ibid.: 162). In the course of his encounters with the local people, interviewed as late as in 1988–1991, Amin is brought face to face with a different world. Amin does not conceal his puzzlement as he hears the following in Naujadi's account, as she responded to his queries about Gandhi:

> Oh regarding Gandhiji! Now you are sitting on this cot towards the south, right! And *sirkar* we are labourers, right!
>
> You see! It was the month of Magh. Everybody is splitting dal [in special chakkis in Mundera Bazaar]. It was a bazaar day, Wednesday or Saturday perhaps. Har-har-har-har [the chakkis goes round and round], everyone is grinding and splitting dal. And then Babu! From *this* very corner—I am not lying, I tell you—from this very side it arose, and then went round and round and round and formed a complete circle. Then it subsided...Like ash, like smoke in the sky it was.
>
> People said it's a python, a python has descended from the hills. There was great commotion. Merchants and brokers, labourers and dal-grinders, all went to see this *tamasha*, this sight, from rooftops. Next day a broom appeared in the southern sky, then a ploughing plank. And then a long twig broom.
>
> God save us now! With this kharhara [the broom] people and their houses will be swept away. No one, nothing will remain, people said. (Amin 1995: 163–164)

The perplexed historian says: 'Unable to understand all of this, I asked Naujadi to elaborate.' Her answer: 'Everyone will die. All will be lost.

It is the end of time [ant kaal].'[8] The historian is rescued in a manner of speaking by the village headman, Sharfuddin, who tries to link this narrative of the end of time to 'the future catastrophe—the riot, the repression, the deaths and imprisonment—which were to destroy the locality a year later', thus giving it some 'sense'. Not fully willing to assimilate Naujadi's narrative into this more comprehensible story, Amin remarks that for Naujadi the omens, though unsettling, were part of a set of strange happenings, for she had heard that shrubs would shoot up into big trees, that and other such happenings would augur Gandhi's arrival in February 1921 (Amin 1995: 164). This is another Shahid Amin, the story-teller or *qissa-go*, a *rasik* of popular Bhojpuri culture and language. And he appears, in the narrative of the book, to be at odds with the historian Amin.

Amin also introduces us to Sita Ahir's narrative of the Mahatma's arrival at Chauri Chaura railway station and in a somewhat similar vein, suspends his 'unwritten rules of historical evidence' (Amin 1995: 166), in order to make sense of his story. For in Sita's account there are references to Gandhi's train waiting in the warehouse that are not corroborated by archival evidence. Often in the course of the book, Amin puts away his historian's mantle and appears before us like a story-teller, sharing his confusions and perplexities and letting his characters speak to us in their own voice. At some places he simply presents before us the voice of the speaker/s without comment, as in the following:

> When Mahatma Gandhi was going back on the night of 8 February from Gorakhpur…there was a huge gathering at Salempur station to have his darshan,' reported a local correspondent in the nationalist weekly *Swadesh*. There was a Barai lad in that gathering. 'It is said that he had asked the wife of a high-caste Brahmin for a cloth wrapper to come to the station. She reprimanded him and refused to give him the blanket. The poor soul came shivering to the station, had darshan of the Mahatma and went back.' But the suffering of that young boy… had become part of a story. Next morning the village was agog with the rumour that shit was raining all over the house of that mean, anti-Gandhian woman who had denied the boy a blanket. This demeaning punishment was not the end of the story: 'In the end, only when she

> kept a fast and did the ritual praying to the Mahatma did peace finally return to her. (Amin 1995: 168–169)

Amin's innovative style is an attempt to deal with a real aporia that might face a historian when dealing with 'evidence' of this nature. There is nothing in the protocols of history-writing that might enable a historian to deal with narratives that are always-already 'mythical'—that is to say, irreducible to the historical. To call these narratives myth-making, fantasy or delusion is, of course, an easy option but one that simply refuses to see that there are two different 'worlds' face-to-face with each other: that of the historian facing the world of Naujadi. Naujadi's is a mode of relating to the world that has its own recollections of the 'event' of Chauri Chaura and of Gandhi's visit, but which has no investment whatsoever in 'total recall'. It has its own recollections of the Mahatma and the catastrophe that came along in his wake, as something that could only have otherworldly resonances—marked by the appearance of 'celestial apparitions' and 'strange stirrings in the sky'. Being lower caste narratives, these recollections are marked simultaneously by reference to the 'broom', 'cleaning up', 'raining shit' (on a Brahmin's house!)—something that did not attract the attention of the historian of Chauri Chaura, the historian's gaze being differently focused.

It is this divide that Ashis Nandy calls attention to in his celebrated (or notorious?) attack on 'History' (Nandy 1995). Nandy's attack combines a complex set of arguments, affects, rhetorics into a performance that serves to highlight something that professional historians usually shy away from acknowledging. While Amin lets his characters speak to us, he scrupulously avoids making a larger statement about history. Nandy, on the other hand, does precisely that. Naujadi, Nandy would say, lives like millions of other Indians (indeed people across the world), *outside History*.

Writing on peasant insurgency in colonial India and with specific reference to the Santhal rebellion, Ranajit Guha wrote that, '(R) eligiosity was by all accounts central to the *hool* [the uprising].' The notion of power that inspired it, he claims, was explicitly religious in character. His search for the autonomy of subaltern consciousness in the early days of Subaltern Studies, led Guha and some other colleagues to grapple with such religious elements of their consciousness:

> Hence the attribution of the rising to a divine command rather than to any particular grievance; the enactment of rituals both before (propitiatory ceremonies to ward off the apocalypse of the Primeval Serpents—Lag and Lagini, the distribution of *tel-sindur*, etc.); the generation and circulation of myth in its characteristic vehicle—rumour (e.g. about the advent of 'the exterminating angel' incarnated as a buffalo, etc.). (Guha 1984: 34)

Notice in this account of a Santhal uprising almost seventy years before Chauri Chaura and in faraway Bengal, the same figures of the apocalypse (*ant kaal*) and the python (the celestial Primeval Serpents) that we have encountered in Naujadi's account. Guha takes up a series of writings by Bengali historians and examines their attempt to deal with such religiosity in terms of tactical maneouvres by Santhal leaders in order to appeal to the consciousness of their followers. He sees in such attempts 'the failure of a shallow radicalism to conceptualize peasant mentality except in terms of an unadulterated secularism' (Guha 1984: 37). He then goes on to argue: 'Hence the rich material of myths, rituals, rumours, hopes for a Golden Age and fears of an imminent End of the World, all of which bespeaks of the self-alienation of the rebel, is wasted on this abstract and sterile discourse' (Ibid.: 39).

Guha's critique of secular modern historiography is brilliant and frank. It points to all the difficulties that a historian might face in dealing with this world of the subaltern. Guha is very suggestive when he deals with these aspects of peasant consciousness, not the least when he places the 'rumour' as structurally of the same order as myth and ritual, indeed as the 'vehicle of myth'. We can see the ways in which 'rumour', even in contemporary societies, functions as the 'myth' that propels action in times of riots, for instance. Yet, there is a profound difficulty in Guha's reading that clearly arises from his modernist Marxist lineage: myths, rituals, rumours remain 'rich materials' for the historian and they eventually simply represent the 'self-alienation of the rebel'. This difficulty however, would remain even if Guha were to give up on his Marxism for that seems to be the only way 'history' and 'historical consciousness', however, self-reflexive, can deal with such ahistorical modes of being. Or so, at least Ashis Nandy would argue.

In a sense, this strain of self-reflexivity reaches it apogee within Subaltern Studies with Dipesh Chakrabarty—in his move away from History to Heidegger and philosophy. In a thoughtful response to critics of Subaltern Studies, Chakrabarty returns again and again to this problem of 'the religious' and the supernatural and its status in historiography (Chakrabarty 2002).[9] If Amin's attempts lead him in the direction of a fiction writer or story-teller, Chakrabarty's lead him towards philosophy. He concludes his essay by posing the problem as one of 'history as democratic dialogue with the subaltern' (Chakrabarty 2002: 33). The question to him now becomes one of finding a way of doing subaltern historiography 'that actually tries to learn from the subaltern'. In the end this can only be done, suggests Chakrabarty, by a radical openness that he expresses in Heideggerian terms as 'the capacity to hear that which one does not already understand'. Such a programme would entail allowing 'the subaltern position to challenge our own conceptions of totalities' and by being open to the possibility of 'our thought systems… being rendered finite by the presence of the other' (Chakrabarty 2002: 36).

What appears in Guha and Chakrabarty as the problem of the religious and the supernatural, of myths and rituals, is posed by Nandy as a problem of Time. Nandy sees these problems of history as arising out of its modern, linear time-consciousness, as something that closes off, by definition, the possibility of relating to other modes of being that are lodged in a different conception of time. This time-consciousness is apparent in the way history constructs 'the Past' and disregards other ways of relating to the past. Time and again, Nandy keeps asserting that though moderns might inhabit history, millions of people across the world live 'outside history' in 'myths'. The figure of linear time is certainly at the core of Nandy's attack but equally, it is the claim to scientificity and to being the only true knowledge about the past that arouses his ire. If Amin, Guha and Chakrabarty critique history from within, Nandy's is an assault from the outside—mounted in the name of those he claims have been 'disenfranchised and marginalized by history'.

These instances of the modes of thinking and being among illiterate peasants from early twentieth-century India (or the mid-nineteenth in Ranajit Guha's case) can be easily set aside as mere remnants or survivals of a traditional mode of popular existence. It is true that they are traditional in the sense that they are not modern, even if they continue into our present as we will see from some instances from late twentieth and early twenty-first century India. Their contemporariness, however, is not really the point here. The point is that once designated as 'irrational', 'backward' and 'unscientific', they are driven out of all spaces of the secular modern, to lead a life of subterranean existence in this 'underground' space that I am calling the paramodern. In the next section I want to discuss the idea of the paramodern in relation to another episode from an early twenty first century metropolis. I will then try and connect this discussion to the concept of 'political society' as expounded by Partha Chatterjee, thus spelling out more clearly what I mean by the paramodern.

The Paramodern—The Rationalist's Quandary

In April–May 2001, the eastern outskirts of Delhi were suddenly gripped by a strange fear, following reports of a creature that was said to be stalking lower-class neighbourhoods. Very few people had actually seen the creature though many claimed to have been injured in its attacks. Generally described by ordinary people as *kala bandar* (black monkey, rendered as 'Monkeyman' in English), the scare of the creature lasted for about a month and a half.

During the period of its existence, the Monkeyman acquired the character of an urban legend, going through many mutations in the many tellings of the stories of its exploits. It was variously described as 'half-monkey, half-man', 'a strange creature with a machine-like body with glowing lights', and in some cases, a 'man with a mask'. According to one news report, although the first complaints, starting from 5 April, were filed at a police station in Ghaziabad, those reports do not show any mention of a 'man wearing a mask'. Except for one, all the complaints were about nocturnal monkey attacks, mainly on people sleeping on terraces, a common practice during summer

(Hebbar 2001: 3). The first complaint that suggested that anything out of the ordinary had happened was made as late as on 30 April, when a local resident claimed that he had been attacked by 'a dark shadow-like creature which seemed like a monkey. His complaint further added that it had hit him 'through his stomach' and the news report corroborated that 'his wounds seemed to correspond with his version.' The police however, claimed that on investigation they found that this person had made a false complaint 'to save himself from arrest as he had actually had a violent fight with his brother and disturbed the peace.' In order to mislead the police, they said, he had created the story of the 'monkeyman'. The report went on to say that this angle was revealed much later, by which time the rumour of the Monkeyman had acquired a life of its own (Ibid.: 3).

As the stories began circulating, with new accretions at every step, the Monkeyman began taking shape in popular imagination. The Hindi daily *Amar Ujala* reported that on 2 May, residents congregated at an open field near Vijaynagar, Ghaziabad (where the original complaints had been filed), after someone claimed having seen 'a monkey-like shadowy figure'. Gradually the terror of the creature built up to such an extent that it created panic and on 10 May, the district administration gave shoot-at-sight orders to bring the situation under control' (Hebbar 2001: 3). From 13 May onwards, the Monkeyman carried on its activities in the eastern outskirts of the capital bordering Ghaziabad.

Interestingly, by this time the creature had mutated into a kind of cyborg—a computerized, robotized being with almost super-natural powers. It was generally claimed that it had green eyes, that it had a springboard under its feet and a green belt with buttons for navigation (Hebbar 2001). Some other reports suggested that at least some of these characteristics had already been acquired by the Monkeyman by the time it had entered Delhi. The Superintendent of Police (SP, City) of Ghaziabad, Mr R.K. Chaturvedi told *The Hindu* reporter that while initially most reports came from Vijaynagar, Raj Nagar and Sanjay Nagar—areas with 'a high simian population'—and people had mostly 'reported attacks by a dark monkey with lips cut', descriptions soon changed to those of a 'masked figure' (Bhatnagar 2001). And very soon, people were speaking of how it 'could jump off tall buildings and move at great speeds', even though, said Chaturvedi, there were no firsthand accounts (Ibid.).

Whatever the point at which these new features may have got added on to the Monkeyman, there is little doubt that by the time its scare became rampant in Delhi, this mutant cyborg was 'in existence'. In my discussions with ordinary folk, I was offered a deductive reasoning for the claim that the creature had intricate, electronically-operated or computerized systems to keep it going. They claimed, for example, that in one house where the Monkeyman attacked, a pitcher of water got spilt in the course of the attack and seeing the water, he took to his heels. Water, they reasoned, would have destroyed his electrical system, which was why he ran away.[10]

In one version, this was then extended into a different narrative that is already available these days for any such oddity, namely the narrative of the Pakistani 'enemy': it was claimed that the creature was a robot with remote control that had been sent in by Pakistan to create terror.[11] The episode thus became the occasion for the externalization of a whole series of latent fears—often of a deeply pathological nature. Some of them were not entirely innocent, as for example the one expressed in the Shiv Sena's bizarre claim that the Monkeyman was a handiwork of the Pakistan secret service, the ISI, which had sent '131 monkeys from across the border to create terror'.[12] So great was the scare that for some days people stopped sleeping on the terraces, night patrols of neighbourhood youth were formed to reinforce the patrolling by the police. *Havanas* and *yagnas*[13] were performed in different parts of the city to exorcise the evil—characteristic of the Puranic mode of being.

Undoubtedly, once the legend took on a life of its own, it seems that a whole series of otherwise unconnected, often innocuous incidents started getting inserted into the larger stories of the Monkeyman's exploits. Descriptions about its height varied, indicating that either people had not seen the creature or that they were generally mistaking different creatures for the elusive Monkeyman. One person in NOIDA claimed, for instance, that he had been attacked by it but when he turned to catch it, it turned into a cat with glowing eyes. Some others claimed that it came on wings and disappeared into thin air when attacked.[14] One of the rare 'sightings' in a well-off middle class colony, for instance, occurred when a gentleman standing on his balcony at 5:30 in the morning, 'saw a speeding Maruti Zen which braked suddenly' and 'a man dressed as a black monkey reportedly stepped out of the car which then sped away.' Injuries that may have been caused by entirely unrelated incidents, now came to be cast within the larger narratives about the Monkeyman.

While speaking to *The Hindu*, the SP of Ghaziabad, Chaturvedi also made some other perceptive observations. Some things, Chaturvedi said, remained unchanged through the changing narratives. For one thing, 'all cases were reported from lower middle class [and] jhuggi clusters with a very high population density.' And in all cases 'the attacks took place within about half an hour of a power breakdown after nightfall.' He further stated that 'all cases were reported from residential areas and there was not a single incident in which a person traveling home alone on a road at night had been attacked.'[15]

This last feature of the Monkeyman's exploits remained unchanged also through all its excursions in Delhi. Settlements of the poor, largely labouring populations, living through prolonged spells of power cuts and darkness, sweating it out on the terraces that join together with those of other houses, was the theatre of its activities. Extrapolating from the life of small towns, where such joined and continuous terraces become, in the monotonous lives of people, a theatre for the playing out of desire, noted Hindi writer Sudhish Pachauri, in fact, perceived a libidinal dimension in this episode. It is not uncommon he suggested, for such transgressive acts to be played out in the darkness of the summer nights.[16]

It is not my intention here to unravel 'the truth' about the Monkeyman, but rather, through it—and through an examination of the rationalist discourse on it—I want to explore a certain chasm that marks the existence of societies like ours.

'The Galloping Spread of Unreason'

The reaction of rationalist public opinion was in some senses classic. The Indian Rationalist Association and its key spokesperson, Sanal Edamaruku dubbed the entire episode as a 'mass delusion'. He was, however, careful to point out that such a 'sudden onset of hallucination' or 'hysteria' 'can acquire epic proportions when people in small or large numbers are charged with extreme fear or anxiety'.[17] Similar opinions were expressed by others too, though not with the same caution as Edamaruku's. *The Hindu*, for example, editorially commented on the entire episode, as did many other newspapers, in the flurry of articles, which appeared subsequently. *The Hindu* editorial represents most succinctly the rationalist consensus that came to be articulated in the wake of this episode.

'It is not for the first time in recent memory', *The Hindu* editorial averred, 'that *civil society in Delhi has shown signs of cracking up*'. It recalled two recent incidents and proceeded to comment thus:

> It was not very long ago that one found people rushing out to the neighbouring provision stores in panic just to buy common salt. It was a rumour about shortage of that commodity. One had also seen men and women, *including those from the affluent sections*, moving about with glasses of milk; this was how they responded to rumours on that day that idols consumed milk. The fear and panic that has now caught the city is indeed, no way different from all those instances when rational behaviour took a beating. And *the instruments of the state*—the police in particular—seem to be adding to the crisis by way of beaming images of a monster on the television screens rather than doing their bit to scotch the rumours and restore a sense of confidence *among the people* about the state and its machinery.[18]

The editorial went on to give a rational explanation of what might have happened and added that, 'The only way to put a stop to such things is to deal firmly with the rumour mongers.' However, it also recognized that this will not be sufficient. Therefore, it is important '*to infuse the fundamentals of a scientific temper among the people* so that they learn to react in a rational manner.' It concluded by observing that '*this is where institutions of civil society, including the cadre of various political parties will have a role to play*.... A vibrant civil society is the only way out of such situations.' The *Indian Express* editorial too, expressed concern at the 'galloping spread of unreason' which it saw as a global phenomenon.[19]

And so, civil society—or its conscience keepers—lashed out at the institutions of the state to force it to intervene, to reign in 'the galloping spread of unreason'. And sure enough, the state fell in line—one of the very rare occasions when it showed inclination to do so—when, within a month, the Delhi Police produced a 200-page report debunking the 'monkey business' as a myth.[20]

There are, in this comment, two principal players. One, on whose behalf, the editorial speaks, is the *civil society*, which it sees as the ultimate guarantor of rationality and scientific temper and about whose occasional 'cracking up', the editor seems worried. The worry seems to be amplified because, on the earlier occasion it was not just the poor unlettered masses but 'even affluent sections of society', presumably well educated, who were taken in by the myth of the 'Gods drinking milk'. The other player in this narrative is the state and its instruments like the police, who seem too, to occasionally slip into roles not exactly expected of them. But there is also a third player, unnamed and unspecified, whose appearance here is acknowledged merely as 'the problem': these are 'the people' who figure in this discourse as the objects of the pedagogical activity of the state and civil society—to infuse 'scientific temper'. Their own agency goes unacknowledged for they have to be taught to 'respond to such situations in a rational manner'. One cannot help feeling that in the opinion of the editorial commentator, it is the presence of these very 'people' that vitiates both the civil society and the state's 'instruments', causing them to lapse back into occasional irrationalities: That it is proximity to these 'people' that makes the state—and occasionally, civil society—vulnerable to unreason. It is also significant that the middle class 'cadres of political parties' are included here among the agents who will have to perform the task of educating 'the people' who form the bulk of the followings of their respective parties.

There was, of course, an irony here in this situation that escaped the editorial commentator. For, this time round, it was not some supernatural power—God or evil spirit—but the very omnipotence of Science that seemed to lie at the root of the terror called the Monkeyman. The Monkeyman was a creature in popular imagination of the omnipotence of a science that had in recent years burst forth in all its splendour. It was after all, only recently that the power of science had exploded before common folk, both in its benign and oppressive forms. In its relatively benign form, the explosion of the new media technologies seemed to dazzle and to exhilarate with their sheer power and brilliance. From watching the live telecasts of wars fought far away, to the wonders of the internet which now forms part of the imagination of common folk, the new telecommunications revolution has certainly expanded the horizon of the imaginable.[21] Clearly, science does not, by itself, enable the power of Reason and in certain conditions, can itself acquire a strangely mystical or magical aura.[22]

But the subaltern populations of a metropolis like Delhi have also seen another face of 'Science' in recent years—brutal and ruthless. This face suddenly became evident in the five or six years preceding the episode, through the eruption of a series of new terms like 'pollution' and 'environment' in the vocabulary of daily life. These terms emerged as handmaidens of a technocratic state elite and an 'activist' judiciary, bent upon restructuring Delhi as a city of the rich and the powerful. Their eruption onto the political scene changed overnight, the terms on which the subaltern populations of Delhi could live in the city, suddenly depriving them of their jobs, their livelihoods and their habitat. They first encountered these new terms in the form of the closure of thousands of industries in the end of 1996; they encountered them again in the form of that dreaded word 'CNG' (compressed natural gas), when thousands of vehicles, mainly auto-rickshaws, were ordered to stop plying in the city because they were supposed to be polluting. In 2000 and 2001, they encountered them again when hundreds of squatter settlements were demolished and thrown to the outskirts of the city.[23] To them all these were part of the same deal—the 'cleaning up of the city' for the rich. In the process, lakhs of people also left the city. There was all round destitution and desperation in the city.[24] And behind this was seen to be that other face of science—all the justifications for these actions were cast in a scientific language that was entirely new to the common folk affected by them.

If, as the Rationalist Association spokesperson suggested, mass hysteria can acquire epic proportions when large number of people are gripped by fear and anxiety, we could see them playing out here convulsing subaltern life in a rapidly globalizing city such as Delhi.

However, my point here is not to find a rational explanation for the Monkeyman phenomenon; nor am I interested, unlike the editorial commentator of *The Hindu* cited earlier in trying to arrest the 'galloping spread of unreason' (in the words of the *Indian Express* editorial) through some kind of pedagogical intervention of civil society, state institutions and enlightened cadre of political parties. My intention rather, is to identify this distinctive space of the paramodern that is populated not just by subaltern populations but also by a whole lot of other beings that are driven out of the secular public sphere vis-à-vis which 'enlightened civil society' can have only one response: educate them and develop a scientific temper among those populations. Typically, moderns see this as a problem of backward thinking, as a problem of knowledge that can be simply dealt with by educating them, whereas for large segments of such populations 'thinking' is not separable from 'being'. These are not just backward ways of thinking but embody different modes of being, which call for another kind of response.

It will be helpful for the purposes of understanding what is at stake to discuss the idea of the paramodern alongside the concept of political society as elaborated by Partha Chatterjee. I say this also because I have long tried to think of what I now term the paramodern, precisely in terms of Chatterjee's notion of political society because of the very obvious resonances between the two. Indeed, when I first studied the Monkeyman phenomenon as it occurred in Delhi, it seemed obvious to me that 'political society' was the idea that could provide the conceptual handle to understand a phenomenon such as this. For my purposes then, I deployed the concept of political society but with a modification: I referred to it as the '*underground of civil society*', where the idea again was what had been driven underground but which continued to live another life anyway (Nigam 2005). On other occasions, I have also tried to think of political society as the 'constitutive outside' of civil society—as that 'outside', in opposition to which civil society and modernity define themselves (Nigam 2008). However, over a very long period of engagement, it now seems that it is perhaps better to think of the two together but as distinct conceptual entities.

Paramodern and Political Society

Over two decades ago, Partha Chatterjee embarked on what seems to me to have been a novel journey in the history of political theorizing in India and, perhaps in the postcolonial, non-Western world at large. Bringing together the results of decades of his own intellectual engagement with Indian politics and the question of subalternity in particular, Chatterjee began articulating a concept that has now acquired wide currency: his concept of 'political society'.

In this body of work, Chatterjee has been developing the idea of political society as a central category with which we might grasp the complex nature of politics, especially in postcolonial contexts. He suggested that at the very heart of postcolonial democracies, lies a contradiction—between 'modernity' and 'democracy'.[25] Democracy in the postcolonial world, he says, has been pitted against the search for modernity. Chatterjee never really says what he means by democracy but in my view, the meaning of this formulation can be properly grasped only if we understand 'democracy' as the point where politics meets the popular, rather than as a specific set of institutions, elections, rule of law and so on. Chatterjee sees the sphere of civil society in its 'classical' sense, as the sphere of modern civil institutions governed by contractual relations of entry and exit, of rights, of the discourse of sovereignty and citizenship. This domain that constitutes the high ground of modernity, he argues, represents a very limited sphere in societies like India's. The state, on the other hand, with its welfare functions, targets the majority of people as 'population', and dispenses welfare to those who in practice, do not count as rights-bearing citizens. These people, the majority, often live in different degrees of illegality and negotiate with the state, through the various mobilizational avenues provided to them by democracy.

Chatterjee's idea of political society is now quite well known and I will not dwell on the specific instances through which he elaborates this idea. Suffice it to mention that theoretically, he elaborates the concept by invoking Foucault's idea of 'governmentality', where the semi-legal or illegal nature of large parts of subaltern existence are seen as problems to be managed, rather than settled through a recourse to rights and the law. It is on this terrain of governmental practices that moral claims of the population on matters like housing for instance, are recognized.

However, in at least one instance, the idea of political society was explicated by Chatterjee with reference to an incident that did not involve 'welfare' but rather a more complex matter pertaining to the problem of reason/unreason. This involved a political negotiation over the death of a leader of a religious sect, Balak Brahmachari, whose followers believed that he had merely gone into *samadhi*, and therefore, refused to let his body be removed, even though it started rotting and became a potential health hazard. Strictly speaking, legally the government would have been well within *its* rights to remove the body but there was the compulsion of not antagonising the followers and resort to force. Rationalist public opinion was appalled and wanted the government to act firmly. This was one of those occasions where the elected government chose to negotiate and minimize damage rather than listen to the secular rationalist elite.

It can be seen from this discussion that 'political society' to Chatterjee is another way of conceptualizing the domain of politics in the context of what could have also been called an 'incomplete modernity'—that is to say, a modernity that has failed to colonize and transform large sectors of society. I want to underline here that though Chatterjee himself does not spend much time on this aspect, the fact that to him civil society is the high ground of modernity (and the state presumably its agent), leaves us with a domain (political society) where the hegemony of the modern is seriously in question and continuously contested, though Chatterjee would rather call it a 'domain of many mediations'.

The major departure from conventional Western political theory here is that this move dislocates 'political society' from its more classical usage, as synonymous with the state and transfers it to *another terrain*. This terrain, distinct from both the state and civil society, is the real domain of politics in postcolonial societies. Here, in this always open domain of negotiations with the state, even populations living otherwise semi-legal or illegal lives, form associations, represent themselves and make demands on it.

'Political society', in Chatterjee's hands, was a way of recuperating a sphere of politics that has been a permanent source of anxiety for theorists of Indian (and postcolonial) democracy—the vast domain that existed *outside* the designated spheres of modern politics, where the untutored masses made claims on the state, unmindful of the formal grammar of rights and citizenship. A crucial part of what defines activities in this domain is 'illegality', or at any rate, non-legality/para-legality, where the state itself places the law in suspension in order to recognize the claims of the governed. Thus for instance, squatting by the poor on government land is, strictly speaking, encroachment in legal terms, and can never acquire the status of a 'right'; yet, it is allowed by governments to continue, through the recognition of some kind of moral claim of the poor on governments and society at large.

In the instance of Balak Brahmachari, the religious leader who died but whose followers nonetheless believed that he had merely gone into *samadhi*—we can actually see the kind of phenomenon that we have been discussing earlier in this chapter. However, it is important to point out that neither in the cases of Naujadi and Sita Ahir in Chauri Chaura, nor in the case of the Monkeyman are we dealing with anything spiritual or religious. In the first case, the context is explicitly political, pertaining to Gandhi's visit to Chauri Chaura and in the second really no context that can be fixed at all—even though narratives of Pakistani involvement do get inserted into it. And yet, they share with the Balak Brahmachari episode, a certain imaginative universe that is not available to the secular-modern mind. In Chatterjee's words, they are still governed by 'the imaginative power of the traditional structure of community', though it might be more apposite to say that they embody a different mode of being and thinking.

However, as it turned out, Partha Chatterjee's interest in this phenomenon was not so much in the non-rational, non-modern, community aspect of the situation but with that slice of it where the state and political power come in. Chatterjee's interest is in understanding the implications of different ways in which the modern state might, in pursuance of its governmental functions, have to suspend matters of rights and legality while dealing with such segments of the population. That is why *political* society is the expression he chooses to describe this domain of transactions. In that sense, there is nothing political about the Chauri Chaura or the Monkeyman narratives. In Chauri Chaura, the political part lies in the remote past—some six decades back in time, whereas in the Monkeyman narrative there simply isn't any. It is now clear to me that *political* society is not the concept that can provide us with a handle on this set of questions.

Nevertheless, I do think that the idea of the paramodern has to be seen in relation to a reformulated idea of political society, if we are to understand the moment where the 'fascist element' emerges and circulates. Chatterjee has, in his later writings, conceded that there are 'darker sides' of political society that his own exploration has been unable to illuminate (Chatterjee 2011). The concept of 'political society' becomes limited in Chatterjee's hands because it is hinged exclusively to welfare-governmentality, thus reducing its operations to almost a benign daily brush between subaltern existence and the state. In the course of accepting his failure to account for the darker side of political society, Chatterjee takes on board the issue of masculinity as one such issue that emerges from the work of Ananya Roy and urban violence as another, in Thomas Blom Hansen's work on Shiv Sena in Mumbai. However, even here, Chatterjee's framework does not change at all; it merely incorporates these difficult questions into a 'problem of the political management of violence' (Ibid.: 19–21). It is not possible to undertake a full-fledged discussion of the difficulties with the concept of political society here. I will just refer to three issues here that seem to me to be critical in thinking of 'politics beyond civil society' that are also relevant for our understanding of the paramodern.

In the first place, even the ordinary everyday interactions of the subaltern populations with state agencies like the municipal authorities or the police in many big cities are anything but benign. In a city like Delhi, especially since the 1990s, the intervention by the state has involved continuous policing and indeed, periodic destruction of the livelihoods of the poor—rickshaw pullers, hawkers and vendors—apart from fleecing them with the weekly cuts these people must pay the police and municipal employees. In the same period, we have seen some of the most violent acts in the city in the form of the large-scale demolition of squatter settlements. In my discussion of the Monkeyman earlier, I have indicated how the violence of mass dislocation of subaltern populations produces anxieties and fears—which in other contexts and places have been known to make such populations amenable to mobilization against imaginary enemies.

Second, any attempt to think 'politics beyond civil society' must take into account matters concerned with the paramodern where politics of a particular kind is never very far off. Here again, we get a fleeting glimpse of this kind of a possibility in the Shiv Sena's attempt to displace the Monkeyman question to a matter of a Pakistani conspiracy. We also see the widespread presence of such political forces in different kinds of popular religiosity. This is not to argue that the proliferation of popular religious events like the Kanwar yatras, undertaken mainly by lower caste devotees of Shiv, are a creation of such politics but there is enough evidence of their active presence on these occasions. This active presence may or may not be entirely instrumental but what is important and needs to be recognized is that a large number of recruits for such politics come from and inhabit the same imaginative universe as that of the Kanwarias.

Third, one only has to pick up the newspaper on any given day to be able to see how rampant and violent is the everyday oppression of the lower, Dalit Bahujan castes in different parts of the country—even though the worst cases might still come from the North and Western Indian states. These atrocities are usually visited upon them by the upper castes but with the active or tacit connivance of the police and other state institutions. The now well-known case of the public flogging of four Dalit youth by upper caste men in Una, Gujarat in 2016 actually took place inside a police station. Similarly, take the case of the violent incidents in Shabbirpur, in Saharanpur district of Uttar Pradesh in 2017, where the Rajputs basically could not bear the thought that from among the Dalits there had emerged a young leadership that was defying caste prohibitions imposed on them. Organized as the Bhim Army, led by a young charismatic lawyer Chandrashekhar Azad, this organization's primary work till the clashes began, had been to educate Dalit youth through informal schools run by them.

The point relevant for our discussion here is that such caste practices in defence of traditional hierarchies, and everyday clashes around them are rampant, especially now that the Dalits are no longer willing to take things lying down anymore. Here, every incident is always already political—even in terms of the presence in them of party political equations as well as those of power. In Partha Chatterjee's terms, these would have nothing to do with political society since they have little to do with welfare-governmentality. But if the 'darker side of political society' is to have any meaning, the idea of political society would itself have to be reformulated to bring into its ambit, spaces of conflict and mobilization such as these—not just to be 'managed' and contained by state and governmental power.

In a manner of speaking then, my most serious disagreement with Chatterjee would be with his prioritizing of state/governmental power over what we may, for want of a better term, call the popular, for in my understanding neither historically nor logically do state/governmental power precede the popular. Of course, it can be argued in Chatterjee's favour that it does not matter which came first historically. Nor does it matter that the popular is logically prior to the constitution of political power, for once constituted, there is really no 'outside' to it; everything is and must be determined in relation to this thing called political power. Thenceforth, it is political, that is, governmental power that sets the terms for everything else. Obviously, the answer to this problem cannot be based on any empirical evidence but depends upon the frame through which one prefers to understand politics. The way I read Michel Foucault's move away from the normative paradigm of sovereignty and right towards a paradigm of government, where 'tactics' and 'management' of conflicts for instance is the supreme concern, gives me the opposite sense. It is precisely because of the presence of this recalcitrant 'outside' which refuses to fall in line that the great normative concerns of the state have to be shelved, which is why every governmental or state power has to keep a leeway—what Foucault has called the 'margin of tolerated illegalities'. In a sense, Chatterjee's own concept of 'political society' is premised on the assumption that the majesty of the Law can be observed only in its suspension, where large segments of the subaltern population are concerned. If this is true, it stands to reason to claim that the dynamic of the subaltern/popular domain cannot simply be reduced to an effect of governmentality or state power, that there is something to the initial quest of Subaltern Studies—the quest for elements of subaltern autonomy—that still needs to be understood. Perhaps the problem with the initial framing was in terms of the autonomy of subaltern 'consciousness' that may be a problematic category in itself. And positing subaltern consciousness in opposition to something called elite consciousness may not be wise given that there are many different kinds of elites and one can always show that the subaltern is not free of the influence of at least the more traditional elites. It is in order to circumvent this inexhaustible but tiresome discussion that I prefer to think of this space as the space of the paramodern where the elite/subaltern distinction is not really relevant. Now, apart from the kinds of instances that I have discussed earlier, there are many other kinds of more recent work that draws our attention to the many other dimensions of the paramodern.

Many 'minor practices' like spirit possession studied by Kalpana Ram (2013) or the combined world of humans and jinns as it appears in William Dalrymple's account (1994) or in the recent book by Anand Vivek Taneja (2018) provide us with other windows into the space of the paramodern. The fact is that these 'minor practices' are still quite widespread. Both Ram's and Taneja's researches deal with late twentieth century (Tamil Nadu) and late twentieth and twenty-first century (Delhi) respectively, and alert us to the continued existence of these practices and what might have been lost with their becoming inaccessible to the secular-modern.

In conclusion, let me reiterate that it is not my intention to romanticize the ways of being and thinking associated with these minor practices or with a different notion of life with jinns and other beings that we encounter in so many of these narratives. My question is rather, the reverse, for I wish to ask—is it possible without abandoning the modern project of rights, autonomy and so on, to strike a different relation with these modes of being? In a manner of speaking, it is close to Chakrabarty's idea of a 'democratic dialogue with the subaltern'. However, one must underline that this 'democratic dialogue' is virtually impossible given that our language has no vocabulary to understand the

Puranic, a necessary consequence of modernity's cognitive arrogance. This democratic dialogue can only be made possible by acknowledging a certain equality between different 'ways of thinking' and being, which in the case of the non-moderns is in any case inseparable from their being that goes way beyond a charity extended by moderns.

In political terms, it has to be emphasized that if we are interested in the fate of the modern project of social transformation, experience shows that its success is impossible as long as moderns do not get rid of their cognitive arrogance and accept that 'scientific temper' does not really exhaust the whole range of life-experiences of people. But the question is not simply political in the sense in which post-Enlightenment moderns understand the term—for a world that is totally disenchanted, were it really possible, would be quite an unliveable world. In fact, a recognition of the Puranic universe as part of our living everyday reality, opens up possibilities of redefining what we mean by the political itself and more importantly, what the modern project of social transformation might look like in that case. A case in point here can be seen in the recent intervention by Nivedita Menon (2019), where she brings in precisely the universe I am calling the Puranic, via her engagement with Dalit-Bahujan-Adivasi intellectuals' writings and the debates raised by them on the so-called asuras/asuric (for example Mahishasura) on the one hand, and with feminist writings on the pre-Aryan Devi—the ferocious mother goddess—on the other. Menon discusses these tendencies as counter-narratives to the dominant Hindutva narratives that are occupying centre-stage today, but it is worth pondering what kind of an understanding of 'the political' might emerge from the epic struggles in this thoroughly unsecular (I avoid the term 'enchanted' here) world. It may not be out of place to also underline here that in this world of the Puranic, malign and dangerous powers are usually not directly confronted but propitiated and 'controlled' through *yajnas*—a stance in direct contrast to the modern idea of the political that is predicated on notions of rights and autonomy.

A recognition of the space of the paramodern calls then, not so much for the abandonment of the modern project of transformation as its radical reformulation. At this stage we may not quite know what the elements and dimensions of such reformulation might be but for starters, we could begin by prioritizing the value of equality in dealing with these other modes of being, rather than placing them on the temporal scale or Progress and assigning to them a place in a past that has to be left behind.

Notes

1. I have dealt with this debate at great length in my book (Nigam 2006) and will not restate my understanding of the debate here. Interested readers can find most of the important interventions in Bhargava (1998). In a sense, aspects of this debate still reverberate in the academic field though it needs revisiting. This chapter is not the place to do so though it does connect to that need in some fashion.
2. The expression 'non-synchronous synchronicities' is a slight modification of the early twentieth-century German art historian Wilhelm Pinder's term that in turn influenced Ernst Bloch's reversed use of the expression. The German expression has also been translated, sometimes as 'simultaneity of the non-simultaneous' and sometimes as 'contemporaneity of the non-contemporaneous' (Schwartz 2001). I have found this expression useful for thinking through many aspects of our contemporary experience, especially capital and 'uneven development', which I discuss at some length in the next chapter.
3. In a somewhat later phase, there emerged a 'third' position represented by Rajeev Bhargava—though strictly speaking, it was a variant of the first, that is secularist position. It initially based itself on a reinterpretation of 'Indian secularism' by arguing that it was not a mere repetition of the 'wall of separation' kind of secularism.
4. It is not that this argument and this claim to a certain secularist plank is no longer there, but it has been somewhat overshadowed by the more rampant anti-Muslim stance of the present regime. This argument will always remain an important one in the Hindutva arsenal for it is through it that Hindutva can show that it is the more modern force while Muslims continue to hold on to archaic community laws.
5. So, for instance, we find him saying: 'Today we hear everywhere the clamour for "rights". All our political parties too are rousing the ego in our people by constantly speaking of their "rights". Nowhere is there any stress on "duties" and a spirit of selfless service' (Golwalkar 1966: 27).

6. Thus: 'The other main feature that distinguished our society was the *Varna-vyavastha*. But today it is being dubbed "casteism" and scoffed at. Our people have come to feel that the mere mention of *Varna-vyavastha* is something derogatory' (Ibid.: 107).
7. Though not put quite in these terms, the link between fascism and nationalisms and nation-states has been underlined by many an important scholar of fascism. However, it should also be clarified here that my use of the term 'fascism' moves away from the understandings that emphasize its singularity, where it often becomes difficult to even see Nazism and Italian Fascism as kindred phenomena—not to speak of many others across the world. There is a way in which the term has been used in a more generic sense, often but not necessarily always tied to the discourse of race, that takes away from this notion of singularity of fascism that is Eurocentric insofar as it denies the wider connections between the technologies of colonialism and racism in the making of the singularity of this experience. For an elaborate and fascinating discussion of this position, see Gilroy (2001). In the case of Hindu nationalism, even though there are many significant differences with both Italian and German fascisms, it is important to note the fact that it was not simply born within the larger discursive universe of fascism, it continues to exhibit equally significant similarities in terms of its political culture and its exaltation of the 'nation', intolerance of dissent and such other features.
8. It is interesting that the Puranas too begin with the creation of the universe and are supposed to end with its destruction.
9. Chakrabarty, of course, had encountered the same problem in his writing of working-class history in the Jute industry of Bengal. Thus, for instance, he had argued, very early on, that 'the worker's relationship to the machine, instead of being mediated through technical knowledge, was mediated through the North Indian peasant's conception of his tools, whereby the tools often took on magical and godly qualities' (Chakrabarty 1996: 89).
10. Conversations with a *paan* shop owner in Rajpur Road.
11. Narrated to me by a resident of Shastri Park area.
12. 'Monkeyman gives power to the people: Parties score points', *Hindustan Times*, 17 May 2001, reported that the Shiv Sena's Delhi Unit claimed that, 'The ISI is behind it; 131 monkeys have come across the border to spread terror.' I am grateful to Prakash Upadhyay for this reference.
13. These are Hindu rituals meant to either propitiate the gods or exorcise evil spirits.

14. This last story was told to Sanal Edamaruku of the Rationalist Association, 'It is a mass delusion, say rationalists' *Express Newsline*, 17 May 2001 (p. 3).
15. Ibid.
16. Sudhish Pachauri, 'Naye zamane ki vaanar leela', *Jansatta Ravivari*, 3 June 2001.
17. 'It is a mass delusion, say rationalists', *Express Newsline*, 17 May 2001 (p. 3).
18. *The Hindu*, Editorial, 19 May 2001. All emphasis added.
19. *The Indian Express*, 19 May 2001. I am only referring here to some of the articles out of a much larger number that came out in those days. Also see, for instance, Ashok Vardhan Shetty, 'Imagination on the Prowl', *The Hindu Magazine*, Sunday 10 June 2001.
20. The *Hindustan Times*, 18 June 2001.
21. The internet in those days was increasingly used by the relatively less privileged people too in the urban areas. My own experience was that by then it was being used in a very functional way for getting information about government policies (for instance, the Delhi Government's franchising of electricity supply for 'unauthorized' colonies) children's examination results and such other things. Among youth, cyber cafes were often used for surfing pornographic sites too. In my interactions with people of different strata, I observed that even when they do not directly use the internet, there was a kind of sense that it is something that can give you any information you require. Mobile phones and the proliferation of landlines even in the poorer colonies had made a significant impact on the lives of common people, in ways unimaginable a few years back. The important thing is that while there was greater access to these new technologies, much of their workings still appeared—and perhaps still do—mysterious. What they can and cannot do is still not clear and as we can see in the way the cyborg is imagined, there is an attribution of some mysterious power to these technologies.
22. It is, of course, entirely possible that this imagination drew on a lot of B grade Hollywood films—some of them supposedly science fiction films—that too had become available for consumption to the common people too, thanks to the cable television.
23. See 'Restructuring Urban Habitat—Land Reforms for Whom?', Report of the International Fact-finding Mission to Delhi, Habitat India Coalition and Sajha Manch, New Delhi, March 2001, for details.
24. I was told by a cloth shop owner in the Nand Nagari resettlement colony in February 2001, that the situation had affected his earnings too, quite

drastically: He would manage to make about Rs 15,000 in a month's sales in a good season, now he could barely manage between Rs. 2,500 to 3,000.

25. I have paraphrased this part of his argument in the discussion that follows, from some of the earlier texts by Chatterjee (1997, 1998a, 1998b).

6

Capital and Historical Time

Synchronicity of the Non-Synchronous[1]

> The elements do not exist in history *so that* a mode of production may exist, they exist in a 'floating' state prior to their 'accumulation' and 'combination', each being the product of its own history and none being the teleological product of the others or their history. When Marx and Engels say that the proletariat is 'the product of big industry'...[they] position themselves within the *logic of the accomplished fact of the reproduction of the proletariat on an extended scale*, (emphasis original) not the aleatory logic of the 'encounter' which produces (rather than reproduces), as proletariat, this mass of impoverished, expropriated human beings as one of the elements of the mode of production...[They] *shift from the first conception of the mode of production, an historico-aleatory conception, to a second, which is essentialistic and philosophical*.' L. Althusser (2006: 198, emphasis added)

Time, in the philosophical discourse of modernity, has been understood as tied to the notion of 'totality', such that there can be only one present (the most 'advanced' form), all other social forms being 'residues' or 'survivals' of the past. That is to say, one fine day, life-forms and social forms that have had long lives, their own pasts and their own presents, suddenly find themselves 'incorporated' into something called 'World-History' of which they, unbeknownst to themselves, suddenly become 'the past'. From that point on, they are put on a linear track where their future is laid out for them—a future that has no relationship whatsoever with their multifarious pasts and their presents. This 'temporal relocation' is a violent process and certainly has other precedents in the ways in which certain monotheistic religions seek to eradicate pagan pasts and life-forms but it is something that acquires a completely different and all-pervasive form with the advent of modernity and its philosophical discourse. This is certainly true of various theories of modernity that see no outside to it and operate with notions of Totality like Hegel's 'World-History' or Marx's global Capitalist Mode of Production; it is also true of liberal discourse that apparently concerns itself only with the individual but operates necessarily within certain notions of a larger and inescapably modern condition. And yet, contemporaneous social or life-forms that have been relegated to the status of 'survivals', simply refuse to vacate the stage, posing in the bargain, problems for this philosophical discourse itself.

In the subtitle of this chapter and the last section, I use the expression 'synchronicity of the non-synchronous'—an expression also translated as 'simultaneity of the non-simultaneous' and attributed to the early twentieth-century Marxist thinker Ernst Bloch. In his masterpiece, *Futures Past*, Reinhart Koselleck uses the expression 'contemporaneity of the non-contemporaneous' to refer to this same 'problem' of co-presence of different times, as it were. Koselleck talks of the 'contemporaneity of the non-contemporaneous' as one of the three different modes of temporal experience—the other two being the 'irreversibility of events' and the 'repeatability of events'. However, he also extends the meaning of this expression to refer specifically to experience in the context of the European expansion. This is the experience 'of the non-contemporaneousness of diverse, but in the chronological sense, simultaneous histories.' The 'geographical opening up of the globe', brought into view 'various but coexisting cultural levels which were through the process of synchronous comparison, then ordered diachronically': 'Looking from a civilized Europe to a barbaric America was a glance backward' (Koselleck 1985: 247). Of course, this wasn't true only about countries or societies that existed in faraway lands and within what came to be known as 'nations' too, there were populations that were thus consigned to the past. The use of the expression 'consigned to the past' is a reference to this diachronic ordering but at another level, it can turn out to be quite problematic as it can imply a desire on their part to inhabit the same time of 'the present'—the time of the moderns. This expression can also be very easily incorporated by certain kinds of theorizations that want to do away, correctly, with this negative representation of them as past, and redeem them as our contemporaries–of our modern and capitalist present.

Ernst Bloch, on the other hand, uses the idea of the non-synchronous or the non-simultaneous, precisely in its early twentieth-century sense, to refer to precapitalist and premodern elements that continue to be present in the Germany of the 1920s and 1930s. Bloch is fascinating, despite his problematic understanding of the 'Orient' and 'Mohammedan lands', where his understanding is pretty mainstream. He is fascinating, in the first place, because of his unconventional style of theorizing; but he is also fascinating because he sees Germany, like Gramsci sees Italy, as that part of Europe that has been unable to eliminate these precapitalist elements. Bloch's essay (1977[1932]), therefore, begins with the claim that 'not all people live in the same Now', even though they may be seen around all the time. 'But that does not mean that they are living at the same time as the others' (Bloch 1977[1932]: 22). This is so because 'they carry earlier things with them' (Ibid.: 22). Now, what could these 'earlier things' be but customs, habits, ways of thinking and so on—which in an earlier Marxist discourse would be clubbed together under the rubric of 'superstructural' forms. Bloch acknowledges Marx's debt insofar as his concept of the non-synchronous follows upon and develops the idea that Marx had talked of—that of the 'unequal rate of development', which 'he ascribes to material production in relationship to artistic production' in his Introduction to the *Critique of Political Economy* (Ibid.: 29).

In the history of Marxism, this is a question that has arisen repeatedly—sometimes in the form of 'superstructural' elements like 'culture', 'ideology', 'customs' and even habits, and sometimes in the form of continuing material economic 'structures' coexisting with capitalism. We will encounter some of these both in the theory of the passive revolution and via Kalyan Sanyal's critique below. We also see them in Marx's attempts to explain the 'lagged effect' of social transformation in the domain of ideas and sometimes in the debates over the rise of 'revisionism' in socialist societies after revolution. Of particular significance in this respect was Mao Zedong's insistence on the Cultural Revolution as a permanent revolution because he had argued superstructural changes take far longer to take hold in comparison to transformations in the economic and institutional structures. On other occasions, we can also see forms of non-synchronicity being hotly debated in the context of revolution, one of the early instances of which was the debate over Trotsky's idea of 'world revolution' as opposed to Stalin's 'socialism in one country'. The point at issue in that debate related to whether the Soviet Union could wait indefinitely for the world revolution to happen simultaneously or should it proceed to build socialism in one country? In other words, would all countries of the world reach 'maturation' of the revolutionary conditions at the same time?[2]

Bloch links the non-synchronous remainder with the rise of Hitler and Nazism, in which his understanding of Germany as a 'retarded' capitalism of sorts, plays an important role. 'Times older than the present continue to effect older strata; here it is easy to dream one's way back to older times' (Ibid.: 22). He connects the non-synchronous in the affective and the ideational domain to the material and economic as well:

> Economically and ideologically, the peasants, in the midst of the flexible capitalist century, are situated in an older place. This is no matter how much capitalism has adapted landed property, a pre-capitalist element; no matter how much it has capitalized the peasants and furnished them with its commodities; no matter if even the most remote village is connected to the 'just milieu' by radio. The peasants retain a distorted remnant. They feel better represented by the feudal estates than by the suspicious city. (Bloch 1977[1932]: 25)

Bloch observes that Germany, which unlike England or France, 'did not accomplish a bourgeois revolution till 1918', *is the classic land of non-synchronism*, that is, of unsurmounted remnants of older economic being and consciousness (Ibid.: 29).

It is precisely this that we see being articulated, though from a very different philosophical stance within Marxism, by Louis Althusser when he says that 'the economic dialectic is never active in the pure state; in History, these instances, the superstructures, etc.—are never seen to step respectfully aside when their work is done'. From the first moment to the last, the lonely hour of the 'last instance' [of the Economy] never comes (Althusser 1979: 113). The non-synchronicity between the material/economic and the superstructural thus remains one of the key issues animating not just the practical revolutionaries but also Marxist thinkers through the twentieth century.

Despite its recurring and almost haunting presence everywhere, the continuing 'past', coexisting in our own time (non-synchronicities), often referred to as 'survivals', has not quite been taken head-on, theoretically speaking, by Marxists in general. Many have been horrified at the violence that has often been meted out to forms of life thus decreed to be past, both by the processes of capitalist industrialization in Europe as well as by the Stalinist state in its forced collectivization and industrialization drives. And yet they have not quite cared to look at what Althusser calls its 'theoretical status'. What we have, instead, are just pious platitudes about say, the 'rights of indigenous peoples'. Althusser happens to be perhaps the lone Marxist thinker in the West to have squarely posed this question, given his deep engagement with Lenin and Mao's thought. Thus, his poser, 'what is a "survival"?' Can it be reduced to the survival of certain economic structures like small scale production that the Revolution was unable to destroy with its first decrees? Or does it refer also to political, ideological structures and things like customs, habits, even 'traditions'? (Ibid.: 114).

Althusser went on to suggest that perhaps, 'the new society produced by the Revolution may itself ensure the survival, that is, reactivation of older elements' in a variety of ways (Ibid.: 116). As it happens, in these earlier writings, Althusser too reduces the question of non-synchronicities to superstructural questions alone. Or perhaps, to put it more accurately, that question—of the relative autonomy of the superstructure—was the real question before Marxists at that time. However, it does not really take care of the non-synchronicities in the actual material/economic domain that is the concern of this chapter and which relates to the very philosophy of history that underlies the attribution of the status of 'backwardness' and 'pastness' to life forms that are our contemporaries.

This chapter is concerned centrally with the non-synchronicities in the material/economic domain where the expected course of capitalist development failed to materialize and where, in large parts of the world, different 'modes of production', capitalist and pre-capitalist/

'feudal' continued to coexist within the same societies. Marxism coined the term 'social formation' to refer to such formations where a multiplicity of modes of production coexisted. But the telos of the eventual establishment remained in theory—practical experience could not shake the edifice of theory.

In twentieth century political-Marxist discourse, this difficulty has been signposted as the problem of 'uneven development' but has not led to any significant theoretical departure as the overarching category of the 'totality' continues to hold unchallenged sway within it. My argument in this chapter moves away from the idea of 'capitalism' as a totality—indeed as a structure of any kind. Instead, as I have argued at some length in Chapter 2, I see it as a mode of being, a disposition towards the world that is predicated on the institution of bourgeois private property and the hegemonic domination of what Macpherson has aptly called the philosophy of 'possessive individualism' (Macpherson 1962). This disposition or mode of being is really what accounts for the epochal change that comes to be known as modernity. 'Capitalism' is, therefore, not propelled by any immanent logic of the economy but put in place—and kept in place—through a combination of apparatuses, interventions by practitioners of specialized knowledges and state officials and policy planners, owners of wealth, philosophers and intellectuals in universities, the media and so on.

My interest thus is in the widely acknowledged *failure* of capitalism to develop outside the Euro-American world. Therefore, I am not really interested in definitional sleights of hand that make it sound as if 'capitalism' in the East and the West are exactly the same.[3] I will enter my argument through a brief discussion of a recent controversy among Indian scholars.

In an attack on the Subaltern Studies (SS) scholars' critique of what they call the 'universal history of capital', a Marxist scholar, Vivek Chibber takes them to task for completely misrepresenting 'the relationship between capitalism and modernity, both in the East and in the West'. This they do, he argues, in two ways, the first of which has to do with their 'distorted understanding of what is distinctive of capitalism as a social system,' where 'certain aspects of twentieth century liberal culture are taken as defining features of capitalism itself'

(Chibber 2013: 24). Not surprisingly, says Chibber, once capitalism is defined so narrowly, it is easy to conclude that what we have in the East is not capitalism at all. The second way in which Subaltern Studies scholars misrepresent the relationship between capitalism and modernity, according to him, appears mainly in the work of Partha Chatterjee, who, according to Chibber, 'evacuates capitalism from domains in which its influence has been critical'. The reference here is to Chatterjee's argument that nationalist ideology tended to promote national modernization as a basic goal because 'nationalist elites had internalized Western discourse', to put it in Chibber's words. He claims that he will show this argument to be entirely mistaken because the reason why the nationalists were promoting modernization was 'not because they were the victims of indoctrination but because of the pressures of governing in a capitalist economy. What Chatterjee presents as an effect of discourse was in fact a recognition of real, material pressures from global capitalism' (Ibid.: 24–25).

Chibber's starting premise is stated very clearly at the very beginning of the book—that 'there is no significant difference between the East and the West and, therefore, there is no reason why theories emerging from the European experience' should not be 'up to the task of capturing the basic structure of Eastern development in the modern epoch' (Ibid.: 23). There is an interesting methodological problem here in Chibber's argument, for if we believe that capitalism and modernity acquired the fullness of their meaning at the very moment of their birth in the West, such that those categories are then able to 'capture the basic structure of Eastern development', then later history should be redundant to the task of conceptualizing either capitalism (or modernity). Understandably then, Chibber accuses SS scholars of generalizing on the basis of the twentieth century form, for any recognition that subsequent development was not already immanent in the beginning, jeopardizes the carefully preserved essentialism that maintains 'capitalism' in its place.[4]

In this chapter, I do not seek to defend the SS critique of the 'universal history of capital', despite my general sympathy with SS scholarship, for I too believe there is much to be revisited and criticized, indeed abandoned, in their position in this regard.

Theirs was an important intervention when it was made but many issues and theoretical assumptions underlying their stance seem to now require serious re-examination. However, my differences with the SS position come from a standpoint that is diametrically opposed to Chibber's, almost point by point. In the first place, where Chibber criticizes SS for 'misrepresenting the relationship between capitalism and modernity, both in the East and in the West'—as though this were a settled matter even with respect to the West—my point of departure lies in *opening up* the entire question of what 'modernity' and 'capitalism' really are, and asking whether the familiar narrative of capitalism's (and modernity's) emergence that Chibber holds on to, is at all tenable today.[5] In making this argument, I draw on a whole body of scholarship (some of it recent and some not quite recent) that Marxists deliberately ignore. This scholarship takes the investigation of the rise of capitalism beyond the very provincial 'transition debates' (the Dobb-Sweezy debate and the Brenner debate for instance) and looks at the global histories of what it still sometimes continues to call capitalism (Banaji 2003; Dussel 2002; Hobson 2002; Goody 2006; Quijano 2000, 2007; Robinson 2000).

Second, where Chibber refers to 'capitalism as a social system', obviously necessarily closed, I have already argued in Chapter 2 that it is difficult to sustain, any longer, this idea of 'capitalism' as a structure or a totality or a system that is necessarily governed by some internal logic. As indicated earlier, I, therefore, see 'capitalism' (as distinct from 'capital') as a disposition, a mode of being, a way of relating to the world—just like say, individualism or secularism or nationalism. This is my main point of departure from an understanding that both SS and Chibber share, thanks to SS's continuing investment in Marxism.

Third, in his reading of Partha Chatterjee's rendering of the nationalist fascination with 'national modernization', Chibber makes a distinction between 'mere discourse' and the 'real pressures of governing in a capitalist economy' which I find totally untenable today. For one thing, regardless of whether Chatterjee will himself agree or not, there is no contradiction between these two claims since facing the 'real pressures of governing in a capitalist economy', and being subject to global capitalism, are both consequences of choices made by the nationalist elites. Nobody asked them to build a capitalist economy and subject themselves to its pressures except the choices they themselves made—in other words the discourse they inhabited. But more importantly, as some recent works like those of Timothy Mitchell (2002, 2007, 2014), Callon (2007), Caliskan and Callon (2009), or nearer home, Neeladri Bhattacharya (2018) argue, 'the economy' is *made*—put in place—in a discourse-practice constellation that resists such a facile separation. Bodies of knowledge like 'economics' emerge *as they restructure or rearrange the real world.*

Some Methodological Considerations

Methodologically, I steer clear of all writing that seeks to defend Marxist orthodoxy in the manner of theological scholasticism, where the theory always remains unquestioned, however difficult the questions posed to it by real-life may be. Following a hallowed tradition in the West at least, theory is neither refutable nor falsifiable, and remains blissful in its beatific presence, untouched by the messiness of the real-empirical or the historico-aleatory world. Within Marxism too this notion of theory continues to reign supreme which, therefore, sees all later post-Marx theory itself as impure, contaminated as it is by the real world, the particular and the diverse. The universal claims of theory do not sit well with these new accretions that get attached along the way and thus the anxiety of the ideologue to continuously assert the 'universal truth' of that theory. We could take two instances of this from within contemporary Marxism. For instance, the invocation of the 'true proletarian standpoint' by a philosopher like Slavoj Žižek obviously has nothing to do with the standpoints (since there isn't *one* standpoint) of the actually existing, real working class/proletarian, which has also been known, often enough, in history to respond enthusiastically to fascist or right-wing mobilizations. Likewise, we have theoretical pronouncements about the universalizing and progressive role of capital/ism that ostensibly brings together the whole world that apparently lay unconnected and isolated in its narrow, parochial existence before capitalism's arrival. Capitalism, on this account, arises out of the immanent logic of the economy or society that precedes it but is not apparently affected by that historical context—it is and must everywhere be the same. What is even more interesting is that while all serious Marxists believe that all actually existing capitalists are evil and always act out of nothing but their own naked self-interest, never for a moment does this belief affect their theorization of the 'historical role of the bourgeoisie', which is always liberatory and progressive in comparison with the past. The logic by which this happens is, of course, well known to us all in Hegel's famous 'cunning of Reason' but has a much wider and longer genealogy in theological thinking on theodicy, for instance. The actual existence of evil in the world never ever managed to compromise the idea of an omnipotent, compassionate and just God.

On the other hand, it is important from my point of view, to trace the vicissitudes of theory as it begins its earthly journey, encountering strange beings and forms of life that it did not, in the first place, find important to account for. Most of the 'impurities' that we might encounter in the historical movement of Marxist theory are, to my mind, indications of the fact that the purer, pristine versions are in need of constant amendment and revision. I am not arguing that empirical evidence simply 'proves' or 'falsifies' a theory—'from the outside' as it were. No amount of contrary evidence can either prove or disprove a theory since every theory has its own way of accounting for, or explaining away, exceptions. It is only when sufficient cases of exceptions accumulate and the theory and its practitioners themselves begin to confront their implications from within, in their own terms, that theoretical modifications or breaks occur, in a manner somewhat similar to Thomas Kuhn's idea of paradigm change.

Seen from this point of view, it is not really a matter of logically proving that critics are 'wrong' or that their 'historical sociology is faulty' as Chibber argues, but of reading the symptoms so to speak. After all, it is not just some SS scholars 'influenced by post-structuralism' who have argued that 'capitalist development' encounters serious barriers in the non-West. The debates go back, at least to the 1960s, if not earlier, when dependency scholars began confronting this problem and in their attempt to understand it better within broadly Marxist categories, made significant modifications in their understanding of capitalism itself. Some such scholars saw the problem in 'unequal exchange' and in the prevalence of low wages in the 'Third World'. Indeed, one might even trace the beginnings of the recognition of this problem in the writings of Antonio Gramsci, who proposed the idea of the 'passive revolution', precisely in order to deal with the fact that *even within Western Europe*, there were societies like Italy's where the 'backward South' continued to co-exist with the relatively more industrially 'advanced' North. One can indeed, go even further back to Leon Trotsky's formulations on 'combined and uneven development', writing as he was from the experience of the Czarist empire, encountering the simultaneity and co-existence of different 'modes of production' within the same society. This is what later, in the phase of the encounter with structuralism, came to be formulated in terms of the 'articulation of different modes of production' (capitalist and pre-capitalist) for which the concept of 'social formation' (as opposed to the ideal-type, the 'mode of production') was proposed. Formulations like those of Immanuel Wallerstein regarding the 'world-system' or those of Andre Gunder Frank, broadly within whose frame the former was functioning, saw the metropolitan-satellite relations as bound up within a common logic, development at one end producing underdevelopment at the other. We can go on multiplying the number of instances but let these suffice for now.

The point then is not to maintain, in theological fashion, that whoever questions the 'universal history of capital' is a renegade or a turncoat and has abandoned the doctrine but rather to recognize that all these so-called deviations are signs of a real impasse. So what the Subaltern Studies scholars were pointing towards was something that had long been recognized in the very earthly movement of Marxism.

In what follows, I take up for consideration this problem of 'uneven development' and the question of historical time as it appears within the universe of Marxist discourse, as it repeatedly encounters societies and forms of life that seem resistant to capitalism's supposedly 'inexorable and irresistible' growth. In particular, I take up for discussion the idea of the 'passive revolution' that many Indian scholars, from the 1980s on, deployed as a way of understanding the inability of capitalism to develop in large parts of the world including India. Specifically, I engage with the work of another critic of SS scholars, Kalyan Sanyal, who is also directly concerned with the question of capitalism's inability to develop but rejects the idea of the passive revolution because of the teleological assumptions that are implicit in it. I argue that we need to hold on to Sanyal's notion of 'non-capital' as the 'outside' of capital but not in the way that he himself does it, that is to say, by incorporating it as an effect of the *structural logic* of postcolonial capitalism, for that simply reinstates capital as the only active element, 'past forms' being seen merely as posited by capital itself. In fact, it might not be out of place to mention here that this is precisely the problem that even the formulations of the various communist parties regarding the character of the Indian state and Indian capitalism sought to grapple with, if in their own language. Characterizations of the Indian state as 'bourgeois-landlord, led by the big bourgeoisie' or 'semi-colonial and semi-feudal', however formulaic or derivative they may have sounded, actually attempted to account for the fact that in India, pre-capitalist forms could simply not be eliminated as was to be expected in a full-blooded bourgeois revolution. These characterizations, therefore, provided for a longer term, gradual transformation of precapitalist 'feudal' landlords into capitalist landlords or the state's takeover by a socialist revolution and the destruction of such semi-feudal structures through radical land reforms.

The 'Passive Revolution'—Argument and Critique

The passive revolution argument is internal to Marxist discourse and draws mainly on the writings of Antonio Gramsci. In understanding why capitalist development does not follow the logic of head-on confrontation with feudal and precapitalist forces, as was said to have happened in England and France, Gramsci argued that the *weakness* of the bourgeoisie forced it into compromises and alliances with those forces that necessitated a kind of 'revolution from above'. In this revolution, there was little place for popular involvement. Rather it depended on the ability of the bourgeoisie to slowly transform the precapitalist relations into capitalist ones through a strategy of molecular transformations. As Gramsci put it, 'the 'passive' aspect of the great revolution which started in France in 1789 and which spilled over into the rest of Europe with the republican and Napoleonic armies', resulted 'not in their immediate collapse as in France but in the 'reformist' corrosion of them [the *ancien regimes*] which lasts up to 1870' (Gramsci 1971: 119). Gramsci actually reads the *entire* history of Europe as a history of the passive revolution, for it gestures towards the fact that *even in the 'advanced West'*, the history of capital does not quite conform to the classical Marxist thesis about capitalist development destroying the older social forms in direct revolutionary combat. Crucial in Gramsci's rendering was the point that because of this relative weakness, the bourgeoisie was forced to engage in a long-term 'war of position' where it had to attempt to slowly establish its cultural-moral hegemony over society at large, for that was the precondition of the passive revolution's success.

This idea of 'passive revolution' attracted the attention of many Indian Marxists who were struggling to come to terms with the relative 'underdevelopment' of their own society. It is well known that various studies in the course of the dependency and underdevelopment debates, across the continents of Africa, Latin America and Asia, saw these societies as afflicted by a peculiar predicament that was variously described as 'retarded development', 'arrested development', 'dependent development'. This predicament arose from the growing recognition that Marx's and Marxists' prognostications about the inevitability of capitalist development were being belied in large parts of the world.

This fact was recognized not just by Marxists in the three continents (also called the global South) but even by important voices among Western Marxists. Thus Robert Brenner (1977) opened his important intervention with the recognition that 'the appearance of systematic barriers to economic advance in the course of capitalist expansion—the "development of underdevelopment"—has posed difficult problems for Marxist theory' (1977: 25). He went on to register the 'strong tendency sharply to revise Marx's conceptions regarding economic development' which, he conceded was at least, 'in part…a healthy reaction to the Marx of the *Manifesto*, who envisioned a more or less direct and inevitable process of capitalist expansion' that would undermine old modes of production and replace them with capitalist social production relations (Ibid.: 25).[6] Clearly then, by the late 1970s, *contra* Chibber, the recognition that there were 'systematic barriers' to capitalist expansion, was very widespread.

The passive revolution argument was first put forward in the Indian context by Asok Sen (1976) and later taken up by Partha Chatterjee (1986, 1994) and Sudipta Kaviraj (1984, 1987).[7] Asok Sen (1988) and Kalyan Sanyal (1988) in their contributions to a special number of the *Economic and Political Weekly* on Antonio Gramsci further amplified on this theme—though Sanyal's contribution stands out as an early critique of the teleology inherent in the idea of passive revolution. The point of the exercise was to theorize the specificity of postcolonial capital/ism which was clearly refusing to live up to Marx's (and Marxists') prognostications.

It is in this context that we must see the theory of the passive revolution as an attempt to explain what appeared then to be the 'retarded' nature of capitalist development in the peripheries of 'world capitalism'. The notions of 'retarded' or 'arrested' development do not give up on the hope that someday there will be full-fledged, unrestrained capitalist development. That teleology is implicit in the idea of passive revolution.

In the Indian context, the idea of passive revolution was deployed in order to deal with precisely such a context of a 'weak bourgeoisie' that was seen to be unable to perform its world-historical task of capitalist transformation. Partha Chatterjee's rendering of the Indian nationalist struggle itself was cast in such terms—as a struggle where the Indian bourgeoisie made a series of compromises and alliances with other precapitalist classes as the bourgeoisie did not represent the national-popular. Chatterjee, in fact, went on to argue that this was a model that held not just with respect to the Indian case but bespoke of a more general condition across the global South. 'The characteristic form of 'passive revolution' in colonial countries', he suggested, was one in which '(T)he 'war of position' implies a political-ideological programme by which the largest possible nationalist alliance is built up against the political rule of the colonial power' with the aim of forming an independent nation-state' (Chatterjee 1986: 48–49).

Thus, after the formation of the independent nation-state, the 'reorganization of political order' takes place in a peculiar fashion: the bourgeoisie neither breaks up or disturbs any of the modern institutions set up under colonial rule, nor undertakes 'a full-scale assault on all precapitalist dominant classes'; rather, it seeks 'to limit their former power', 'neutralize them where necessary', attack them selectively and 'bring them around to a position of subsidiary allies within a reformed state structure' (Ibid.: 49).

As a consequence, the strategy of economic development and accumulation that was evolved had to continuously balance the demands of accumulation and the need for political legitimation. The bourgeoisie could no longer carry out the business of industrial development by resorting to the violent process of dispossession that the classic primitive accumulation model involved. Thus, the political logic of the passive revolution called for 'promoting industrialization without taking the risk of agrarian political mobilization' (Chatterjee 1994: 213).

As an aside, we may note that while this accurately describes the stance of the nationalist leadership, it is not quite clear that it can be thus reduced to the logic of capital and its relative weakness in taking on precapitalist landlordism alone. The combined class-caste interests of the nationalist leadership, their position of dominance in the Brahmanical power structure and therefore, their opposition to the struggles of the lower orders (both lower caste and peasant struggles)—all these suggest that for a large majority of them it was simply a question of preserving their own positions of power. It is really difficult to see them as representatives of 'the bourgeoisie' in any real sense of the term. Here and in Kaviraj's argument further, the exclusive focus on class position to the detriment of say caste and community dynamics, must be seen as another mode of evasion of the non-synchronicities that we discussed earlier. Caste and community histories go much further back in history and have very different trajectories from histories of class formation in modern times. But that actually tells us only half the story. Histories of caste and community are also meshed with histories of modern 'capitalist' class formation which really leaves us without a capitalist class of the kind we are looking for. If there is no universal history of 'capital', there is also no universal, pure capitalist class that apparently has the same interests and the same dispositions to the extent of wanting to rewrite the same script everywhere.

Sudipta Kaviraj, unlike Chatterjee, locates the imperative of the passive revolution strategy in India, in the context of a certain realignment that the Congress party went through in the period between 1946 and 1950. 'The departure of the reformist elements from the Congress' he says, 'led to a feeling among the small elite around Nehru of being encircled within their own party' and that created the pressure towards, a 'passive revolution' strategy (Kaviraj 2010: 114).

Kaviraj argues that the 'Indian capitalist class' exercises its control over society through a strategy that is distinct both from 'a moral-cultural hegemony of the Gramscian type' as well as of 'the purely coercive type' seen in many newly independent countries. Rather, this control is exercised 'by a coalitional strategy carried out partly through the state-directed process of economic growth, and partly through the allocational necessities indicated by the bourgeois-democratic political system (Ibid.: 106).

Within this strategy of the Nehruvian leadership, the programme of 'serious bourgeois land reforms' was abandoned as a result of a combination of 'feudal resistance, judicial conservatism, and connivance of state Congress leaderships' (Ibid.: 114). One of the key moves of the Nehru leadership, in this respect, was the demobilization of its own movement. Rather than push it towards radicalization, which could have broken down conservative resistance, it decided to rely on the bureaucratic apparatus for carrying out its reformist initiatives (Ibid.: 114–115). As mentioned previously, here again, 'breaking down' the 'conservative resistance' was not, and could not be, simply a matter of mass mobilization against the bourgeoisie, which might have been a relatively simpler affair. The 'conservative resistance' was once again a matter of the class-caste power of the modernizing Brahmanical elite which had established its hegemony over conservative Hindu society that had started its political journey with the mass mobilization of the late 1890s against the Age of Consent Bill and reached its apogee with the defeat of the Hindu Code Bill piloted by B.R. Ambedkar with Nehru's backing. In the event, Ambedkar had to resign as Nehru decided to push through the reforms piecemeal.

However, Kaviraj is right in arguing that while the Congress was willing to accept the continuance of 'semi-feudal rural power', it did adopt 'massive plans for capitalist development', clearly rejecting 'a trajectory of satellite growth' that seems to have become a common destiny of many newly independent countries.

Apropos Chibber's argument mentioned earlier, it should be evident that my difficulty with the passive revolution argument is that it is class reductionist and simply unable to read the complex dynamic of mass nationalist mobilization that was always 'overdetermined', with class, caste, community combining in different combinations at different points of the anticolonial struggle, which itself was never coterminous with nationalism.

A Critique of the Argument

In an early critique, Kalyan Sanyal (1988) had argued against the teleology implicit in the passive revolution idea and the 'historicism' inherent in the capital/pre-capital distinction that undergirded it.

Sanyal sets up his argument against 'the concept of economic development', whereby 'the process of economic development ultimately leads to a full transformation of the economy from pre-capitalism into capitalism' (Sanyal 1988: PE-27). 'The main ideological thrust of bourgeois development economics', he argues, 'thus lies in its identification of economic development with the expansion of the domain of capital' (Ibid.: PE-27).

As against this, Sanyal claims,

> 'Even casual observations reveal that capitalist development in most of the third world countries has reinforced the capital/pre-capital dualism rather than destroyed it...*it has failed to incorporate the entire economy within the ambit of capitalist development: the rest of the economy remains outside the domain of capital.*' (Sanyal 1988: PE-28, emphasis added)

He therefore, does not see this problem as one of a 'transition' that will bear fruit one day, but rather as a *structural limitation* of what he will later identify as postcolonial capitalism. One of the key elements here is the way in which, avenues for endless expansion for third world capitalism are limited because there is always a need for poverty-eradication. The economy essentially stands divided between a high accumulation enclave economy and a vast hinterland where need-based consumption determines production (Ibid.: PE-29).

For Sanyal, as long as one continued to see 'precapital' as something that lay in a time prior to capital, the question would continue to be posed in the way in which Chatterjee, in particular, was posing it. In his more recent work, Sanyal (2007) countered the 'transition narrative' implicit in the position of Chatterjee and others, by underlining the need 'for a characterization of capitalist development *that theoretically rules out the possibility of capital superseding pre-capital*' (Sanyal 2007: 39).

Very briefly, Sanyal's argument is that while 'primitive accumulation', that is the violent separation of the immediate producer from the means of production, is a necessary concomitant of the arising of capital, there is something else that postcolonial capitalism must deal with. Unlike capitalism in Britain and Europe, populations thus uprooted and dispossessed cannot simply be dispensed with, for in today's world, governments must show that they take care of their populations and instead of leaving them to die, they undertake various 'developmental' activities through poverty alleviation and income generation programmes. He links this aspect of the 'development discourse' to the idea of governmentality that involves taking charge of the population's well-being. These interventions basically mean reversing the effects of primitive accumulation, providing the dispossessed, once again, with some means of livelihood. These populations, who inhabit the sprawling informal economies of the global South, constitute the vast domain of 'non-capital', in Sanyal's view. They are not remnants of the past and therefore, not pre-capital, since they are a result of the way postcolonial capitalism works.

The problem with Sanyal's argument is that he sees the entire process—primitive accumulation *and* its reversal, as internal to 'capital' itself—to postcolonial capitalism, to be specific. We can see why he makes this move: By seeing 'non-capital' as something that is posited by capital itself, he makes the supersession of such 'pre-capital'/'non-capital' by capital an impossibility. If non-capital is produced by capital, as its necessary outcome, then there can never be any point when capital entirely supplants non-capital. However, in doing this, Sanyal has to carry out a twofold operation: first, he must reinstate the idea of a totality or structure that is clearly governed by an 'internal logic'. Thus he says: 'In short pre-capital's… conditions of existence *flow from the internal logic of the expanded reproduction of capital*' (Sanyal 2007: 39). Second, even more problematically, he must include even 'governmental rationality' and 'development discourse'—and the state itself—as internal moments of postcolonial capitalism's structure.

While Sanyal's intervention provides an interesting way of reading the history of 'postcolonial capitalism', his insistence on seeing the existence of non-capital as a product of postcolonial capital's internal logic immediately takes away what he has gained. In attempting to provide a non-teleological account of capitalism's development, Sanyal ends up working out a solution that reintroduces the idea of a totality/structure with its own internal logic that Chatterjee's argument had the advantage of avoiding, dealing as it does with the contingent arrangement and deployment of forces.

Sanyal also joins issues with the widely prevalent 'tendency to subsume under the term "capitalist development" all developmental possibilities of a market economy' that he ascribes to a way of seeing 'capitalism as the dominant form of the economy'. In this representation, he goes on to argue, 'capitalism's dominance overshadows other possible, *existing forms of production that are always already present, thus pushing the heterogeneity that inheres in the economy to the background.*' (Sanyal 2007: 4, emphasis added).[8] Though this is an argument that can be made about all modern economies in general, Sanyal is concerned here with 'the economic formation of the third world' that is traditionally seen as marked by the co-presence of the capitalist and pre-capitalist forms of production (Ibid.: 4). In contrast, Sanyal sees the dependency (and world system) theories as having effected a much-needed departure that viewed third world capitalism as a different kind of formation, which expectedly, invited strong criticism from Marxists. However, while the adherents of dependency and world-system theories explicitly recognized that in the peripheries, 'along with a capitalist industrial sector, a wide range of *traditional, archaic systems* of production' exist as an integral part of the global market network, they nevertheless gave these forms little importance, *seeing them as subsumed within the exchange relations, which they designated as capitalist* (Ibid.: 11, emphasis added).

This then is the key question: what is the theoretical status of these 'traditional and archaic systems' of production? Can they simply be reduced to appendages of capitalism—functional to or posited by capital? I have argued elsewhere that this is the status analogously also ascribed to the pre-modern or non-modern, by theorists who proclaim that once we are 'in modernity', all other modes of being are subsumed within it as 'modern'.[9] There is then no longer any 'outside' to either modernity or capitalism.

In a critical engagement with those who argue from the standpoint of the articulation of the capitalist and pre-capitalist modes of production in the third world (for example Ernesto Laclau), that 'feudal relations exist not as survivals of the past *but as an inseparable part of the capitalist mode to form an 'indissoluble unity'* (Ibid.: 15), Sanyal asks why they nonetheless continue to exist at all. His claim is that the answer is to be sought beyond the economic realm and that the 'centrality of the "economy" in the Frankian and post-Frankian literature on underdevelopment must be rejected in favour of an analytical framework that recognizes the specificity of the non-economic instances and *foregrounds the question of agency: who are the agents of change*? And what are the conditions under which they can act?' (Ibid.: 25, emphasis added).

I have italicized the key issue of agency identified by Sanyal in the previous passage because this is precisely why I find Sanyal's own resolution of the issue problematic.

For in making his key theoretical move, building upon an important empirical phenomenon, when he argues that capitalism itself is essentially a complex of capitalist and non-capitalist production, he asks us to see *capitalist development as a process that necessarily produces non-capitalist economic processes in its own course* (Ibid.: 7). Agency then simply shifts back to capital: pre-capital becomes non-capital because it has no agency of its own, for it is simply posited by capital.

My argument is that the chronological priority of certain forms cannot be wished away, making the 'outside' itself a function of capital. This becomes quite clear, once again, if we look at the land struggles against dispossession that mark the map of contemporary India: the displacement of land-owning peasants or forest-dwelling Adivasis (indigenous people) cannot be seen as 'posited by capitalist development' whatever that may mean, for they see themselves and must be understood, therefore, as standing in radical alterity to capitalist relations.

The 'Simultaneity of the Non-Simultaneous'

In the remaining part of this chapter, I want to argue that the difficulty in all the positions discussed earlier, especially Sanyal's that comes closest, in my view, to overcoming a teleological transition narrative, is that they are still complicit with a particular, broadly Marxist mode of theorizing that is unable to extricate itself from the larger assumptions bequeathed by the Western narrative—that is to say, by the entire complex of the material and discursive universe of the rise of capitalism and modernity in the West. Theories of modernity and capitalism in the West did not merely *describe* a state of affairs but actually produced them as normatively desirable, because they ostensibly embodied Progress and Reason. We have already seen, in Chapter 2, how an entire range of recent scholarship has established quite convincingly that neither modernity nor capitalism were exactly endogenous developments within Europe but were assembled out of elements sourced from various different parts of the world. Technologies like print, gunpowder or the compass, so crucial to the development of both colonialism and modernity came from China; mathematics based on the decimal system, so critical for capitalist accounting, from India via the Arab world; the great traditions of rationalist thought and science were nurtured and developed in the medieval Arab world; not to speak of the wealth plundered from the global South. As argued earlier, it is well-nigh impossible to hold on, any more, to the story of a world that lay in darkness, waiting to be illuminated by the light of the Enlightenment. That origin myth of modernity as we know it is seriously thrown into question by now. However, it is worth repeating here that by invoking this scholarship, I do not intend to argue that capitalism and modernity in their extant form/s were global products, in the sense of having been produced in some kind of benign global collaboration. Europe and the West, more generally, remain the key agents insofar as the emergence of the new constellation is concerned—giving birth to an entirely new discourse of Modernity as Emancipation and Progress, expressed in notions of individual autonomy and the language of rights and 'capitalism' as the new mode of being. With the emergence of capitalism as a particular mode of being, predicated on the arrival of the self-maximizing (or self-aggrandizing) possessive individual, orientation to accumulation, endless production of wealth and consumption became instituted as the norm, as the desirable state that all societies must aspire to. This new 'ontology of the economic' wasn't the outcome of any objective economic logic at work. Modern states, armed with this new philosophical discourse, set about reorganizing societies in the most 'rational' and 'progressive' way possible. If James Scott's *Seeing Like a State* gave us one aspect of the story, then from somewhat different angles, Timothy Mitchell's *Rule of Experts* (2002) and Neeladri Bhattacharya's *The Great Agrarian Conquest* (2018) show us some other dimensions of the same story of transformation by the state, in both its avatars—colonial and postcolonial.

However, that is not what I want to discuss here. What interests me here, in the context of our present discussion, is the way in which modes of being chronologically prior to but contemporaneous with, modern forms like capitalism are, through a peculiar intellectual operation, transformed into forms simply 'posited by capital'. In the theoretical discourse of Marxism, this relationship between capitalism and precapitalist forms, their co-presence in the same time, has a specific name: 'uneven development' or in Trotsky's formulation, 'combined and uneven development'. Why 'uneven' development? Because there is the prior assumption of the Totality—so that what were simply different and non-contemporaneous forms can now only be seen as 'unevenness', of 'forward' and 'backward' or 'early' and 'late', since they are placed within the same structural whole now. Not all Marxists would hold the position that precapitalist forms are simply 'retroactively posited by capital' but this understanding often derives from Marx's claim in the *Grundrisse* and *Capital Vol. I,* that 'the anatomy of man is key to the anatomy of the ape' and that 'pointers to higher species of animals in the lower species can only be understood if the higher species is already known.' Thus says Marx, in this celebrated passage, 'the bourgeois economy provides the key to the economy of antiquity'. In Marx, this was an epistemological claim, which established legitimacy of the present's claim over the past but in the hands of some theorists it actually became an *ontological* claim—about the very being of the 'lower species' or 'lower social forms'.

Recapitulating our earlier discussion in Chapter 2, let me put this in the words of Slavoj Žižek:

> Such co-existence [of different life-worlds] holds not only for India but is present everywhere, including in the most developed societies. It is here that *one should apply the properly dialectical notion of totality*: capitalism functions as a 'totality', in other words, *elements of pre-existing life-worlds and economies (including money), are gradually re-articulated as its own moments*, 'exapted' with a different function. What this means is that the line separating H1 and H2 is by definition blurred: parts of H2, found by capitalism to be external to it, become permanently re-articulated as its integral elements. (Žižek 2011: 284, emphasis added)

The reference to H1 and H2 here is to a specific formulation made by Dipesh Chakrabarty in his well-known *Provincializing Europe*. Chakrabarty bases his distinction between 'two kinds of history', H1 and H2, on his reading of Marx himself:

> 'I try to develop a distinction that Marx made between two kinds of histories: histories 'posited by capital' and histories that do not belong to capital's 'life process'.' (Chakrabarty 2000: 50)

Histories that are 'posited by capital' are called H1 by Chakrabarty and histories that do not belong to its 'life-process', H2. It is Žižek's point here that we will continue to misunderstand this distinction unless we take recourse to a 'properly dialectical notion of totality' for that alone makes it possible to understand life-worlds that existed before the arrival of capitalism as its 'own moments'. We know that Marx himself, once he was through with his empirical researches and sat down to write *Capital*, started re-reading Hegel. How to make sense of the actual empirical evidence that was before him was the issue and neither Hegel nor the 'properly dialectical notion of totality' were constitutive elements of his understanding of capital till the process of distillation i.e. writing began. Hegel simply provided that seductive argument whereby the opposing element of the contradiction was internalized as a moment of the unfolding Absolute Idea. One can wager that had Marx taken recourse to a Spinoza rather than a Hegel, his results would have been altogether different. It is not surprising then that Chakrabarty too, despite talking of H2 as history that does not belong to capital's 'life-process', nevertheless titles his chapter 'Two Histories of *Capital*'. Because of his still being trapped within this discourse, despite his gestures to poststructuralism and its critique of totality, we find him arguing about the resistance of pre-capitalist forms thus:

> From where does such resistance arise? Many labour historians think of resistance to factory work as the result of either a clash between the requirements of industrial discipline and *preindustrial habits of workers in the early phase of industrialization* or a heightened level of worker consciousness in a later phase...Marx, in contrast, *locates this resistance in the very logic of capital.* That is to say, he locates it in the structural 'being' of capital rather than in its historical 'becoming'. (Chakrabarty 2000: 58–59, emphasis added)

The circular logic of this notion of a dialectical totality becomes evident even in Chakrabarty's own text that Žižek perhaps needlessly attacks. Needlessly, because Chakrabarty is entirely in agreement with him on this point, as will be evident from the following statement that comes at the end of the long discussion, and where Chakrabarty states his own position very clearly:

> In other words, History 1 and History 2, considered together, *destroy the usual topological distinction of the outside and the inside that marks*

> *debates* about whether or not the whole world can be properly said to have fallen under the sway of capital. *Difference, in this account,.is not something external to capital.* Nor is it something subsumed into capital. It lives in intimate plural relationships to capital, ranging from opposition to neutrality. (Chakrabarty 2000: 65–66, emphasis added)

That difference is not really external to capital is what I take from the somewhat circuitous discussion undertaken by Chakrabarty. The point that I want to underline here is that regardless of whether such modes of being live in relationships of opposition or neutrality, in Chakabarty's reckoning too, they are not external to capital, and indeed he seems to accept what he says is Marx's argument—that these are pasts posited by capital itself, for once one understands the logic of capital one can no longer see them, despite being historically prior, as independent entities.[10]

The crucial methodological point here relates to our earlier discussion of the relationship of theory's earthly journey to the way in which it confronts the empirical-historical world on the one hand, and the idea of a supposedly objective 'logic of capital'. But theological stances can only be preserved in their pristine purity by insulating them from the messy empirical world of actual practices. Thus, the 'logic of capital' has to be insulated from the actual processes of history.

If on the other hand, we take the position that there is nothing really objective about the 'logic of capital' and that antagonisms and resistance are not given by the structure (or totality) itself but by the way in which political subjectivities shape up, discursively, in any given historical context, we might come up with completely different conclusions. Let us take, for example, the point made by Ernesto Laclau and Chantal Mouffe about the changing character of workers' struggles in Europe itself:

> There were without a doubt *radically* anti-capitalist struggles in the nineteenth century, but they were not struggles by the proletariat—if by the 'proletariat' we understand the type of worker produced by the development of capitalism, rather than the artisans whose qualifications and modes of life were threatened by the establishment of the capitalist system of production. (Laclau and Mouffe 2001: 156)[11]

As opposed to these, the struggles of the modern working class produced by capitalism, argue Laclau and Mouffe, turn out not to challenge capitalist relations of production but are struggles that Marxists would term 'reformist' (Ibid.: 157). In making this point, Laclau and Mouffe do not tie themselves up in knots in trying to prove that what is chronologically prior is not in fact, prior, for in their understanding resistance is not a matter of some objective, immanent 'logic of capital' but of the discursive construction of antagonisms.

From the point of view of my argument, however, it is important to recognize that there *are* chronologically prior forms/modes of being that are nevertheless contemporaneous with capital and for that reason, cannot be considered past forms. Their relations with capital/ism—like those of Laclau and Mouffe's artisans—are relations of externality unlike say the relations of the modern working class and the bourgeoisie, which can be seen as 'legitimate differential positions in a unified discursive space' (Laclau and Mouffe 2001: 157). Laclau and Mouffe are, of course, concerned with precapitalist communities that eventually perished and disappeared into the pages of history but our reference points here are modes of being that continue to be with us, contemporaneously, in the global South. My point here is that in designating these modes of being (or modes of life, in Laclau and Mouffe's terms) either as 'non-capital' and presenting them as appendages of capital, or as pasts that are retrospectively posited by capital, we do violence to them.

Interestingly, from within Western Marxism, we have another reading of the same story that becomes possible by simply doing away with the Hegelian dialectical totality. As early as in *Reading Capital*, Louis Althusser and Etienne Balibar wrestle with the problem of historical time and the question of the 'totality'. The discussion in the book is shot through with notions like 'transition', 'survivals', 'under-development' and the problem of 'periodization.' In Balibar's contribution we see the theme of the birth of capitalism tackled through a close reading of the *Grundrisse* and *Pre-Capitalist Economic Formations* in particular. Here Balibar underlines that 'the elements combined by the capitalist structure *have different and independent origins*. It is not one and the same movement that makes free labourers and transferable wealth' (Althusser and Balibar 1977: 281, emphasis added). This means that 'instead of being thought at the level of structures, the transition is thought at the level of the elements (Ibid.: 280). What is, however, even more important is the recognition that,

> Thus the unity possessed by the capitalist structure once it has been constituted is not found in its rear. Even when the study of the pre-history of the mode of production takes the form of a genealogy...even then *the pre-history can never be the mere retrospective projection of the structure.* (Althusser and Balibar 1977: 281, emphasis added)

In his posthumously published *Philosophy of the Encounter*, Althusser returns to this question. He underlines that Marx repeatedly claims that the capitalist mode of production arose from the 'encounter' between 'the owners of money' and the proletarian stripped of everything but his labour-power. What is crucial, he argues, in this conception is '*the aleatory character of the "taking-hold" of this encounter, which gives rise to an accomplished fact* whose laws it is possible to state' (Althusser 2006: 197, emphasis original). The laws and the 'totality' do not exist prior to the aleatory character of the encounter.

In this text, Althusser in fact distinguishes between a 'historico-aleatory' conception of the development of capitalism and an 'essentialistic and philosophical' one (Ibid.: 198). The point of bringing in this discussion of Althusser and Balibar here is not just to marshal support for my argument but rather to illustrate how, from within the Western Marxist tradition, a departure from Marx's Hegelian trappings could open the pathway to a different understanding of the 'mode of production'—which no longer appears as a closed totality, positing its own past, as it were. It is, of course, not a mere coincidence that for Althusser, the rejection of the Hegelian totality came through his deep engagement with the writings of Mao Zedong and Lenin and the meditation on the question of so-called 'survivals' and 'uneven development' as a consequence.[12]

To return, in conclusion then, to the key point we have been discussing, it seems that in moving away from the linear time of modernity and capital that sees all past forms as belonging to the past, scholars such as Sanyal and Chakrabarty—like many Western

Marxists—end up doing another kind of violence to their being: they reduce them to mere appendages of capital's history. My argument here is that it if we do not want to reduce these modes of being to passive entities, simply subsumed and posited by capital as its own past, it is necessary for us to hold on to the idea of their chronological priority and externality to capitalism. The fact that they emerge chronologically before the rise of capitalism should not and cannot be reason enough to delegitimize their existence and their agency—for they continue to offer resistance to capitalism throughout its history and into the present moment.

Notes

1. The expression 'simultaneity of the non-simultaneous' is attributed to Ernst Bloch (1977[1932]), who does not quite use the expression though he does talk about non-simultaneity and co-presence. The terms are often translated as 'synchronicity' and 'non-synchronous' as well, and I prefer this to other alternative expressions. A parallel expression, 'contemporaneity of the non-contemporaneous', appears in Reinhart Koselleck's classic (1985) also but refers to Bloch's use of the expression because it ties up with our discussion of Marxism and 'capitalism' that are both reference points for Ernst Bloch as well. I will discuss the idea at length in the last section of this chapter.
2. I have discussed some of these issues at great length in my chapter 'Time and the Revolutionary Imagination' in Nigam (2010) and will not repeat the discussion here. Interested readers may read that chapter in particular.
3. It may be useful to keep in mind that at the beginning of the twenty-first century, this is recognized by many an important ideologue of capitalism itself. In particular, the work of Hernando de Soto is important and worth considering, since the very subtitle of his book says it in so many words: *Why Capitalism Triumphs in West and Fails Everywhere Else.*
4. Chibber calls it 'twentieth century liberal culture' but there is a problem in leaving unspecified the nature of its relationship to capitalism, in the way SS scholars read it. On their reading, the intellectual-cultural formation is of a piece with the specific form that capitalism takes in these societies.
5. See Chapter 2 for an elaboration of this argument. I have also made this argument at length in an unpublished paper titled, 'Capital, Time and

Difference: Modernity and the European Episteme' (presented at the Global Capital and Social Difference Conference, Centre for the Study of Social Systems, Jawaharlal Nehru University, October 2016).

6. Brenner is obviously referring here to *The Communist Manifesto* that presented the idea of capitalism's inevitability and the bourgeoisie's historically progressive role in highly celebratory terms. In a well-known passage, it had claimed that, 'The bourgeoisie cannot exist without constantly revolutionizing the instruments of production, and thereby the relations of production' and that 'by the rapid improvement of all instruments of production…it draws all, even the most barbarian, nations into civilization…. In one word, it creates a world after its own image'.
7. The dates mentioned refer to the original publications though I have used the subsequent reprints in Kaviraj 2010—all reference henceforth shall be to this volume.
8. This part of Sanyal's argument is clearly indebted to the pioneering argument about 'capitalocentrism' made by J.K. Gibson-Graham, extending insights from feminist and queer theory to the field of the economy (Gibson-Graham 2006).
9. See Note 3.
10. Lest I be misunderstood, here is the quote: 'It goes without saying that it is not the actual process of history that does the "presupposing"; the logical presuppositions of capital can only be worked out by someone with a grasp of the logic of capital' (Chakrabarty 2000: 63).
11. Laclau and Mouffe continue: 'The strongly antagonistic character of the struggles of these "reactionary radicals"—in Craig Calhoun's phrase—their calling into question of the whole of the capitalist system, are explained by the fact that these struggles expressed resistance to the destruction of artisanal identities and the whole set of social, cultural and political forms which went with them.' (2001: 56).
12. The key texts in this respect are the well-known essays 'Contradiction and Overdetermination' and 'On the Materialist Dialectic—On the Unevenness of Origins', in *For Marx* (1979).

Conclusion

In conclusion then, let me draw together, however briefly, the different strands of the argument made in this book. First of all, I have tried to steer clear of the stance of simply criticizing Eurocentrism, for I argue that though criticism was an important first step, we are now in a different conjuncture. The criticism of Western knowledge and Eurocentrism has had its moment and it has produced important work globally, as well as in India. It has opened out the space for many of us to think further, in terms of doing theory in the global South. The time now, however, demands something else of us; it demands that we undertake the task of actually reconfiguring social and political theory by moving away from received modes of relating to theory. In the Introduction, I have called this way of relating to theory as the colonial mode of knowledge production, where theory and theoretical infrastructure based in metropolitan academies and their overseas subsidiaries, somewhat like manufactories, source raw material from all over the world, process them, package and return them for consumption to 'native' markets. This endlessly reproduces the pattern where the Non-West simply serves as the 'field' from where 'data' is collected and the market where the goods are sold. Both the questions with which the researcher approaches the field, as well as the subsequent ways of processing that data, come out of theoretical frameworks that are born in other time-spaces, basically Europe in another time.

It is hardly surprising then that the answers that we get when we pose questions to this theory regarding most problems confronting the Non-West today simply point to the ways in which these societies may be deficient and lacking in the proper ways of being modern.

Given this, the project of decolonization demands that we produce our own infrastructures of theory, if in import-substituting mode, which in a modest sort of way this book has tried to do. I make no claim to having accomplished any such thing as decolonizing theory; rather the attempt has been to bring other perspectives from historical or anthropological scholarship into the business of 'doing theory' and thus opening up a space for understanding practices and conceptions in the Non-West not as 'lacks', and not in terms of why they did not or could not take the way shown by Europe. The general stance adopted in this book has also found no use for various kinds of Indian or South Asian exceptionalism that claim for themselves a special status where the universalisms of social and political theory or philosophy supposedly fail to apply to them because *they* are special. Not only are stories of such past greatness often greatly exaggerated, but they are also results of colonial, Orientalist histories that had their own reasons for playing up the 'uniqueness' of these cultures. Moreover, such claims are better avoided as they are often excuses for evading the bigger challenge of engaging Western theory in a dialogue of equals and producing alternative conceptual frameworks.

Further, to recall the more general point made in the Introduction, this book has moved away from the mode of agenda-setting and laying out programmatic perspectives, about how to do theory. The time for that too is long past. The task of reconfiguring theory is seriously on the agenda today and there are myriad ways in which this is being done by different people in different parts of the world, some of which I have referred to in Chapter 1. In a sense, the key issue, as I see it, is about intervention in our own times, for that is what theory is all about. It has to be able to help us, like torchlight, find our way on uncharted seas rather than sit aside and talk of how great our ancestors were when our ship might actually fall over the precipice any moment. Needless to say, it is also not about endlessly regurgitating theories borrowed from other space-times and mindlessly 'applying' them to our contexts. We seriously need to think across traditions in more ways than one.

The unstated background assumption behind this impulse towards the decolonization of thought is also the growing realization worldwide that the European episteme has brought the world to the brink of an unprecedented disaster and something needs to be done to seriously reverse this direction of things. The ecological disaster that is now already upon us, is certainly a concern that has been animating the thinking of many people across the world. It has also been animating my own thinking about both capitalism and modernity for close to three decades and I was repeatedly forced into the realization that we were in a complete dead end as far as theory was concerned. The more I read and tried to understand the writings of Western Marxists, the more I realized, how dangerously blinkered and limited their vision was. Many like Žižek could even joke that it is easier to imagine the end of the world than to imagine the end of capitalism. It took me a very long time to understand that the problem with the Marxist theorizations of capitalism were of a piece with general theorizations about modernity and the state/the political and so on: *there was simply no 'outside'* to the enclosed, self-developing totality: modernity, capitalism, History were all all-encompassing, all were apparently driven by some objective 'internal logic'. Even theoretical frameworks that did not invoke totalities or an immanent logic of History, such as liberalism, pretty much took the narrative of Progress and the all-encompassing, *universal* nature of modernity's claims as unquestionable. The need to theoretically specify this possible 'outside' therefore, became the central concern that is evident throughout this book.

In the most optimistic and radical accounts of the totality called capitalism, the 'internal logic' was said to be inevitably driving it towards some utopia of abundance and material prosperity for all, when we could all see with our naked eyes that within our own lifetime the world had run out even of resources we thought were simply there for all, forever: air and water. There are regions in India that have run out of water, populations have migrated out of them; there are areas where groundwater has become toxic forcing people out again. There are big cities in India that will run out of water in the next two years. And yet, not only do our political elites continue to fantasize about smart cities and Western-style development, even our Marxist intellectuals have not found a way out of the industrialization imagination. It is all still seen as historical inevitability and any attempt to question the inevitability of industrialization is still dubbed 'romantic', 'backward-looking' and so on. The only difference is that *they* are being taken increasingly less seriously now.

The very possibility of this theoretical question of the 'outside', however, arises only because of the prior recognition that runs through this book—that of the legitimacy of non-synchronous synchronicities, that is, with modes of being that were once consigned to the past. The moment we do away with the idea of the inevitable logic of history and the historical necessity of industrialization, we are forced to deal with the question of how we relate to these modes of being as contemporaries *and as* equals. When E.P. Thompson wrote of rescuing 'the poor stockinger, the Luddite cropper, the "obsolete" hand-loom weaver, [and] the "utopian" artisan' who perished in the storm of industrialization, 'from the enormous condescension of posterity', he was dealing with modes of being that had already passed into history—uprooted and destroyed (Thompson 1968: 13). As a Marxist, he nevertheless had to concede, even as he undertook this heroic task, that 'their crafts and traditions may have been dying; their hostility to the new industrialism may have been backward-looking; their communitarian ideals may have been fantasies; their insurrectionary conspiracies may have been foolhardy…' (Ibid.: 13). How could he as a Marxist have said anything else? How could any modernist, even the most critical among them? All that Thompson had by way of his defense was his recognition that 'they lived through these times of acute social disturbance, we did not' (Ibid.). And as a historian, he was recording this painful if inevitable history of those modes of being so erased from the contemporary map of his times. But similar modes of being are very much part of our present in the twenty-first century in India, as in many other parts of the world—and we no longer believe that it is not only their destiny but also their duty to make way for what I have called modern, capitalist modes of being. Today the question is not just of extending them the charity that Thompson retrospectively could; today it is also a matter of recognizing the larger question of justice and indeed, 'epistemicide' (de Sousa Santos) and epistemic justice that is on the table as an ethical question.

These being really the animating concerns behind this exercise, I have argued in this book that the question of decolonizing theory is, for us in the global South today, not a mere academic question but one that relates to our very existence. Chapter 6 takes up this question head-on, especially via an engagement with Kalyan Sanyal's work and places itself outside the philosophy of history that lays the basis of teleological arguments regarding the inevitability of capitalism. Sanyal's wasteland of postcolonial capitalism is that vast metaphorical space where the uprooted are thrown but where most governments today must intervene as part of their governmental responsibility to 'reverse the effects of primitive accumulation'. This is the population of those non-synchronous life forms who cannot be transported to Australia, New Zealand or to the Americas as in the 'classic case' (that is England) of industrialization.

An exploration of the question of modernity that is the key concern in Chapter 2, also became inescapable in the context of these larger sets of concerns. The all-enveloping character of the modern seemed equally stifling from the point of view of the literally millions of people who were being dispossessed and turned into beggars and criminals but handed over a discourse of rights and autonomy as compensation. Something here has not seemed quite right. The divisions and the lines of demarcation presented to us by the received narrative of modernity were just too sharp and unfathomable: Was everything premodern bad? Did ordinary people have to be dispossessed and made into destitutes, criminals and beggars (within nation-states), and transported as slaves across continents globally? And why did entire continents have to be subjected to the genocide of indigenous populations? The ostensible justification of everything was that this was the onward, irresistible march of Reason and Progress—older modes of being simply had to make way for the moderns who were now the 'masters of the universe'.

What after all, is modernity then? This naturally became an urgent question to explore, as one realized that actual histories of the world hardly supported the story of a world lying in darkness, backwardness and superstition before the Enlightenment. That seemed to be such a specific story of Europe under medieval Christianity but how easily and rapidly did it become the way we all were to start narrating our 'universal past'. The work of historians and historians of ideas showing the great strides that science, mathematics, philosophy and culture had made in say the Arab world, India and China in ancient and medieval times, simply seemed to have no effect on the theoretical narrative of modernity and Progress that emerged in Europe after the Enlightenment. It became necessary to disentangle that story and Sudipta Kaviraj's recent proposal of a revisionist theory of modernity opened out the possibility of further unpacking the history of modernity. The idea of seeing modernity as a constellation of different processes, proposed by Kaviraj, actually suggested something far more radical: constellations are not 'real entities' but placed in proximity, different stars suggest a pattern that is then recognized as such, simply by convention. It also suggested that the different elements/processes of the constellation could have and indeed have different histories and chronologies going back to different time-spaces. What then was Europe's distinctive contribution? I have identified this as the discourse of individual autonomy and rights that ties up neatly—indeed facilitates—the emergent new mode of being called capitalism.

Chapter 3 is a direct engagement with some aspects of the work of Slavoj Žižek—the initial impetus for which had come in response to a sharp exchange in the columns of *Al Jazeera* between the Spanish philosophy professor Santiago Zabala and Iranian–American scholar Hamid Dabashi joined later by others. It was interesting that just a couple of years before this exchange, Žižek had visited India and delivered lectures in different cities. What he wrote about India and Indian civilization seemed to me to be symptomatic of what precisely was wrong with the attitude of Western philosophers and thinkers in dealing with non-Western societies. They had all their frameworks ready and all they needed were 'facts' that they could pick up from anywhere—often in the most cavalier fashion—in order to offer profound theorizations. The implicit assumption there was that no thought was really taking place in these societies, so you could just pick up facts and interpret them in whatever way you wanted to. What people in these societies, who lived these 'facts' thought of them was of no consequence whatsoever. As it happened, I had actually attended a conference in London a few years before his India visit, where a galaxy of Western Marxist philosophers spoke on the idea of communism. I had written about what I thought was quite an amazing display of smug self-satisfaction. It was white male European philosophers speaking to a white audience about what the world should be doing—the radical agenda for the rest of the world. That conference in 2009 was when I actually first began thinking of the problem of the 'outside of capital' and it seemed to be important to bring together all that by way of this critique of Žižek.

The questions of 'the political' and 'the secular' (and secularism) are so central to the story of modernity that they naturally form the other two chapters (Chapters 4 and 5) in the book. The political is usually spoken of, following Western conventions deriving from the European experience, in terms of sovereignty. The notion of sovereignty, as we know, has been understood as indivisible and unitary—both in relation to the state's internal relations to its people and to its external relation to other states. This idea arises from the experience of absolutism and the sovereign state system—though the idea of sovereignty actually harks back to God and his deputy, the monarch in Latin Christendom. This is once again very different from the various different relations in which the political and the social stand in different societies across the world outside Europe. Many modern Indian thinkers, especially in the early twentieth century, including Gandhi and Tagore, have consistently argued that politics and the state, in particular, were never central to the way Indian society was organized and that it was the samaj or society (as distinct from the state) that had been central in its imagination. This idea has been recognized by many later scholars and thinkers but the actual constitution of 'the political' has not really been specified. Nor has the question been posed as to what the ingredients of the modern state in India were and whether it was able to wipe out past forms and practices without trace or residue? Chapter 4 tries to explore this aspect, very tentatively and suggestively. In order to do this I take up two aspects of the Indian formation—the *mandala* or a circle or galaxy and the idea of the 'social polity', suggested in the writings of Bhupendranath Datta. Though the instance I take up is that of India, variations of the *mandala* form, in particular, are in evidence through much of South and South East Asia, as scholars have noted. The idea of the social polity was used by Datta specifically to refer to the polity or power structure, distinct from the state that was the caste order.

The question of the secular or the non-religious becomes the key reference point in Chapter 5, where I propose two related categories—the 'paramodern' and the 'Puranic'—in order to create a conceptual space for understanding another kind of non-synchronous synchronicity that is very much a part of our living present. The chapter is actually quite centrally concerned with what one might call a 'postsecular secularism' in that it recognizes that there is something in the secular project that needs to be salvaged but in a way that cannot shun the issue of religion and spirituality. By not recognizing the fact that what I call the Puranic mode of being is a way of living with gods and goddesses, jinns and spirits—benign and malign—and ancestors, the secular modern simply banishes these modes into other spaces that constitute what I call the paramodern. It is also a part of the argument of this chapter that the 'fascist' revolt against the secular modern actually feeds on this fertile soil of the epistemically and culturally dispossessed and breeds in these spaces that have become out of reach for the rational secular modern. My use of the term 'fascism' or 'fascist' is more generic and not quite in tune with the insistence of theorists of Fascism or Nazism regarding the singularity of the Fascist/Nazi phenomenon. It is not really about a particular form that can be identified only when it finally 'matures' into Hitler's or Mussolini's kind of state machine. Indeed, that kind of a fuehrer figure was absent in the Hindu Right for most of its almost hundred-year history as was the obsessive concern with state power that characterizes European fascisms. But there is a way in which modern fears of the other, of loss of the secure comfort of traditional ways of living and the feeling of being culturally marginalized, often get easily inserted into aggressive and violent mobilizations of a nationalist type. These are very modern pathologies linked to the exaltation of the 'nation' as the source of all authenticity.

If these are the broad arguments and concerns of this book, I do not want to end with restating these alone. It is necessary to reiterate here what I have tried to underline at length in Chapter 1—that there cannot be a single right way or strategy by which one can decolonize theory and that we need a multiplicity of ways of doing theory for our purposes which allow us to think our present independently. To reiterate the point made in the Introduction, if we are to start from where we are, we need to think of the work of decolonizing theory as analogous to import-substituting industrialization (though industrialization itself is something we might want to drastically rethink). The point really is that we need to recognize that we begin this journey not from scratch but from a point where we are already lodged within a certain configuration of power and already produced by our Western education and training. For many of us, the task of 'thinking across traditions' may not be immediately possible, even if we so desire, because of our exclusive training in a single tradition.

Does that mean that we stop thinking about our complex times till we are able to decolonize in the specific sense of thinking across traditions and largely through Non-Western categories? That does not seem to be an option really if we recognize that modernity and modernity/coloniality have meant large scale dislocation and migration of populations. I mention the blacks who were transported from Africa as part of the Atlantic slave trade, the indentured labourers from different parts of the world and the indigenous populations of the Americas and elsewhere who perished in the genocides that the settlers carried out. For many such people, as well as many others who migrated over the past few centuries—and for a very large number of scholars who come from such communities—the language of the colonialists and settlers are the only languages that are available, at least in the foreseeable future. Precisely for that reason, it does not make sense for us to insist on any single strategy of decolonization. 'Authenticity' is not really the category through which we can possibly think of the vast range of work that, to my mind, takes place in different locations and sites that are critically important in our being able to think outside the colonial frame.

As a matter of fact, this is not only a question of scholarship from diasporic communities but equally of scholars working in Africa and Asia whose societies have been subjected to long years of colonial rule. Is it at all possible for us to think of such work as part of the decolonizing move in any way? In this context, it is useful to recall the work of Kalyan Sanyal once again, whose work is discussed in Chapter 6. Sanyal works entirely within the categories and frameworks of Western theory and yet is able to provide us with a way of looking at the large sectors of the wasteland and the informal economy with a perspective that is uniquely Non-Western. The same must be said of the immensely generative work of Partha Chatterjee that has opened up newer avenues in our study and understanding of postcolonial politics.

Ashis Nandy does only marginally better in terms of drawing some of his key concepts from Tagore and Gandhi and occasionally, some formulations from the epics. By and large, however, his categories too come from psychology and the social sciences.

To end then, it seems our first and most important task is the very enunciation of the theoretical or philosophical question. Where do our questions arise from? How do we formulate them? As I have indicated at length in Chapter 1, even when there has been excellent scholarship on societies like India, if the questions they are responding to are of the nature 'was there feudalism in India?' or 'how secular is Indian secularism?', or 'what are the barriers to capital accumulation in India?', then clearly our answers will take us in a direction where Europe and its very 'provincial' experience will remain our primary reference points.

How we then frame our questions and proceed to answer them seem to me to be questions of critical importance here.

Bibliography

Abu-Lughod, Janet L. 1989. *Before European Hegemony: The World System A.D. 1250–150*, New York and Oxford: Oxford University Press.

Althusser, Louis. 1979, *For Marx*, London: Verso.

———. 2006. *The Philosophy of the Encounter: Later Writings, 1978–1987*. London and New York: Verso.

Althusser, Louis and Etienne Balibar. 1977. *Reading Capital*, London: NLB.

Alvares, Claude. 1991[1979]. *Decolonizing History: Technology and Culture in India, China and the West: 1492 to the Present Day*, New York: The Apex Press and Goa: The Other India Press.

Ambedkar, B.R. 2007[1937]. *Annihilation of Caste*, Delhi: Critical Quest.

Amin, Samir. 1985. *Delinking: Towards a Polycentric World*, trans. Michael Wolfers, London: Zed Books.

Amin, Shahid. 1995. *Event, Metaphor, Memory: Chauri Chaura 1922–1992*, New Delhi: Oxford University Press.

———. 2015. *Conquest and Community: The Afterlife of Warrior Saint Ghazi Miyan*, New Delhi: Orient Blackswan.

Anderson, Perry. 2012. *The Indian Ideology*, New Delhi: Three Essays Collective.

Arkoun, Mohammed. 2002. *The Unthought in Contemporary Islamic Thought*, London: Saqi Books and The Institute of Ismaili Studies.

Asad, Talal. 2003. *Formations of the Secular: Christianity, Islam, Modernity*, Stanford California: Stanford University Press.

Badiou, Alain. 2008. 'The Communist Hypothesis', *New Left Review*, 49, January–February, pp. 29–42.

Bahuguna, Rameshwar Prasad. 2013. 'Religion and State in Eighteenth Century Rajasthan: Sawai Jai Singh and 'Reformed' Vaishnavism,' *Proceedings of the Indian History Congress*, Vol. 74, pp. 353–362.

Banaji, Jairus. 2003. 'Islam, Mediterranean and the Rise of Capitalism', *Historical Materialism*, Vol. 15, No. 1, pp. 47–74.

Belting, Hans. 2011. *Florence and Baghdad: Renaissance Art and Arab Science*, Cambridge, Massachusetts: The Belknap Press of Harvard University Press.

Bernal, Martin. 1991. *Black Athena: The Afroasiatic Roots of Classical Civilization*, London: Vintage.

Bhargava, Rajeev, ed. 1998. *Secularism and Its Critics*, New Delhi: Oxford University Press.

Bhattacharya, K.C. 2011[1928]. 'Svaraj in Ideas', in *Indian Philosophy in English: From Renaissance to Independence*, edited by Bhushan and Garfield, pp. 102–110, New York: Oxford University Press.

Bhattacharya, Neeladri. 1991. 'Myth, History and the Politics of Ramjanmabhumi', in *Anatomy of a Confrontation: The Babri Masjid–Ramjanmabhumi Issue*, edited by Sarvepalli Gopal, pp. 122–140. Pp. 122-140, New Delhi: Viking.

——. 2018. *The Great Agrarian Conquest: The Colonial Reshaping of a Rural World*, Ranikhet: Permanent Black, in association with Ashoka University.

Bhushan, Nalini and Jay L. Garfield, eds. 2011. *Indian Philosophy in English: From Renaissance to Independence*, New York: Oxford University Press.

——. 2017. *Minds Without Fear: Philosophy in the Indian Renaissance*, New Delhi: Oxford University Press.

Bloch, Ernst. 1977[1932]. 'Nonsynchronism and the Obligation to its Dialectics', translated by Mark Ritter, *New German Critique*, No. 11 (Spring), pp. 22–38.

Brenner, Robert. 1977. 'The Origins of Capitalist Development: A Critique of Neo-Smithian Marxism', *New Left Review*, I/104, July–August, pp. 25–92.

Bronkhorst, Johannes. 2011. *Language and Reality: On an Episode in Indian Thought*, Leiden: Brill Academic Publishers.

Calasso, Roberto. 2015. *Ardor*, Great Britain: Penguin Books.

Caliskan, Koray and Michel Callon. 2009. 'Economization, part 1: Shifting Attention from the Economy Towards Process of Economization', *Economy and Society*, Vol. 38, No. 3(August), pp. 369–398.

Callon, Michel. 2007. 'What Does it Mean to Say That Economics is Performative?', in *Do Economists Make Market? On the Performativity of Economics*, edited by MacKenzie et al., pp. 311–357, Princeton and Oxford: Princeton University Press.

Chakrabarti, Arindam. 2014. 'Just Words: An Ethics of Conversation in the *Mahabharata*', in *Mahabharata Now: Narration, Aeshetics, Ethics*, edited by Arindam Chakrabarti and Sibaji Bandyopadhyay, pp. 244–283, London and New Delhi: Routledge.

Chakrabarti, Arindam and Ralph Weber. 2015. *Comparative Philosophy Without Borders*, London: Bloomsbury.

Chakrabarti, Kunal. 2001. *Religious Process: The* Puranas *and the Making of a Regional Tradition*, New Delhi: Oxford University Press.

Chakrabarty, Dipesh. 2000. *Provincializing Europe: Postcolonial Thought and Historical Difference*, Princeton and Oxford: Princeton University Press.

Chatterjee, Partha. 1986. *Nationalist Thought in the Colonial World—A Derivative Discourse?* Zed Books and United Nations University, Tokyo and London.

Chatterjee, Partha. 1994. *The Nation and Its Fragments: Colonial and Postcolonial Histories*, New Delhi: Oxford University Press.

———. 1997. 'Beyond the Nation? Or Within?', *Economic and Political Weekly*, Vol. 32, Nos. 1–2, January 4–11, pp. 30–34.

———. 1998a. 'Community in the East', *Economic and Political Weekly*, Vol. 33, No. 6, Feb. 7, pp. 277–282.

———. 1998b. *Wages of Freedom: Fifty Years of the Indian Nation-State*, Delhi: Oxford University Press.

———. 1998c. 'Secularism and Tolerance', in *Secularism and Its Critics*, edited by Rajeev Bhargava, New Delhi: Oxford University Press.

———. 2008. 'Democracy and Economic Transformation in India', *Economic and Political Weekly*, Vol. 43, No. 16, April 19, pp. 53–62.

Chatterjee, Partha, Sudipta Kaviraj and Nivedita Menon. 2015. *The Indian Ideology: Three Responses to Perry Anderson* (With an Introduction by Sanjay Ruparelia), Ranikhet: Permanent Black in association with Ashoka University.

Chattopadhyay, Brajadulal. 1995. 'Political Processes and the Structure of Polity in Early Medieval India', in *The State in India: 1000–1700*, edited by Hermann Kulke, pp. 195–232, New Delhi: Oxford University Press.

Chen, Kuan-Hsing. 2010. *Asia as Method: Toward Deimperialization*, Durham and London: Duke University Press.

Chibber, Vivek. 2013. *Postcolonial Theory and the Specter of Capital*, New Delhi: Navayana/Verso.

Chinn, Ewing. 2001. 'Nagarjuna's Fundamental Doctrine of Pratityasamutpada', *Philosophy East and West*, Vol. 51, No. 1, (Jan 2001), pp. 54–72.

Chinnaiah, Jangam.2013. 'The Story of a Jailed Prince: Feudal Roots of Democratic Politics in Andhra Pradesh'. *Economic and Political Weekly*, Vol. 48. No. 25, pp. 11–15.

Colmo, Christopher. 1998. 'Alfarabi on the Prudence of Founders', *The Review of Politics*, Vol. 60, No. 4 (Autumn 1998), pp. 719–741.

Comaroff, Jean and John L. Comaroff. 2016. *Theory from the Global South: Or, How Euro-America is Evolving Toward Africa*. London and New York: Routledge

Cooper, Garrick, Charles W. Mills, Sudipta Kaviraj and Sor-hoon Tan. 2017. 'Responses to James Tully's "Deparochializing Political Theory and Beyond"', *Journal of World Philosophies 2*, (Summer 2017), pp. 156–173.

Copland, Ian. 1999. *The Princes of Indian in the Endgame of Empire*, New Delhi: Foundation Books/Cambridge University Press.

Dabashi, Hamid. 2011. *The Arab Spring: The End of Postcolonialism*, London: Zed Books.

Dabashi, Hamid. 2013. 'Can Non-Europeans Think?', *Al Jazeera*, 15 January 2013, https://www.aljazeera.com/indepth/opinion/2013/01/2013114142638797542.html (last accessed on 8 September 2019).

———. 2015. *Can Non-Europeans Think?* London: Zed Books.

Dallmayr, Fred. 1997. 'Towards a Comparative Political Theory', *The Review of Politics*, Vol. 59, No. 3, Non-Western Political Thought (Summer 1997), pp. 421–427.

Dallmayr, Fred and Zhao Tingyang. 2013. *Contemporary Chinese Thought: Debates and Perspectives*, New Delhi: KW Publishers Pvt Ltd.

Datta, Bhupendranath. 1983. *Studies in the Indian Social Polity*, Calcutta: Nababharat Publishers.

Datta, Pradip Kumar. 1999. *Carving Blocs: Communal Ideology in Early Twentieth Century Bengal*, New Delhi: Oxford University Press.

———. 2010. *Heterogeneities: Identity Formation in Modern India*, New Delhi: Tulika Books.

D'Entreves, Maurizio Passerin and Seyla Benhabib. 1996. *Habermas and the Unfinished Project of Modernity*, Cambridge and Oxford: Polity Press.

Dirks, Nicholas B. 1987. *The Hollow Crown: Ethnohistory of an Indian Kingdom*, Cambridge and Bombay: Cambridge University Press and Orient Longman.

Doornbos, Martin and Sudipta Kaviraj, eds. 1997. *Dynamics of State Formation: India and Europe Reconsidered*, New Delhi and London: SAGE Publications.

Duerlinger, James. 2005. *The Indian Buddhist Theories of Persons: Vasubandhu's 'Refutation of the Theory of a Self'*, London and New York: Routledge Curzon.

Dunk, Herman von der. 1997. 'The Formation of Modern States in Europe', in *Dynamics of State Formation: India and Europe Reconsidered*, edited by Doornbos and Kaviraj, pp. 56–73, New Delhi and London: SAGE Publications.

Dussel, Enrique, 'World–System and "Trans"–Modernity', *Nepantla: Views from the South*, Vol. 3, No. 2, pp. 221–244.

Eisenstadt, S.N. 2000. 'Multiple Modernities', *Daedalus,* Winter 2000, Vol. 129, No. 1. Research Library Core, pp. 1–29.

Eisenstadt, S.N. and Harriet Hartman. 1997. 'Historical Experience, Cultural Traditions, State Formation and Political Dynamics in Indian and Europe', in *Dynamics of State Formation: India and Europe Reconsidered*, edited by Martin Doornbos and Sudipta Kaviraj, pp. 27–55, New Delhi and London: SAGE Publications.

Eisenstadt, Shmuel N., and Wolfgang Schluchter. 1998. 'Paths to Early Modernities: A Comparative View', *Daedalus*, Vol. 127, No. 3, pp. 1–18.

Fakhry, Majid. 1997. *Islamic Philosophy: A Beginner's Guide*, London: Oneworld.

Fakhry, Majid. 2001. *Averroes (Ibn Rushd): His Life, Works and Influence*, Oxford: Oneworld.

Fracchia, Joseph. 1991. 'Marx's *Aufhebung* of Philosophy and the Foundation of a Materialist Science of History', *History and Theory*, Vol. 30, No. 2, (May), pp. 153–179.

Frank, Andre Gunder. 1996. 'India in the World Economy, 1400–1750', *Economic and Political Weekly*, Vol. 31, No. 30 (July 27, 1996), pp. PE50–PE64.

———. 1998. *ReOreint: Global Economy in the Asian Age*, Berkeley/Los Angeles/London: California University Press.

Ganeri, Jonardon. 2011. *The Lost Age of Reason: Philosophy in Early Modern India 1450–1700*, Oxford University Press, Oxford.

———. 2016. 'Why Philosophy Must Go Global—A Manifesto', (Comprising the text of 'Manifesto for a Re:emergent Philosophy', and 'Reflections on Re:emergent Philosophy'), *Confluence: An Online Journal of World Philosophies*, June 2016: pp. 134–141 and 164–186.

Garfield, Jay L. 1994. 'Dependent Arising and the Emptiness of Emptiness: Why Did Nagarjuna Start with Causation?', *Philosophy East and West*, Vol. 44, No. 2, (April 1994), pp. 219–250.

———. 2015. *Engaging Buddhism: Why it Matters to Philosophy*, New York: Oxford University Press.

Garfield, Jay L. and Graham Priest. 2003. 'Nagarjuna and the Limits of Thought', *Philosophy East and West*, Vol. 53, No. 1, pp. 1–21.

Geertz, Clifford. 1980. *Negara: The Theatre State in Nineteenth-Century Bali*, Princeton: Princeton University Press.

Ghoshal, U.N. 1959. *A History of Indian Political Ideas: The Ancient Period and the Transition to the Middle Ages*, Bombay and London: Oxford University Press.

Gilroy, Paul. 2001. *Against Race: Imagining Political Culture Beyond the Color Line*, Cambridge (Massachusetts): The Belknap Press of Harvard University Press.

Godrej, Farah. 2009. 'Towards a Cosmopolitan Thought: The Hermeneutics of Interpreting the Other', *Polity*, Vol. 41, No 2 (April 2009), pp. 135–165.

Golwalkar, M.S. 2015[1939]. *Golwalkar's 'We or Our Nationhood Defined'*, With a Preface and Introduction by Shamsul Islam, New Delhi: Pharos Media and Publishing Pvt Ltd.

———. 1966. *Bunch of Thoughts*, Bangalore: Vikrama Prakashan.

Goody, Jack. 2006. *The Theft of History*, Cambridge UK: Cambridge University Press.

Gowans, Christopher W. 2003. *Philosophy of the Buddha*, Routledge, London and New York.

Gramsci, Antonio. 1971. *Selections from the Prison Notebooks of Antonio Gramsci*, edited by Quentin Hoare and Geoffrey N. Smith, New York: International Publishers.

Guha, Ranajit. 1998. *Dominance without Hegemony: History and Power in Colonial India*. New Delhi: Oxford University Press.

Guha, Ranajit. 1984. *Elementary Aspects of Peasant Insurgency in Colonial India*. New Delhi: Oxford University Press

Gundimeda, Sambiah. 2009. 'Dalits, Praja Rajyam Party and Caste Politics in Andhra Pradesh'. *Economic and Political Weekly*, Vol. 44, No. 21, pp. 50–58.

Habermas, Jurgen. 1987. *The Philosophical Discourse of Modernity*, Cambridge and Oxford: Polity Press.

Halbfass, Wilhelm. 1990. *India and Europe: An Essay in Philosophical Understanding*, Delhi: Motilal Banarsidass.

Harper, Katherine Anne and Robert L. Brown, Eds. 2002. *The Roots of Tantra*, New York: State University of New York Press.

Hobson, John M. 2004. *The Eastern Origins of Western Civilization*, Cambridge UK: Cambridge University Press.

Hoskote, Ranjit and Ilija Trojanow. 2011. *Confluences*, Yoda Press, Delhi.

Hui, Wang. 2011. *The Politics of Imagining Asia*, Cambridge (Mass.) and London: Harvard University Press.

———. 2014. *China from Empire to Nation-State*, Cambridge, Massachusetts: Harvard University Press.

Iqbal, Muhammad. 2011. *The Reconstruction of Religious Thought in Islam*, Delhi: Shivalik Prakashan.

Jayaswal, K.P. 1943. *Hindu Polity: A Constitutional History of India in Hindu Times (Parts I and II)*, Bangalore: The Bangalore Printing and Publishing Co. Ltd.

Jayatilleke, K.N. 1963. *Early Buddhist Theory of Knowledge*, London: George Allen and Unwin.

Jullien, Francois. 2004. *A Treatise on Efficacy: Between Western and Chinese Thinking*, translated by Janet Lloyd, Honolulu: University of Hawai'i Press.

Kautilya. n.d. *Arthashastra*, translated into English by R. Shamashastry, [Publisher not given], https://csboa.com/eBooks/Arthashastra_of_Chanakya_-_English.pdf (last accessed on 26 September 2019).

Kautilya. 1925. *Kautilya Arthashastra*, in Sanskrit with Hindi translation by Udaiveer Shastri, Lahore: Sanskrit Pustakalay.

———. 1972. *The Kautilya Arthashastra, Part II*, translation and critical, explanatory notes by R.P. Kangle, Delhi: Motilal Banarsidass.

Kaviraj, Sudipta. 1995. 'Democracy and Development in India', in *Democracy and Development*, edited by Amiya Bagchi, London: St Martin Press.

Kaviraj, Sudipta. 1996. 'Dilemmas of Democratic Development in India', in *Democracy and Development: Theory and Practice*, edited by Adrian Leftwich. Cambridge: Polity Press.

———. 1997. 'The Modern State in India', in *Dynamics of State Formation: India and Europe Reconsidered*, edited by Doornbos and Kaviraj, pp. 225–250, New Delhi and London: SAGE Publications.

———. 2005. 'An Outline of a Revisionist Theory of Modernity', *European Journal of Sociology*, Vol. 46, No. 3, pp. 497–526.

———. 2009. 'Marxism in Translation: Critical Reflections on Indian Radical Thought', in *Political Judgement: Essays for John Dunne*, edited by Richard Bourke and Raymond Guess, pp. 172–199, Cambridge, UK: Cambridge University Press.

———. 2010[1987]. 'The Passive Revolution and India: A Critique', Kaviraj, *Trajectories of the Indian State—Politics and Ideas*, Ranikhet: Permanent Black.

———. 2010. *The Trajectories of the Indian State: Politics and Ideas*, Ranikhet: Permanent Black.

Khan, Razak. 2015. 'Local Pasts: Space, Emotions and Identities in Vernacular Histories of Princely Rampur'. *Journal of the Economic and Social History of the Orient*, Vol. 58, No. 5, pp. 693–731.

Kimura, Masaaki and Akio Tanabe, eds. 2006. *The State in India: Past and Present*, New Delhi: Oxford University Press.

Koselleck, Reinhart. 1985. *Futures Past: On the Semantics of Historical Time*, Cambridge (Mass.) and London: The MIT Press.

Kothari, Rajni.1994. 'Rise of Dalits and the Renewed Debate on Caste'. *Economic and Political Weekly*, Vol. 29, No 26, pp. 1589–1594.

———. 1970. *Politics in India*, Hyderabad: Orient Longman.

———. 1964. 'The Congress 'System' in India'. *Asian Survey,* Vol. 4, No 12, pp. 1161–1173.

Kulke, Hermann, ed. 1995.*The State in India, 1000–1700*, New Delhi: Oxford University Press.

———. 2006. 'The Integrative Model of State Formation in Early Medieval India: Some Historiographic Remarks', in *The State in India: Past and Present*, edited by Masaaki Kimura and Akio Tanabe, pp. 59–81, New Delhi: Oxford University Press.

Laclau, Ernesto and Chantal Mouffe. 2001. *Hegemony and Socialist Strategy: Towards a Radical Democratic Politics*, London and New York: Verso.

Long, Jeffrey D. 2005. 'Claiming the Buddha for Hinduism: Swami Vivekananda and the Rediscovery of Buddhism in India', in *The Cyclonic Swami: Vivekananda in the West*, edited by Sukalyan Sengupta and Makarand

Paranjape, pp. 113–120, New Delhi: Samvad India Foundation in association with Center for Indic Studies, University of Massachusetts at Dartmouth.

Loy, David. 1993. 'Indra's Postmodern Net', *Philosophy East and West*, Vol. 43, No. 3, pp. 481–510.

Lyons, Jonathan. 2010. *House of Wisdom: How the Arabs Transformed Western Civilization*, New York and London: Bloomsbury.

MacKenzie, Donald, Fabian Muniesa and Lucia Siu. Eds. 2007. *Do Economists Make Market? On the Performativity of Economics*, Princeton and Oxford: Princeton University Press.

Macpherson, C.B. 1962. *The Political Theory of Possessive Individualism: Hobbes to Locke*, Ontario: Oxford University Press.

Madan, T.N. 1987. 'Secularism in its Place', *The Journal of Asian Studies*, Vol. 46, No. 4, (Nov, 1987), pp. 747–759.

Mahajan, Gurpreet. 2013. *India: Political Ideas and the Making of a Democratic Discourse*, London: Zed Books.

———. 2014. 'The Divisiveness of Secularism', *The Indian Express*, 31 May 2014, https://indianexpress.com/article/opinion/columns/the-divisiveness-of-secularism/ (last accessed on 29 December 2019).

Maldonaldo-Torres, Nelson. 2007. 'On the Coloniality of Being: Contributions to the Development of a Concept', *Cultural Studies*, Vol. 21, No. 2, pp. 240–270.

Marder, Michael. 2013. 'A Post-colonial Comedy of Errors', *Aljazeera*, 13 April 2013, http://www.aljazeera.com/indepth/opinion/2013/03/201331411225576l369.html (last accessed on 28 February 2020).

Marks, Laura. 2012. 'A Deleuzian *Ijtihad*: Unfolding Deleuze's Islamic Sources Occulted in the Ethnic Cleansing of Spain', in *Deleuze and Race*, edited by Arun Saldanha and Jason Michael Adams, Edinburgh: Edinburgh University Press.

Marks, Robert B. 2017. The Origins of the Modern World: A Global and Environmental Narrative from the Fifteenth Century to the Twenty First Century, Lanham and London: Rowman and Littlefield.

Marx, Karl. 1971. *Capital—A Critique of Political Economy*, Vol. III, Moscow: Progress Publishers.

——. 1976. 'Theses on Feuerbach', in *Ludwig Feuerbach and the End of Classical German Philosophy*, edited by Frederick Engels, pp. 61–65, Beijing: Foreign Languages Press, Peking.

McCrea, Lawrence. 2009. *The Teleology of Poetics in Medieval Kashmir*, Harvard: Harvard University Press.

Menon, Dilip. 2018. 'Thinking About the Global South: Affinity and Knowledge', in *The Global South and Literature*, edited by Russell West-Pavlov. Cambridge (UK): Cambridge University Press, pp. 34–44.

Menon, Nivedita. 1998. 'Women and Citizenship', in *Wages of Freedom*, edited by Partha Chatterjee, New Delhi: Oxford University Press.

———. 2010. 'The Two Žižeks', response to Žižek after his talk in Delhi, http://kafila.online/2010/01/07/the-two-Žižeks/ (last accessed on 8 September 2019).

Menon, Nivedita. 2019. 'Beyond the Euro-centrism—Indigenism Binary: Counter-narratives to Hindutva Claims'. *Economic and Political Weekly*, Vol. 54, No. 38, pp. 37–45.

Menon, Nivedita and Aditya Nigam. 2007. *Power and Contestation: India After 1989*, Zed Books, London.

Mignolo, Walter. 2002. 'Geopolitics of Knowledge and the Colonial Difference', *South Atlantic Quarterly*, Vol. 101, No. 1, Winter 2002, pp. 57–96.

———. 2007. 'Delinking', *Cultural Studies*, Vol. 21, No. 2, pp. 449–514.

———. 2011. *The Darker Side of Western Modernity: Global Futures, Decolonial Options*, Duke University Press, Durham and London.

———. 2013. 'Yes, We Can: Non-Western Thinkers and Philosophers', *Aljazeera*, 19 February 2013, http://www.aljazeera.com/indepth/opinion/2013/02/20132672747320891.html (last accessed on 28 February 2020).

———. 2018. 'Decoloniality and Phenomenology: The Geopolitics of Knowing and Epistemic/Ontological Colonial Differences'. *The Journal of Speculative Philosophy*, Vol. 32, No. 3 (Special issue with the Society for Phenomenology and Existential Philosophy), pp. 360–387.

Mitchell, Timothy. 2002. *Rule of Experts: Egypt, Techno-politics, Modernity*, Berkeley: University of California Press.

———. 2007. 'The Properties of Markets', in *Do Economists Make Market? On the Performativity of Economics*, edited by Donald MacKenzie, Fabian Muniesa and Lucia Siu, pp. 244–275, Princeton and Oxford: Princeton University Press.

———. 2014. 'Economentality: How the Future Entered Government', *Critical Inquiry*, Vol. 40. No. 4, pp. 479–507.

Mookerji, Radha Kumud. 2003. *The Fundamental Unity of India*, New Delhi: Bharatiya Vidya Bhavan and Chronicle Books.

Nandy, Ashis. 2003. *The Romance of the State and the Fate of Dissent in the Tropics*, New Delhi: Oxford University Press.

———. 2001. *Time Warps: The Insistent Politics of Silent and Evasive Pasts*, Delhi: Permanent Black.

———. 1995. 'An Anti-secularist Manifesto', *India International Centre Quarterly*, Vol. 22, No. 1, (Spring 1995), pp. 35–64.

Nasr, Seyyed Hossein. 2006. *Islamic Philosophy From its Origin to the Present: Philosophy in the Land of Prophecy*, New York: SUNY Press.

Nayak, G.C. 1979. 'The Madhyamika Attack on Essentialism: A Critical Appraisal', *Philosophy East and West*, Vol. 29, No. 4, pp. 477–490.

———. 2000. 'Nagarjuna, Chandrakirti and Wittgenstein: A Critical Evaluation of Certain Significant Aspects', *Annals of the Bhandarkar Oriental Research Institute*, Vol. 81, No. 1/4, pp. 123–133.

Ndlovu-Gatsheni, Sabelo J. 2015. 'Genealogies of Coloniality and Implications for Africa's Development', *Africa Development*, Vol. 40, No. 3, Transforming Global Relations for a just World, pp. 13–40.

Nigam, Aditya. 2005. 'Civil Society and its "Underground": Explorations in the Notion of "Political Society"', in *Civil Society, Public Sphere and Citizenship*, edited by Rajeev Bhargava and Helmut Reifeld, Delhi: SAGE Publications.

———. 2006. *The Insurrection of Little Selves: The Crisis of Secular-Nationalism in India*, Oxford University Press, New Delhi.

———. 2008. 'The Implosion of "the Political"', *Journal of Contemporary Thought*, No. 27, Summer.

———. 2010. *After Utopia: Modernity, Socialism and the Postcolony*, Delhi: Viva Books.

———. 2014. '"Molecular Economies": Is there an Outside to Capital?', in *Critical Studies in Politics: Exploring Sites, Selves, Power*, edited by Nivedita Menon, Aditya Nigam, Sanjay Palshikar, Hyderabad: IIAS Shimla and Orient Blackswan.

———. 2016. 'Afro-Asian Solidarity and the "Capital" Question: Looking Beyond the Last Frontier', (*Inter-Asia Cultural Studies*, Vol. 17, No. 1, pp. 33–51.

Nishitani, Keiji. 1983. *Religion and Nothingness*, Berkeley: University of California Press.

Nkenkana, Akhona. 2015. 'No African Futures without the Liberation of Women: A Decolonial Feminist Perspective', *Africa Development*, Vol. 40, No. 3, pp. 41–57.

Nusseibeh, Sari. 2017. *The Story of Reason in Islam*, Stanford: Stanford University Press.

O'Brien, Peter. 2011. 'Islamic Civilization and (Western) Modernity', *Comparative Civilizations Review*, No. 65, Fall 2011, pp. 18–32.

Olivelle, Patrick. 2013. *King, Governance and Law in Ancient India—Kautilya's* Arthashastra (A new and annotated translation by Olivelle), New Delhi: Oxford University Press.

Palshikar, Sanjay. 2014. *Evil and the Philosophy of Retribution: Modern Commentaries on the Bhagavad-Gita*, New Delhi: Routledge.

Park, Peter K.J. 2013. *Africa, Asia, and the History of Philosophy*, New York: SUNY Press.

Perlin, Frank. 1984. 'State Formation Reconsidered', *Modern Asian Studies*, Vol. 19, No. 3, Special Issue: Papers Presented at the Conference in Indian Economic and Social History, Cambridge University, Cambridge: Cambridge University Press, pp. 415–480.

Pinch, William. 1996. *Peasants and Monks in British India*, Delhi: Oxford University Press.

Pollock, Sheldon. 2009. *The Language of Gods in the World of Men*, California: University of California Press.

Pomeranz, Kenneth. 2000. *The Great Divergence: China, Europe, and the Making of the Modern World Economy*, Princeton and Oxford: Princeton University Press.

Quijano, Anibal. 2007. 'Coloniality and Modernity/Rationality', *Cultural* Studies, Vol. 21, No. 2–3, pp. 168–178.

——. 2000. 'Coloniality of Power, Eurocentrism and Latin America', *Nepantla: Views from the South*, Vol. 1, No. 3, pp. 533–580.

Ram, Kalpana. 2013. *Fertile Disorder: Spirit Possession and its Provocation of the Modern*, Honolulu: University of Hawai'i Press.

Rathore, Akash Singh. 2017. *Indian Political Theory: Laying the Groundwork for Svaraj*, London and New York: Routledge.

Richter, William L. 1971. 'Princes in Indian Politics'. *Economic and Political Weekly*, Vol. 6, No. 9, pp. 535–542.

Robinson, Cedric J. 2000. *Black Marxism*, Chapel Hill: The University of North Carolina Press.

Rocher, Ludo. 1986. *The Puranas*, Weisbaden: Otto Harrassowitz.

Roy, M.N. 1950. *India's Message*, Calcutta: Renaissance Publishers Ltd.

——. 1981. *The Historical Role of Islam*, Delhi: Ajanta Publications.

Rudolph, Lloyd I. and Susanne Hoeber Rudolph. 2010. '*Federalism as State Formation in India: A Theory of Shared and Negotiated Sovereignty*'. *International Political Science Review*, Vol. 31, No. 5, pp. 553–572.

Ruparelia, Sanjay, Partha Chatterjee, Sudipta Kaviraj and Nivedita Menon. 2015. *The Indian Ideology: Three Responses to Perry Anderson*, New Delhi: Orient Blackswan.

Saliba, George. 2007. *Islamic Science and the Making of the European Renaissance*, Cambridge (Massachusetts) and London (England): The MIT Press.

Samuel, Geoffrey. 2009. *The Origins of Yoga and Tantra: Indic Religions to the 113th Century*, New Delhi: Cambridge University Press.

Sanyal, Kalyan. 1988. 'Accumulation, Poverty and State in Third World: Capital/ Pre-Capital Complex', *Economic and Political Weekly*, Vol. 23, No. 5, January 30, pp. PE27–PE30.

Sanyal, Kalyan. 2007. *Rethinking Capitalist Development: Primitive Accumulation, Governmentality and Post-Colonial Capitalism.* London, New York: Routledge 2007.

Savarkar, V.D. 2009. *Hindutva: Who is a Hindu?*, New Delhi: Hindi Sahitya Sadan.

Schwartz, Frederic J. 2001. 'Ernst Bloch and Wilhelm Pinder: Out of Sync', *Grey Room*, No. 3 (Spring 2001), pp. 54–89.

Scott, James C. 2010. *The Art of Not Being Governed: An Anarchist History of Upland Southeast Asia*, New Delhi: Orient Blackswan.

Sen, Asok. 1976. 'Bureaucracy and Social Hegemony', in *Essays in Honour of Prof S.C. Sarkar*, pp. 667–688, New Delhi: People's Publishing House, New Delhi.

——. 'The Frontiers of the "Prison Notebooks"', *Economic and Political Weekly*, Vol. 23, No. 5, January 30, 1988, pp. PE31–PE36.

Sharma, Jyotirmaya. 2005. 'Ideological heresy?', *The Hindu*, Sunday Magazine, 19 June 2005, front page.

——. 2015. *Hindutva: Exploring the Idea of Hindu Nationalism*. Chennai: Context, an imprint of Westland Books.

——. 2019. *M.S. Golwalkar, the RSS and India*. Chennai: Context, an imprint of Westland Books.

Sheth, D.L. 2018. *At Home with Democracy: A Theory of Indian Politics*, edited with an Introduction by Peter Ronald de Souza, Singapore: Palgrave Macmillan/Springer Nature.

Shulman, David. 2012. *More than Real: A History of the Imagination in South India*, Harvard: Harvard University Press.

Singh, Mohinder. 2014. 'Crisis and Critique: Diagnosis of the Present in the Nationalist Discourse in Hindi (1870–1908)', in *Critical Studies in Politics: Exploring Sites, Selves, Power*, edited by Nivedita Menon, Aditya Nigam, Sanjay Palshikar, pp. 419–447, New Delhi: Orient Blackswan.

Southall, Aidan. 1988. 'The Segmentary State in Africa and Asia', *Comparative Studies in Society and History*, Vol. 30. No. 1, pp. 52–82.

Sousa Santos, Boaventura de. 2016. *Epistemologies of the South: Justice Against Epistemicide*, London and New York: Routledge.

Spodek, Howard. 1973. 'Urban Politics in the Local Kingdoms of India: A View from the Princely Capitals of Saurashtra under British Rule'. *Modern Asian Studies*, Vol. 7, No. 2, pp. 253–275.

Sreenivasan, Ramya. 2014. 'Rethinking Kingship and Authority in South Asia: Amber (Rajasthan)', ca. 1560–1615. *Journal of the Economic and Social History of the Orient*, Vol. 57, No. 4, pp. 549–586.

Srinivasan, T.N. ed. 2007. *The Future of Secularism*, New Delhi: Oxford University Press.

Stein, Burton. 1995. 'The Segmentary State: Interim Reflections', in *The State in India, 1000*–1700, edited by Hermann Kulke, pp. 134–161, New Delhi: Oxford University Press.

Tambiah, Stanley Jeyaraja. 2013[1973]. 'The Galactic Polity in Southeast Asia' (reprint from *Culture, thought and social action*), *Journal of Ethnographic Theory*, Vol. 3, No. 3, pp. 503–534.

———. 1998. 'The Crisis of Secularism in India', in *Secularism and Its Critics*, edited by Rajeev Bhargava, pp. 418–453, New Delhi: Oxford University Press.

Taylor, Charles. 2007. *A Secular Age*. Harvard: Harvard University Press.

Tejani, Shabnum. 2007. *Indian Secularism: A Social and Intellectual History 1890–1950*, Permanent Black, Delhi/Ranikhet.

Thapar, Romila. 1984. *From Lineage to State: Social Formations in the Mid-First Millennium B.C. in the Ganga Valley*, Bombay: Oxford University Press.

———. 2004. *Cultural Pasts Essays in Early Indian History*, New Delhi: Oxford University Press.

Thompson, E.P. 1968. *The Making of the English Working Class*, London: Penguin.

Trautmann, Thomas R. 2012. 'Does India Have History? Does History Have India?', *Comparative Studies in Society and History*, Vol. 54, No. 1 (January 2012), pp. 174–205.

Tripathi, Radhavallabh. 2016. *Vada in Theory and Practice*, Shimla and New Delhi: IIAS and DK Printworld.

Tully, James. 2016. 'Deparochializing Political Theory and Beyond: A Dialogue Approach to Comparative Political Thought', *Journal of World Philosophies*, Vol. 1, (Winter 2016), pp. 51–74.

Urban, Hugh. 2003. *Tantra: Sex, Politics and Power in the Study of Religion*, Berkeley: University of California Press.

Vaikuntham, Y. 2004. *People's Movements in Princely States*, Delhi: Manohar.

Vatsyayan, Kapila. 1996. *Bharata: The Natyashastra*, New Delhi: Sahitya Akademi.

Vijaisri, Priyadarshini. 2015. *Dangerous Marginality: Rethinking Impurity and Power*, Delhi: Primus Books in association with Indian Council of Historical Research.

Visvanathan, Shiv. 2006. 'Official Hegemony and Contesting Pluralisms', in *World Anthropologies: Disciplinary Transformations Within Systems of Power*, edited by Gustavo Lins Rebeiro and Arturo Escobar, Oxford and New York: Berg.

Vivekananda. 2018. *The Definitive Vivekananda*, New Delhi: Rupa.

Walser, Joseph. 2018. *Genealogies of Mahayana Buddhism: Emptiness, Power and the Question of Origin*, London and New York: Routledge.

White, David Gordon. 2006. *Kiss of the Yogini: 'Tantric Sex' in its South Asian Contexts*, Chicago and London: The University of Chicago Press.

Wong, R. Bin. 1997. *China Transformed: Historical Change and the Limits of European Experience*, Ithaca and London: Cornell University Press.

Wood, Dan. 2015. 'Political Philosophy and the Vestiges of Colonialism: A Critical Analysis of Žižek's Leftist Plea for Eurocentrism', *Radical Philosophy Review*, Online First: August 11, 2015.

Yamazaki, Gen'ichi. 2006. 'State and Kinship in the Period of the Sixteen *Mahajanapadas* in Ancient North India', in *The State in India: Past and Present* edited by Masaaki Kimura and Akio Tanabe, pp. 37–58, New Delhi: Oxford University Press.

Zabala, Santiago. 2013. 'Slavoj Žižek and the Role of the Philosopher', *Aljazeera*, 25 December 2012, http://www.aljazeera.com/indepth/opinion/2012/12/20121224122215406939.html (last accessed on 28 February 2020).

Žižek, Slavoj. 1998. 'A Leftist Plea for "Eurocentrism"', *Critical Inquiry*, Vol. 24, No. 4. Summer, pp. 988–1009.

———. 2000. *The Fragile Absolute—or, why the Christian Legacy is Worth Fighting For?*, London: Verso.

———. 2002. 'A Plea for Leninist Intolerance', *Critical Inquiry*, Vol. 28, No. 2 (Winter 2002), pp. 542–566.

———. 2004. 'The Ongoing "Soft Revolution"', *Critical Inquiry*, Vol. 30, No. 2 (Winter 2004), pp. 292–323.

———. 2008. *In Defense of Lost Causes*, London: Verso.

———. 2010. *First as Tragedy, Then as Farce*, Delhi: Navayana.

———. 2011. *Living in the End Times*, London/New York: Verso.

Index

Note: The letter 'n' locators refers to notes.

N

O

P

About the Author

Aditya Nigam is Professor at the Centre for the Study of Developing Societies (CSDS), Delhi. His main areas of interest are political philosophy and social theory.

His recent work has been concerned with the decolonization of social and political theory. He has earlier worked on ideological and discursive formations and their relationship with the emergence and constitution of political subjectivities. The engagement with discursive formations has led to the need for greater attentiveness to the actual thought-worlds and imaginations of social agents and the need to step outside theoretical frames provided by standard theory, derived primarily from Western experience.

In particular, Nigam is interested in theorizing the contemporary experience of politics, populism and democracy in the non-West—treating the non-West as the ground for 'doing theory', rather than a field for application or testing of standard frameworks derived from the Western experience.

A parallel and related part of Nigam's work has been concerned with interrogating the received 'philosophical history' of capital, once again from the vantage point of the experiences of India and the non-West.

Aditya Nigam has also been associated with a group of South Asian scholars from Sri Lanka, Pakistan, and India, working around the idea of the 'post-national condition'.

He also works with the CSDS's Indian Languages Programme and is on the editorial board of its Hindi journal *Pratiman*. He comments regularly on contemporary political issues on the blog, kafila.online

He is the author of *The Insurrection of Little Selves: The Crisis of Secular Nationalism in India* (2006), *Power and Contestation: India Since 1989*, with Nivedita Menon (2007), *After Utopia: Modernity and Socialism and the Postcolony* (2010), and *Desire Named Development* (2011).

